P9-ARC-545

POWER AND GENDER

IN ONEOTA CULTURE

Power and Gender

Thomas Edward Berres

in Oneota Culture

A Study

of a Late

Prehistoric

People

NORTHERN ILLINOIS UNIVERSITY PRESS DeKalb

© 2001 by Northern Illinois University Press

Published by the Northern Illinois University Press, DeKalb, Illinois 60115

Manufactured in the United States using acid-free paper

All Rights Reserved

Design by Julia Fauci

Library of Congress Cataloging-in-Publication Data

Berres, Thomas E.

Power and gender in Oneota Culture: a study of a late prehistoric people /
Thomas Edward Berres.

p. cm.

Includes bibliographical references and index.

ISBN 0-87580-587-6 (pbk.: alk. paper)

1. Oneota Indians (Great Plains)—Social life and customs. 2. Indians of North
America—Rock River Valley (Wis. and Ill.)—Antiquities. 3. Rock River Valley
(Wis. and Ill.)—Antiquities. 4. Social archaeology. I. Title.

E99.O5 B47 2001

977.3'301—dc21   00-058232

This book is dedicated to the memory of

Bernard A. Berres and Florence A. Berres,

for their spirituality and

focus on tradition.

Contents

List of Tables and Figures

Acknowledgments

This work could not have been written without assistance from many people who have greatly influenced my career. Many thanks to Dr. Tom Dillehay (University of Kentucky) who introduced me to the peer polity interaction model and pointed out the futility of looking for the elite (the "big man") in small-scale Native American societies of the Midcontinent. Tom also taught his students the value of good argumentation and to not accept any statement of other archaeologists on faith alone. I thank Dr. Douglas J. Brewer (director of the Spurlock Museum) for his support, encouragement, and guidance during my graduate years at the University of Illinois at Urbana-Champaign as well as for providing invaluable assistance with faunal analysis and interpretation. His stress on the importance of reliability and validity in scientific research will never be forgotten. Dr. David C. Grove expanded my horizons regarding symbolism, ritual, and power and, from a Mesoamerican perspective, showed how the Mayan people flourished for centuries without the need for "lords." Dr. Mark W. Mehrer (Northern Illinois University) provided insights regarding American Bottom archaeology, especially the importance of examining "the community," necessary for discussions on problems related to Mississippian interaction. I am especially indebted to Dr. Norman E. Whitten, Jr., whose courses on peoples and cultures of Greater Amazonia completely changed my perception of Native American cosmology, creativity, cultural transformations, adaptation, and their resistance to sociopolitical domination. The true meaning of *culture* was presented as embodying aboriginal dreams, festivals, songs, rituals, and aesthetics filled with symbolism and was not restricted to

material culture and settlement-subsistence patterns.

Drs. James A. Brown, M. Catherine Bird, Robert J. Jeske, and Rochelle Lurie deserve a special thanks for providing their expertise on Langford material culture and adaptations. Although we may not agree with each other's arguments, the challenges posed can only lead to better questions and interpretations of prehistory in northern Illinois. James A. Brown (Northwestern University) also provided helpful comments regarding festivals, Fisher ceramics, and the "horizon" concept necessary for an understanding of the late prehistory within the Prairie Peninsula and its environs. Dr. David M. Stothers (University of Toledo) provided me with materials that found their way into the book. I benefited greatly from his focus on "loyalty to the data" and concern for "tradition."

Others who answered inquiries and/or provided helpful information included but were by no means limited to Larry R. Abbott, Ferrel Anderson, Charles J. Bareis, Kenneth A. Barr, J. Joe Bauxar, Robert F. Boszhardt, Lawrence A. Conrad, Joseph P. Craig, Duane Esarey, William Flesher, Andrew C. Fortier, Elizabeth B. Garland, Dale R. Henning, R. Eric Hollinger, Lynda Johnson, Douglas W. Jones, Paul P. Kreisa, Robert G. McCullough, Kevin P. McGowan, Terrance J. Martin, Ronald J. Mason, Doug Miller, Cheryl A. Munson, John T. Penman, G. Michael Pratt, Dick Reece, Thomas J. Riley, Greg Walz, Thomas R. Wolforth, and Carol Yokell. I very much appreciate their help.

The artifact photographs and some of the illustrations are by Linda Alexander; her work and creativity are much appreciated. Other art work is by Susan Brannock-Gaul (several maps) and Paula Luesse (several illustrations). Finally, I owe a debt of gratitude to the three anonymous reviewers for raising questions and offering many incisive comments and helpful suggestions that contributed to a significant improvement in the organization and clarity of the book.

POWER AND GENDER

IN ONEOTA CULTURE

CHAPTER ONE

Interpreting Oneota

A new culture was to emerge on the Midcontinent about 1,000 years ago, known to archaeologists as Oneota. If we could travel back to those times, we would see villages on high ground overlooking rivers, lakes, or marshes, whose inhabitants could trek by foot or canoe in small groups or individually on hunting, fishing, and collecting expeditions. Early in their history, villages were rather small and consisted of perhaps 10 to 20 houses. Two popular house types were built as single family units, including a small, rectangular semisubterranean (pit) structure and a mat and pole wigwam style dwelling. Interspersed among the houses were numerous deep storage facilities, basin-shaped processing pits, and hearths for cooking and heating. Fortifications were rarely constructed around such villages, which were often situated on exposed terraces covered by prairie grasses. During the latter part of their history, however, Oneota society changed as reflected by differences in settlement size, organization, and location. Villages sometimes grew very large, covering more than 20 acres, and consisted of long houses capable of accomodating several families. Some were placed in defensive positions and strongly fortified with palisades and ditches. What were once rather peaceful times turned chaotic, a precursor to when a different phase of warfare would dominate the landscape, created by the struggle between the French and English for domination of trade and territory.

Oneota is a name given to the culture of the Native American people who occupied much of the midwestern United States from the late tenth through early seventeenth centuries A.D. Evidence of this culture can be found throughout the Midcontinent, including portions of Illinois, southwestern Michigan, northwestern Indiana, Iowa, Wisconsin, southern Minnesota, northern Missouri, and eastern Nebraska. Oneota encompassed a multitude of distinctive, localized traditions that shared many of the same stimuli and engaged in cultural interaction at various levels and intensities. For instance, the Oneota people shared ideas about the way tools, ornaments, and ritual items were to be manufactured and utilized as well as beliefs about how people should live together and interact with their environment. Evidence suggests that their cosmology, or worldview, consisted of an ordered, perpetually self-repeating system of meaningful relations (life-death-rebirth) serving as a foundation for proper conduct toward the physical environment and the supernatural (see Ingold 1993:41; Redfield 1952; Wright 1987). Their tribal or uncentralized egalitarian sociopolitical organization rested on authority distributed among a number of small groups similar to that found among historic native Midwest tribes of the seventeenth through early nineteenth centuries, such as the Iliniwek, Miami, Sac, Fox, Ioway, Ojibway, Oto, Ottawa, Winnebago, Menominee, and Potawatomi (Benn 1989:237; Callender 1978; Hall 1997:142; Kreisa 1993). In a manner similar to historic groups, male and female Oneota leaders may have helped direct many ritual and economic activities, while the consensus of the group would have played a vital role in decision-making matters. Such shared decisions resulted in behavioral uniformity within social groups.

The Oneota villagers were horticulturists who maintained diverse, or broad-spectrum, subsistence economies that involved slash-and-burn cultivation of maize supplemented by a wide range of seasonally available wild foods from the forest and prairie. White-tailed deer of the deciduous forest were an important part of the Oneota economy, but the rich and varied aquatic/wetland resources near the villages (e.g., fish, waterfowl, mussel, and turtle species) were the main target of exploitation (Gibbon 1986). The people made distinctive globular jars, often tempered with crushed shells of freshwater mollusks and decorated on the shoulder with geometric motifs like curvilinear trailed lines and chevrons. Their stone tool kits were dominated by small triangular projectile points with some miscellaneous stemmed and unstemmed knives, and end scrapers (Overstreet 1997). Other key traits include a complex assortment of tools, ornaments, and ritual paraphernalia made of bone, antler, shell, and copper.

Within Oneota societies, relations of power could be observed in the imagery and creativity associated with events, like festivals and rituals, and objects (pottery, textiles, and metalwork) embellished with symbols communicating inner personal and community strengths. These strengths could result, in part, from dreams and visions involving personal spiritual interaction with supernatural powers, like the mythical avian creature of the upperworld, the thunderbird, or the horned hairy serpent and long-tailed underwater panther of the underworld. Such power relations were vital parts of Native American traditions, with men and women actively engaged in the beauty and *experience* of being alive. They provided a means of renewing time and reaffirming life in culture, a sharing of the whole sacred drama of life. Traditions of freedom, equality, and the ability to dream were paramount in their lifeways, as they have been among peoples of small-scale societies throughout history (Black Elk and Lyon 1991; Johnston 1995; Lame Deer and Erdoes 1972; Steltenkamp 1993).

Like other tribal societies, each Oneota group probably saw themselves as the "true" human beings occupying the sacred center of the universe, superior to all others. Many historic Native American societies named themselves "The People" in their own language, a symbolic phrase transmitting their notion of "us" versus "them." For example, the Cherokee called themselves *Ani-yunwiya,* "Real People" (Spence 1911:503), the Eskimos are properly named *Inuit,* or "People," and the proper name of the Navajos is *Dine,* "People" (Furst and Furst 1982). The Lakota called themselves "allies" while all other Indian people were *toka,* "enemies" (DeMallie 1988:9). The power to interpret and mediate the forces of untamed nature comes from the cultural center, a culturally safe place where imagery, creativity, and wisdom produce aesthetic expressions (i.e., art, folklore [covering legends, sacred stories or myths, tales, proverbs, and texts of songs and chants], and ceremonies) communicating knowledge or power to "others." That knowledge is passed on through successive generations or traditions and serves to remind the Indian that each creature is part of a living whole, related to all others by virtue of their participation in the harmony, balance, or wholeness of the universe (Allen 1986; Darnell 1988).

What is truly remarkable about Oneota is its long-term success or durability over such an immense area (Figure 1). Aided by an increasing suite of radiocarbon dates and artifact collections, contemporary archaeologists have shown that this major cultural tradition existed from roughly A.D. 950 through the end of the protohistoric period, about A.D. 1650 (Benn 1989; Boszhardt 1989; Brown and Sasso 1992; Dobbs 1982; Henning 1995; Overstreet 1997). Thus, long after power began to wane for the great Middle Mississippi center of Cahokia about A.D. 1200, Oneota societies thrived through successive generations. As such, they should be considered healthy, open entities that were continually created, maintained, and transformed through interactions with peer polities (see Bender 1990:262; Cobb 1991:173–74; Hodder 1991:39; Kohl 1989:218; Kowalewski 1995:148; Nassaney and Sassaman 1995:xxvii; Paynter 1989:376; Spielmann 1991:2; Trigger 1986a:257, 1989:25–26). The peer polity interaction approach provides a way of interpreting events and processes that occurred among the small, autonomous, nonhierarchical Oneota groups (as comparable units) spread across the landscape. The archaeologist Penelope Drooker (1997:37) aptly describes the positive aspects of the model:

> This approach emphasizes the nonisolation of autonomous political entities, and de-emphasizes "relations of dominance and subordination" (Renfrew 1986:1). It also emphasizes the importance of style as an essential component of communication systems, and symbolic systems as links among political peers (Renfrew and Cherry 1986:vii–viii). Material, technological, and symbolic systems are seen as interacting and changing together, within a particular social matrix.

The environment is important in the peer polity concept and in how settlements are distributed over whole regions or culture areas. One seeks evidence of spatial redundancy or patterning that may reflect the abundance and predictability in space and time of subsistence resources and similarities in human-environmental interactions.

Oneota groups are distinguished from other Mississippi societies, such as Cahokia of the American Bottom and the Fort Ancient tradition of the Middle Ohio River region, by their successful adaptation to a biogeographical region exhibiting a mosaic of grassland, forest, and aquatic/wetland resources. This region is commonly known as the Prairie Peninsula, which extended in a wedgelike form from the short grass prairie of the central Great Plains into the deciduous forests of eastern North America (Geis and Boggess 1968; Transeau 1935). Whether near a lake or river, the Oneota main settlements were never far from forest, prairie, and aquatic/wetland resources. Certainly, the Prairie Peninsula can be viewed as a culture area as defined by the anthropologist Harold E. Driver: "A culture area is a geographical area occupied by a number of peoples whose cultures show a significant degree of similarity with each other and at the same time a significant degree of dissimilarity with the cultures of the peoples of other areas" (1961:12). Indeed, the pioneer archaeological work of James A. Brown (1965, 1991) has demonstrated that the Prairie Peninsula is a valid culture area where human adaptations to the abiotic and biotic environments occurred along parallel trajectories among autonomous groups from Hopewell to Mississippi times. This was especially evident in his study of the similarities and differences in ceramic style zones.

Archaeologists are still puzzled about many aspects of Oneota. How did this major cultural tradition originate (could it have developed through the transformation of resident Late Woodland populations influenced by Middle Mississippian interaction?), and what happened to them shortly before historic contact in the seventeenth century? There also is a lack of knowledge concerning what languages were spoken and what they might have called their land, villages, and homes. However, their archaeological remains—ceramics, in particular—are easily recognized on

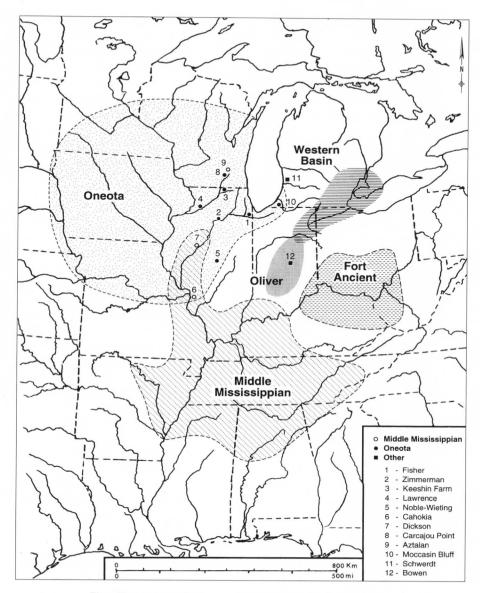

Figure 1 Location of Oneota, other cultures in the Midcontinent, and sites mentioned in the text.

the ground surface and in site excavations (Emerson and Brown 1992; Henning 1970, 1995; Overstreet 1997; Staeck 1995).

Oneota is frequently known among archaeologists as a "pottery culture" (Boszhardt 1994:185; Gibbon 1986:319; Mason 1981:357; O'Brien and Wood 1998:345). Ceramic vessels provide the main criterion for Oneota recognition and internal diversity. Archaeologists believe that the similarities and differences between ceramic vessel types, styles, or attributes reflect cultural historical relationships through time and space. Thus, ceramic similarities between areas are viewed as indicative of cultural contact (via trade, migration, or conquest) or exchange of knowledge; conversely, differences reflect the absence of such cultural contact (Arnold 1988). The typical Oneota ceramic vessel is a squat, globular or *spherical* cooking/storage jar often exhibiting straight or everted rims, rounded to angular shoulders, and rounded bottoms. Thus, they are easily distinguishable from the semiglobular Powell Plain and Ramey Incised jars with their inslanted rims and sharply angled shoulders found at the Middle Mississippian centers of Cahokia near East St. Louis, Illinois, or Aztalan in the Upper Rock River valley. They also sharply contrast with the uncollared and collared rims and elongated-bodied vessels with slight shoulders characteristic of the Late Woodland Western Basin tradition of the western Lake Erie region (Mason 1981:Plate 8.26; Stothers 1995; Stothers and Graves 1983:113; Stothers and Pratt 1981:Figure 5) and with the Mississippian Fort Ancient tradition of the Central Ohio Valley (Henderson et al. 1992:Figure XVIII-2).

From this perspective, one should find in Oneota a shared culture among basically similar adaptive systems, which can then be distinguished from other culture areas based on differences in ceramic vessel form and decoration. I will show in this work that the similarities between Fisher, Langford, and other early Oneota cultures extend to many cultural aspects including material culture, settlement-subsistence strategies, mortuary ritual, reciprocal exchange systems, and limited warfare. It is important to note that the observed patterns are the result of similar relations of power in cultures that have a long tradition, especially those regarding religious practices most resistant to change.

FISHER AND LANGFORD ONEOTA CULTURES

The Fisher and Langford cultures of northern Illinois were situated along the northeastern portion of the Prairie Peninsula (Figure 2) and are the primary focus of this volume. Both are considered here to be peer polities within the major Oneota cultural tradition existing in the same culture area. They were contemporaneous, shared many common beliefs and practices, and actively interacted, as determined by the similarities in their ceramic traditions. Unlike our Western tribal models in which territories were divided and defended by *discrete ethnic groups,* the Fisher and

Langford folk possessed overlapping, amorphous boundaries. The only "real" difference between the two is that Fisher peoples manufactured ceramic vessels tempered with shell, like most other Oneota groups, while Langford peoples manufactured vessels tempered with grit. Their members may have recognized themselves as a separate regional or kin group within Oneota culture on this basis, an identity that could have been situational (utilized in some contexts and not in others) (see Rosman and Rubel 1995:303). This would show that social choice or resistance to power existed in the Langford tradition leading to variability in Oneota as a major cultural tradition. Howard Harrod (1987:39) states, "In some societies it is the value and power of the past, of tradition, which illuminates the meaning of the future and shapes what is believed ought to occur in the present. The future, in such societies, becomes largely a projection of the shared traditions of the past, so that present and future are seen as continuous with that which has gone before."

The Fisher phase (ca. A.D. 1000–1400/1500) is concentrated primarily in the southern Lake Michigan area, particularly the relatively flat Chicago Lake Plain of extreme northeastern Illinois and northwestern Indiana. But sites are also found in the Upper Illinois Valley and some of its tributaries as exemplified by those near Starved Rock in the Upper Illinois Valley and throughout the Lower Des Plaines and Kankakee Valleys. They are conspicuously absent from the Fox, Du Page, and Upper Des Plaines Valleys (Emerson and Brown 1993; Hart and Jeske 1987; Markman 1991b). Fisher occupations also have been encountered at western outlier sites, like the Lawrence site in the Middle Rock Valley, Illinois, and in eastern outlier sites, like the Moccasin Bluff and Wymer (20BE132) sites in the Lower St. Joseph Valley, southwestern Michigan (Emerson and Brown 1993; Garland 1991). The best-documented Fisher components are present at the Fifield (Faulkner 1972), Fisher (Griffin 1944, 1946, 1948; Langford 1927, 1928, 1930), Griesmer (Faulkner 1972), Horton (or Butterfield Creek) (Rackerby and Struever 1968), Hoxie Farm (Herold et al. 1990), Plum Island (Fenner 1963), Rader (Faulkner 1964), and Yahl (Faulkner 1972) sites. The limited number of sites investigated leaves the Fisher phase culture poorly understood, with the exception of its chronological relationships.

The Fisher phase represents an early manifestation within a single tradition known as the Fisher-Huber tradition. Its chronology is fairly well established, being roughly contemporaneous with the Langford tradition. The earliest recognizable Fisher components at the Yahl site in Lake County, Illinois (Faulkner 1972:159–160), and the Moccasin Bluff and Wymer sites, Berrien County, Michigan (Bettarel and Smith 1973; Fitting 1975:162; Garland 1991), date between A.D. 1000 and 1100. Apparently, the Huber phase developed out of an early Fisher ancestor sometime between A.D. 1400 and 1500 and subsequently extended into protohistoric times (Jeske 1990; Kullen 1994).

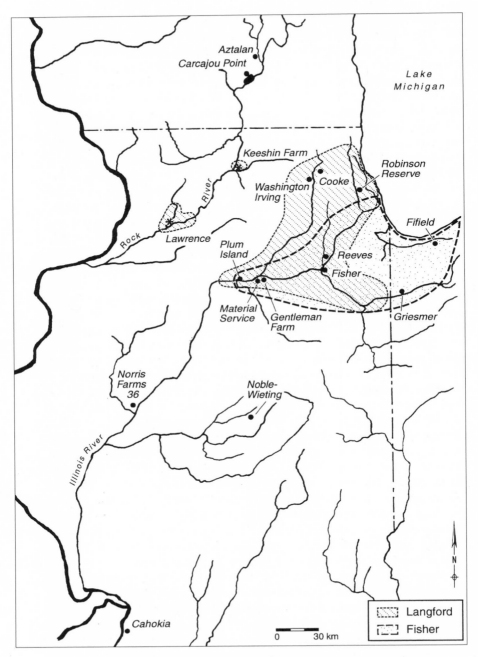

Figure 2 Location of the Fisher and Langford cultures, Lawrence and Keeshin Farm sites
(asterisks), and selected sites discussed in the text.

The ceramic markers of the Fisher phase include shell-tempered, globular jars that often exhibit everted rims, flattened lips, and rounded shoulders. The exterior surface finishes are primarily smoothed-over cordmarked, although cordmarked and smoothed surfaces also occur. Such vessels may exhibit lip modification in the form of punctations on superior surfaces and tool-impressed exterior surfaces. A series of curvilinear trailed designs bordered by punctates may also occur on the upper shoulder design field. Other shoulder designs, such as Langford, consist of chevrons, festoons, and geometric plats. Appendages occur in low frequency and include lugs, loop handles, and strap handles (Emerson and Brown 1992; Faulkner 1972; Swartz 1973).

Langford tradition sites (ca. A.D. 1000–1400/1500) are located predominantly in the Middle Rock Valley and the Upper Illinois River basin, including the Fox, DuPage, Kankakee, and Des Plaines river valleys. Significant Langford components contributing to our knowledge of this tradition are reported from the Cooke (Markman 1984, 1991a, 1991b), Fisher (Griffin 1946; Langford 1927, 1930), Gentleman Farm (Brown et al. 1967), Material Service Quarry (Bareis 1965), Noble-Weiting (Schilt 1977), Oakwood Mound (Skinner 1953), Plum Island (Fenner 1963), Reeves (Craig and Galloy 1995), Robinson Reserve (Fowler 1952; Lurie 1987), Washington Irving (Jeske 1990), and Zimmerman (Brown 1961) sites. Almost all of these sites have been excavated and published from localities in the Upper Illinois River basin, with the exception of the Noble-Weiting site located along Kickapoo Creek of the Upper Sangamon River drainage. Small upland sites also have been commonly reported in the drainage basins noted above (Birmingham 1975; Early 1970, 1973) but are poorly understood because of the absence of archaeological excavations.

The Langford tradition emerged from local Late Woodland societies between about A.D. 1000 and 1100. Ceramic criteria and clearly dated deposits show that the earliest calibrated radiocarbon dates for Langford cluster around A.D. 1000 as determined for components at the Cooke and Zimmerman sites (Markman 1991a). The ceramic assemblages from the components include a mixture of Late Woodland types such as the Aztalan/Starved Rock ceramic series (see Fowler 1952; Hall 1987) and early wares consisting of Langford Plain, Langford Cordmarked, and Langford Trailed (see Brown et al. 1967; Fenner 1963) vessels. Many wares within the early Langford series exhibit either rim collars or lip folds. Thus, the Langford ceramic tradition is considered a development out of the collared vessels of the so-called Des Plaines Complex (Gillette 1949), a Late Woodland manifestation centered in northeastern Illinois. This complex, in turn, appears preceded by manifestations producing mafic-tempered globular jars characteristic of Canton, Maple Mills, and Tampico wares centered in west-central Illinois (Hall 1987a; Markman 1991a). The termination of the Langford tradition may date as late as

A.D. 1500 (Brown and Asch 1990:150, 154; Doershuk 1988:125; Emerson and Brown 1992:82; Jeske and Hart 1988:181–185). However, Brown (1990) points out that this assay was taken on bone collagen from a human burial feature at the Zimmerman site and may prove excessively young. Despite the long duration interpreted for Langford, Jeske (1990) suggests a more restricted range between A.D. 1200 and 1450. In contrast, Sampson and Esarey (1993) propose dating Langford between about A.D. 1000 and 1350. One should note that these ranges may be biased by the paucity of dated deposits and restriction to dating a few sites located in the Upper Illinois Valley.

Grit-tempered, globular jar forms dominate Langford ceramic assemblages, with bowls and pinch pots present in low frequency. The jars often exhibit straight or everted rim forms with rounded shoulders. Many Langford types have folded rims but lack noticeable collars. Lip forms are either flattened or rounded and lip decoration is usually absent. The exterior-surface finishes vary from cordmarked to smooth or smoothed-over cordmarked. Though rare, a red-slipped surface finish may occur on interiors (Brown et al. 1967:21). Trailing on jar shoulders occurs as arches, festoons, chevrons, V-shapes, or curvilinear decorative motifs (Markman 1991a). Appendages are occasionally found, consisting of lugs, loop handles, and crude strap handles (Fenner 1963; Jeske 1990).

The nature and definition of the Fisher and Langford traditions continue to be problematic for archaeologists for several reasons. First, there is a limited data base, drawing from a small number of excavated sites and published site reports. Second, there has been continual revision in what the name "Oneota" represents, whether in terms of taxonomy, origins, demise, traits, or interaction. Third, earlier research efforts have attempted to compare Fisher and Langford to other Mississippian cultures (i.e., Cahokia and Fort Ancient) in a very general sense while often disregarding important changes taking place through time as defined by horizons (characterized by a particular artifact or set of artifacts that can be recognized over a wide area and may cross cultural boundaries), phases within regional Oneota cultural traditions, and adaptations within the Prairie Peninsula—a geographical area subjected to a significant climatic shift about A.D. 1150–1200 that brought droughty conditions with associated changes in plant and animal distributions (e.g., an influx of bison east of the Mississippi River). Finally, theoretical changes in the archaeology discipline have shifted the focus from a concern for chronology to a focus on ecological- and economic-human relationships and, currently, to an emphasis that stresses relations of power in Native American societies. Therefore, Fisher and Langford cultures are now viewed as natural, open entities that were continually created and re-created by people as *agents* involved in interaction, by symbols as central to human existence through communication, and by material culture as an instrument in creating meaning and order in the world.

Oneota Terminology:
Origin, Development, and Problematics

Oneota was known from the 1930s through the 1950s as an Upper Mississippi phase manifestation of the Mississippi Pattern using the Midwestern Taxonomic Method. It was thought to consist of several distinct foci or phases occupying a restricted area of northeastern Iowa and southern Wisconsin. With new data collected from regional surveys and site excavations along with the aid of radiocarbon dating, Oneota subsequently became recognized as a major cultural tradition evolving over several centuries from the tenth to the early seventeenth century. It is associated with numerous localized traditions covering an immense area of the Midwest; each had an independent history yet closely interacted with other groups through trade, exchange, and migration. Their evolution is identified primarily by changes in ceramic styles within broadly defined horizons.

The Oneota concept originated in the work of Charles R. Keyes in Iowa and Will C. McKern in Wisconsin during the late 1920s and early 1930s. Keyes (1927:214–229) was the first to introduce the word "Oneota" in archaeological contexts, which was applied in a very restrictive geographic–cultural material sense as compared to subsequent applications. He used the term to designate shell-tempered ceramics and related archaeological finds that were collected from a number of sites by Ellison Orr (1914:231–239) along the Upper Iowa River in extreme northeastern Iowa—a river known to the Oneida Iroquois as "Oneota" or "people who sprang from a rock" (McKusick 1973:4). During the late 1930s, the concept of Oneota was revised because of McKern's archaeological work in Wisconsin that revealed new Oneota finds (hence Oneota covered a much wider landscape) as well as his principal effort in formulating the Midwestern Taxonomic Method for culture classification.

The Midwestern Taxonomic Method was in vogue in the Midcontinent and eastern United States during the 1930s and 1940s. It was created as a response to the problem of large archaeological collections, available in museums, universities, or private hands, with little provenience information except for site location or region. Archaeological remains were classified in order of increasing inclusive categories based on their shared similarities in cultural traits, the five taxonomic levels being component, focus, aspect, phase, and pattern. In the method's "genetic-taxonomic" scheme, Oneota was interpreted as an "aspect" of the Upper Mississippi Phase of the Mississippi Pattern. It was thought to consist of only three foci that, in spite of differences, shared many traits: the Orr focus of northeastern Iowa and extreme western Wisconsin, and the Grand River and Lake Winnebago foci of eastern Wisconsin (McKern 1931, 1933, 1945). Another closely related focus defined in northeastern Illinois, the Fisher focus, completed McKern's early Oneota aspect composition (Glenn 1974).

Upper Mississippi is the general term pertaining to late cultures of the Midwest, including the Oneota tradition of the Upper Midwest and the Fort Ancient tradition of the Middle Ohio River region. The peoples led a semisedentary lifestyle, engaged in horticultural activities on a part-time basis for a basic, storable food supply, located their habitation sites on prominent flat elevations overlooking rivers and lakes, sometimes constructed low conical mounds for mortuary purposes, and manufactured relatively good pottery, small triangular projectile points, and end scrapers (McKern 1933:85, 1945:170). Pottery is the most definitive criterion used to establish the presence of an Upper Mississippi site. The typical clay vessel form is a wide-mouthed, grit- or shell-tempered jar, while Middle Mississippi cultures, like Cahokia in the American Bottom, produced a variety of shell-tempered forms. Problems would develop in interpreting cultural relationships when archaeologists attempted to lump the Upper Mississippian cultures as a single unit and insisted that they all must have a shared ancestry, probably from a Middle Mississippian cultural base, or heartland, and were geographically and culturally "marginal" or "peripheral" to the Cahokia cultural core with its hierarchical social organization, intensive horticultural subsistence strategies, prestige-goods economies, and temple mound and plaza complexes (Griffin 1943:302, 1960, 1967; Stoltman 1986; Stoltman and Baerreis 1983).

McKern's method had deliberately excluded problems of the antiquity and development of Oneota culture because there was little chronological control of the data (Boszhardt 1994:174; Willey and Sabloff 1974:112). At the time, there was a lack of deep refuse sites in the Midcontinent suitable for stratigraphical sequence dating, and the formulation of the Midwestern Taxonomic Method preceded radiocarbon dating (the carbon-14 technique for organic materials was first presented informally in 1950). These are basic tools in archaeology without which chronologies and sequences of events cannot be constructed.

The archaeologist's perception of "Oneota" has undergone continual revision. This is partly attributable to expanding collections of cultural material from archaeological site investigations with datable contexts. In search of statistical measures of truth, archaeologists have had to rely on small sample sizes of observations of artifacts to make inferences. Inferences become more accurate or more versatile with greater sample sizes. A sample statistic is only as reliable as the sample is large (Bailey 1987:80–81; Levin and Fox 1991:183). Thus, it was inevitable that, with the identification of more Oneota sites over a wider geographic area and cases of subsequent excavations, the increase in artifact sample sizes would result in increased variation in Oneota ceramic types, styles, and attributes as well as other aspects of material culture. Importantly, the accumulation of data would also highlight formal similarities or patterns between phases (foci) reflecting a shared culture history and *perhaps* cultural origins.

By 1960 archaeologists recognized that they needed to replace the static terminology of the Midwestern Taxonomic Method and the lumping of regional Oneota cultures within an "Upper Mississippi phase." Organizing the data by using this method contributed to confusion in the development of chronologies since it was devoid of any temporal or genetic meaning. At an Oneota conference convened at Columbia, Missouri, the participants (Robert T. Bray, Carl H. Chapman, Robert L. Hall, Dale R. Henning, Mildred Mott Wedel, and Waldo R. Wedel) determined that Oneota should be reinterpreted by adopting the terms "tradition" and "phase" to replace "aspect" and "focus," respectively. Thus, Robert Hall (1962) renamed the Oneota aspect as Oneota tradition, which was placed in a dynamic evolutionary framework by segmenting it sequentially into Emergent, Developmental, and Classic time horizons. A "horizon" is defined by Willey and Phillips (1958:33) "as *a primary spatial continuity represented by cultural traits and assemblages whose nature and mode of occurrence permit the assumption of a broad and rapid spread.* The archaeological units linked by a horizon are thus assumed to be *approximately* contemporaneous." Each horizon exhibits certain characteristics that are used to facilitate comparisons with other geographic areas and time periods. The panregional Oneota time horizon concept has enabled archaeologists to approach problems of origins, intergroup relationships, and development more systematically and directly (Boszhardt 1994; Overstreet 1997:255; Staeck 1995). John P. Staeck (1995:3) observes that "it still serves as the foundation for many of our current perspectives on Oneota."

Oneota can be viewed as a major or "full cultural tradition," the most inclusive archaeological unit on all developmental stages (Willey and Phillips 1958:48–51). Jennings (1974:9–10) refers to an archaeological culture as "the idea of the unity of, or similarity of, a series of site collections which seem to imply or to prove the existence of a widespread lifeway, involving the same level of technology and a shared exploitative or ecologic base." Chapman (1975:23) refers to an archaeological culture as "an arbitrary unit of cultural form placed in definite categories of space and time by reference to its preserved content and whatever of the common social and philosophical tradition that can be inferred therefrom." Although most archaeologists view Oneota as strictly an archaeological culture, I will show in this study that Oneota is truly a culture in the ethnographic sense with its set of learned behaviors, beliefs, attitudes, values, and ideals that are characteristic of a society.

There are a number of regional traditions that compose the Oneota cultural phenomenon. A "tradition" is conceptualized as a socially transmitted cultural form that exhibits both a long duration and extreme spatial fluidity (Willey and Phillips 1958:37–38). It is an integrative unit for expressing relationships between phases. Thus, a tradition has greater geographical and chronological dimensions than a phase. Willey and

Phillips (1958:22) define a "phase" as an archaeological unit, comparable ideally to a social unit in ethnography (comprising a number of communities), that emphasizes a very high degree of cultural similarity in a relatively small geographic area and in a relatively brief period of time. It is a manageable classificatory unit. This usage of the term conforms to its application by most American archaeologists (Chapman 1975:23–24; Willey 1971:3).

A major problem confronting Langford and Fisher research relates to the temporal framework used to define these regional manifestations, which involves using the terms "phase" and "tradition" interchangeably to define similar archaeological units. Both manifestations may be better defined as localized traditions within the major Oneota tradition. They could then be subdivided within an Emergent (ca. A.D. 950–1150) and Developmental (ca. A.D. 1150–1400) horizon time sequence (Table 1) as originally proposed for the Eastern Prairies region by Brown and Sasso (1992), which is comparable to those created for eastern Wisconsin (Hall 1962; Overstreet 1978, 1995, 1997), the La Crosse locality in southwestern Wisconsin (Boszhardt 1989), and the Mississippi Alluvial Plain of southeast Iowa (Henning 1995). The validity of the use of the horizon model for facilitating comparisons between regions can only be tested when published data on excavated Langford sites in northeastern Illinois become available and more Fisher sites are excavated, creating larger sample sizes. It is assumed that the dates for each horizon will vary slightly in northern Illinois and in other regions.

THEORETICAL APPROACHES TO THE STUDY OF ONEOTA: CHANGING PERSPECTIVES

The nature of Oneota culture in the Prairie Peninsula has been the subject of considerable debate among archaeologists advocating various schools of thought, including culture historical, processual, and post-processual approaches. In the continual development of the discipline, the different perspectives are based on variation in a dialectical understanding of the culture/nature and ideal/material distinctions. Time and circumstance have sharpened our perception of reality. Contemporary archaeologists are demonstrating through their research that Oneota and other Mississippian cultures were indeed open entities that actively interacted with one another and were continually transformed or re-created through such interaction. Thus, there is a stress on *cultural traditions* and the interactions of Native American peoples within the contexts of adaptations to the Prairie Peninsula cultural-biogeographical area that was originally pioneered by James A. Brown (1965). Archaeologists also have provided important chronological data (calibrated carbon-14 dates) to explore changes that took place in the Midcontinent through various communication channels and migrations of peoples.

Until the early 1970s, most Oneota research was oriented toward constructing a series of regional cultural chronologies, explaining the function of tools, and identifying regional art styles. Archaeologists held that "culture" comprised members sharing a configuration of behavior, language, technology, beliefs, values, and customs. Four problems figured prominently in the studies of this time. The first such problem involved defining the spatio-temporal distribution of Oneota cultural groups based on the presence or absence of material cultural traits, particularly ceramic styles and tempering agents. Second, there was a need to formulate alternative hypotheses concerning Oneota "origins" that involved either a Middle Mississippian migration from a particular core area like Cahokia in the American Bottom (without any real understanding of how migration worked as patterned behavior) followed by readaptation in a new environmental setting (Griffin 1960) or the *in situ* transformation of regional Late Woodland antecedents located on the hinterlands and frontier in response to specific external stimuli (e.g., political and economic pressures) from a single or multiple Upper Mississippi phase heartlands (heartland-hinterland-frontier or core-periphery models). Third, defining the Oneota economy within the contexts of an agriculturally marginal environment that determined culture. The Upper Mississippi River basin was seen as marginal because of the supposed limiting factors of either climate (Griffin 1967:15) or inaccessibility to year-round exploitation of floodplain resources due to flooding (Stoltman 1985:32), both adversely impacting horticultural pursuits. A fourth concern was the search for connections between Oneota phases and ethnographically "named" Native American groups, which have been rarely demonstrated (Emerson and Brown 1992:105–106; Staeck 1995:4–5). In the 1960s, there was little understanding of the dynamics of internal cultural development, so those problems were avoided. Archaeologists came to question the effectiveness of their empirical approaches, which often emphasized the classification of artifact types and construction of local chronologies or cultural sequences but did not expose and explore the dynamics of human behavior (Benn 1995; Ingersoll and Bronitsky 1987:9; Trigger 1986:208).

During the era of the New Archaeology (also called scientific archaeology, processual archaeology, or systems archaeology) extending from the late 1960s through the 1980s, most research efforts employed various analytical tools (many of them interdisciplinary) to model human populations as components of economic and ecological systems. The New Archaeology was largely a product of Lewis R. Binford, a very influential American archaeologist who transformed the discipline. The general goal was to link the static archaeological record with the dynamics of past human behavior through explicit description, hypothesis testing, and modeling (Binford 1965). Archaeology was to be like other natural sciences, proving to the public (and the National Science Foundation) its

Table 1.

Oneota Tradition chronological models for the Mississippi period.

NORTHERN ILLINOIS ONEOTA TRADITION
(Adapted from Brown and Sasso 1992)

Horizon (Time Scale)	Tradition/ Phase	Component	
CLASSIC (A.D. 1400-1650)	Huber	Anker	Fifield
		Hoxie Farm	
		Knoll Springs	Fisher
		Oak Forest	Huber
		Zimmerman	
		11CK105	Palos
		Comstock-Trace	Rader
		Griesmer	
DEVELOPMENTAL (A.D. 1150-1400)	Langford	Zimmerman	
		Washington Irving	
		Robinson Reserve	
		Noble-Weiting	
		Reeves	
		Gentleman Farm	
	Fisher	Griesmer	
		Fisher	
		Jehalo (11GR96)	
		Wymer?	
		Lawrence	
EMERGENT (A.D. 1000-1150)	Langford	Keeshin Farm	
		Material Service	
		Noble-Weiting	
		Zimmerman	
		Cooke	
	Fisher	Yahl	
		Moccasin Bluff	

WISCONSIN ONEOTA TRADITION
(from Overstreet 1998)

Horizon *(Time Scale)*	Phase	Locality
CLASSIC (A.D. 1350–1650)	LateBrice Prairie	La Crosse
	Pammel Creek	La Crosse
	Valley View	La Crosse
	Late Koshkonong	Lake Koshkonong
	Lake Winnebago	Middle Fox River Passageway
	Green Bay	Door Peninsula
	Lake Winnebago	Door Peninsula
DEVELOPMENTAL (A.D. 1150–1350)	Early Brice Prairie	La Crosse
	Grand River	Middle Fox River Passageway
	Adams *(Blue Earth–like)*	Lake Pepin
	Green Bay	Door Peninsula
	Mero Complex *(Late)*	Door Peninsula
EMERGENT (A.D. 950–1150)	Silvernale	Lake Pepin
	Early Koshkonong	Lake Koshkonong
	McKern	Middle Fox River Passageway
	Mero Complex *(Early)*	Door Peninsula

usefulness by predicting human behavior patterns and formulating laws. It was Science with a capital "S" as the discipline sought intellectual power and prestige associated with objective knowledge relevant to the modern world (Shanks and Tilley 1992:31). But the approaches sometimes appeared obsessed with statistics (i.e., precisely measuring nutrient requirements of human populations, edible meat weight yields, number of person-hours dedicated to an activity, population density, and input/output fluxes of the ecosystem) hoping that rigorous measurement could guarantee irrefutable precision in data interpretation. Many archaeologists chose an emotionally detached and antihistorical attitude toward their data, thus ignoring the importance of social, religious, and political action in human history. Native American peoples were treated as *objects* rather than *subjects* worthy of research (Marquardt 1992; Trigger 1980). The New Archaeologists waived their right to include religion, gender, cosmology, and ideology in their models.

With the neoevolutionary perspective of culture as an "extrasomatic means of adaptation" (White 1959:8) advocated by the New Archaeologists, cultural change was interpreted as a behavioral response to environmental conditions (see Binford and Binford 1968; Fritz and Plog 1970; LeBlanc 1973; Reidhead 1981; Watson et al. 1971). They were indifferent to concepts of migration and diffusion, interpreting similarities between populations as simply adaptations to similar natural environments, with societal interaction perceived as minimal and restricted. Cultures were often analyzed as isolated, tightly integrated, and clearly bounded systems (Trigger 1984:279–280). In settlement-subsistence pattern studies, the catchment area (habitats within a particular radius of a site) became the primary unit of analysis, thus neglecting whole "core" regions or culture areas. Regarding migration, David W. Anthony (1990:895) has stated that "systems-oriented archeologists, in rejecting migration, have thrown out the baby with the bathwater." They did not incorporate the movement of peoples into their explanation of culture change because of its apparent unpredictability and the difficulty of tracking it archaeologically (Adams et al. 1978; Anthony 1990).

Researchers of Oneota societies did make significant progress in delineating adaptations to various environments throughout the Prairie Peninsula, which included systematic surveys within regions, subsistence analyses of individual sites, and site territory (catchment) analyses to make predictions concerning food-procuring strategies associated with each settlement (a series of concentric catchments are sometimes used that are roughly circular, with radii of 1, 2, 3, 4, or 5 km, and encompass a variety of habitat types with resources closest to the settlement thought to have been procured first by the inhabitants) (Birmingham 1975; Gibbon 1982; Stevenson 1985). Their results indicated that Oneota subsistence strategies were successful within a wide range of environments having the same suite of essential resources from upland, prairie, and wetland habitats (Brown 1982). However, the interpretations regarding human behavior were sometimes flawed by misapplying optimal foraging models. Researchers viewed such human adaptations as an optimal mixture of hunting, gathering, and horticulture within artificially bounded systems that were pursued in a rational manner by societies to maintain homeostasis (analogous to any organism). It was generally understood that individuals sought to maximize or optimize resource exploitation and utilization with the least effort and risk under the Principle of Least Effort (see Roper 1979:11–12). Keene (1983:145) notes that there is a major problem with this assumption: "The investigative framework becomes both teleological (adaptive systems seek optimal levels of performance) and tautological (optimal behavior is adaptive behavior; all creatures optimize, and it is our task to figure out what they are optimizing)." Unintentionally or not, flesh-and-blood peoples were being equated with wild animals living in a home range or territory, "that area traversed by the individual in its normal activities of food gathering, mating, and caring for the young" (Vaughn 1986:321). Humans were just another biological population seeking their niche in the ecosystem (White 1984:184).

There has been a theoretical revolt against established archaeological scientific thought because of its lack of success in improving the quality of archaeological explanation. This movement of mostly British and some American archaeologists was led primarily by Ian Hodder and is usually referred to as "postprocessualism." It places much more emphasis on studying the symbolic and cognitive life of past peoples than did earlier approaches. Hodder states, "Culture and mind contribute something; we don't just respond to the environment the way animals do" (Balter 1998:1444). Postprocessualism also rests on an openness to other avenues and perspectives that "see" the same world in different ways (pluralism), thus escaping the monoculture of modern Western science. Archaeologists acknowledge biases in their research that may reflect a personal ideological stance, sampling techniques, or inherent shortcomings in the archaeological record due to differential preservation of organic remains. The discipline attempts to avoid ethnocentric interpretations by being more sensitive to Native American issues, as experienced by the Native American Graves Protection and Repatriation Act (NAGPRA) and the ethical debate over Indian mascots at universities, so that we might bridge the differences between peoples. Meanwhile, feminists have identified myriad instances of gender (the cultural values inscribed on sex) bias that have persisted in the archaeological discipline in the name of "good science" or "science as usual" (Wylie 1998:64–65), which must be overcome if we are to know anything definite about the past or human behavior. As a result, some archaeologists, like David W. Benn (1995:92–93), have encouraged other researchers to explain cultural interaction as the actions of people, not artifacts, and to focus on the vital role women played in community activities.

It must be noted that the postprocessual movement is not all that new or revolutionary, just as the New Archaeology was not. Will C. McKern (1956:360–361) made a very provocative statement (a challenge to archaeologists) in his review of Willey and Phillips's (1955) "Method and Theory in American Archeology":

> We are attempting to reconstruct realistically the actual cultural status in the history of a departed people, employing every source of information available to us, whether archeological, geological, ethnological, historical, or available from other humanly formulated disciplines. We are after "historical reality," not just that portion of the picture which can be reconstructed from data secured by means of the archeological approach.

For better or worse, archaeology is often a political enterprise, one that is engaged in creating a past that is thought to be expedient for, or dictated by, present interests. Today, anthropological archaeologists are trying to implement a holistic approach by uniting two worlds: the humanities, which lie at the cultural center of Western civilization, and the natural sciences, which have always been perceived as a bit outside society's inner circle (Kepecs 1997). There is a stark realization that modern science cannot solve all of our problems. Science offers no security, for there are no absolute truths about the real world. As the evolutionary biologist Edward O. Wilson (1998:2049) states, "The time has come to look at ourselves closely as a biological as well as a cultural species using all the intellectual tools we can muster." This new sense of interconnectedness is applicable to our search for an understanding of Oneota culture, an interconnectedness that the archaeologist Will C. McKern acknowledged decades ago.

RESEARCH OBJECTIVES

The word *culture* has been used differently by archaeologists over time. In contrast to the passivity of culture associated with the normative or adaptationist approaches, culture is now viewed as human action embedded in an individual's interaction and social negotiation with other people in his or her kin or lineage group or with other societies (Hodder 1992). Cultures are perceived as open entities with fluid group boundaries. The structuring principles of society are continually reproduced, negotiated, and transformed through cultural interaction (Nassaney and Sassaman 1995) along with human-environment reciprocal relationships couched within the cosmology of the society. Natural resource management and use are socially constructed and culturally mediated (Hastorf and Johannessen 1991). As such, they can be considered the statistical outcome of numerous individual decisions, some of which worked while others failed (Trigger 1989).

This study attempts to provide a better understanding of the dynamism and creativity of Oneota culture in the Prairie Peninsula by examining relations of power among Fisher and Langford peoples occupying the Middle Rock River region of northern Illinois. It is important to explain cultural similarities and differences that better fit archaeological, ethnohistorical, and ethnographic data applicable within the contexts of the "culture area" (Prairie Peninsula), regional (Middle Rock River), and local (Lawrence and Keeshin Farm) scales of analysis. Cultural development and identity were predicated on their individual histories occurring within local and extralocal spatial dimensions (Cobb and Nassaney 1995; Lightfoot and Martinez 1995). Cultural interaction will be examined primarily through ceramic vessel and faunal data recovered from feature contexts at the Lawrence (Fisher phase) and Keeshin Farm (Langford tradition) sites (Figure 2), which are both riverine habitation sites. The data are used with comparative Oneota assemblages to examine interactions of men and women, of people with the environment, and of people with the supernatural, which are viewed as occurring within the context of historical conditions that constrain and facilitate human action.

An analysis of ceramic vessels from the Lawrence and Keeshin Farm sites is critical to understanding power among Oneota societies. Household ceramics served both as utilitarian objects and as a medium of communication (Braun 1991). This study addresses three primary questions using vessels. First, what are the patterns or trends in the attributes of vessels within and between Oneota assemblages, and how do they compare to those of other cultures? Second, what kind of messages were conveyed by a particular artistic style? Style refers to the specific artistic character (i.e., the unique way component elements of art are combined) and dominant form trends noted during specific periods of history (Ocvirk et al. 1968:5; Rosman and Rubel 1995:239). Third, who were the artists creating powerful imagery on Oneota ceramics, and how did they receive their inspiration?

In this study, analyses of faunal remains from Lawrence and Keeshin Farm, both located in similar ecological settings, are used to determine the similarities and differences in Fisher and Langford exploitation and utilization behavior. It has often been assumed that Oneota cultures practiced a broad-spectrum subsistence strategy with a focus on aquatic/wetland resources. Using this investigation as a case study, taxonomic abundance is measured by ratio and ordinal scales (or levels across faunal samples) using the number of identified specimens per taxon (NISP). This informationn is used in concert with analyses of taphonomic agents to examine late prehistoric diet breadth. Because variability at sites may be reflected in local resource availability, subsistence strategy, site function, and/or a group's interaction with other societies couched within Oneota cosmology, these factors are examined as part of the investigation of patterns in faunal exploitation and utilization practices.

The primary objective of this work is to interpret and explore the dimension of "power relations" in the small-scale, kin-based Oneota societies. Power is not a metrically measurable quantity (Barnes 1988:63), and so its study was avoided by the New Archaeologists. The concept of power is viewed in a very generalized sense as a force that, throughout societal history, permeates social relationships and the practices of everyday life (Bell 1992:204; Black-Rogers 1988:45; Foucault 1983; Jones and Porter 1994:117; Tilley 1993:199). In other words, it is largely embedded in routines and organized interaction (Barnes 1988). Power, as stated by Hodder (1991:39), "is not simply a 'thing' that is wielded by those in certain positions within social structures but is a relational process whereby structures (of various forms) are actively brought into play in relation to events." Power relations revolve around the ambiguity, insecurity, and uncertainty associated with access to social and natural resources along with esoteric knowledge (Bean 1992; Upham 1990:11). This interpretation is also given by Arens and Karp (1989:xii): "The concept of 'power' as it is used by all peoples encodes ideas about the nature of the world, social relations, and the effects of actions in and on the world and the entities that inhabit it." It is power in a positive sense involved in creating, shaping, and molding individuals. Power continually acts on individuals, who are its *subjects* (Barker 1993:78). To explore power is to explore principles of freedom (in the sense of accessible options) and, thus, resistance to domination (Bell 1992:201). As a result, archaeologists are challenged to view power in terms of its heterogeneous nature in which all men and women have "power over" others as well as the "power to" (as a transformative capacity) alter or intervene in a given set of events (Hodder 1992:258–259; Klein and Ackerman 1995; Miller 1989; Paynter and McGuire 1991:6–7), as in the power to transmit and receive resources through kinship or the power to enforce some rules and not others. One may associate the heterogeneity of power with social regulation within the cultural tradition (consensus, social norms) and resistance to it.

The term *hegemony* has sometimes been used by archaeologists to interpret Cahokia relations of power in the Midwest during Mississippian times (see Pauketat 1994; Pauketat and Emerson 1997), but it will not be used here. Hegemony is a slippery term that was used widely by the Italian communist Antonio Gramsci in the early twentieth century to revise previous Marxist theory related to domination. Gramsci argued that controlling public institutions and the press (historical blocs) in modern capitalist societies enabled those in power to exercise hegemony over others without actually, formally ruling them. From this insight, it was off to the races (Frederick E. Hoxie, personal communication, 1998; Lears 1985). Undoubtedly every organized society is directed by a hegemonic group. However, historians and political theorists warn that hegemony should *not* be used in a narrow, restrictive sense in which elites, as individuals, exercise cultural as well as economic and political power over an entire society (Barnes 1988:6; Bell 1992:198; Jones and Porter 1994:117; Lears 1985:579; Villa 1992:713) and ideology is simply a tool of the dominant classes (Balkin 1998:111–121; Bell 1992:188–192).

CHAPTER TWO

Cultural Comparisons

Historical Reality

A review of some of the salient attributes of Oneota culture is now in order, focusing on sociopolitical organization, sexual division of labor, cosmology, dreams and visions, material culture traditions, settlement-subsistence strategies, mortuary ritual, reciprocal exchange systems, and evidence for warfare. Through these and related elements, one can gain an understanding of what "Oneota" represents, in terms of widespread regional similarities, before examining the similarities and differences in Fisher and Langford cultures. In cases regarding sexual division of labor, cosmology, dreams, mortuary ritual, and exchange systems, the ethnohistoric and ethnographic analogues regarding human culture generally, and tribal societies specifically, are presumed to hold for the prehistoric past within the contexts of historicity or cultural continuity through time and space (Native American cultural traditions) and cultural universals that exist despite immense behavioral diversity (see Arnold 1988:6–8; Bock 1974:430–434; Grieder 1975; Leach 1976; Levi-Strauss 1963; Murdock 1955:4–5; Redfield 1952). The cross-cultural similarities are found within a uniform system of power relations, involving people engaged in patterned behaviors motivated by common beliefs in their relations to the world around them, including other peoples and the supernatural.

SOCIOPOLITICAL ORGANIZATION: A TRIBAL WORLD

Oneota societies consisted of various forms of tribal sociopolitical organization (Benn 1989; Gibbon 1972;

Hall 1991; Kreisa 1993; Stevenson 1985). A tribe is an uncentralized, nonhierarchical political structure in which decisions affecting the community occur primarily through consensus established from a network of individual and group relations (Braun and Plog 1982; Ember and Ember 1990:391; Lewellen 1983:24–26). It may consist of an intermarrying group of bands sharing a common language and culture, like the numerous independent bands making up the Sioux and other Plains "tribes" (Bodley 1994; Rosman and Rubel 1995:302). The bands were united by kinship ties as well as common traditions and rituals so that the members could think of themselves as part of the same "people." Among many Native American tribal societies, there were different kinds of leaders for different types of activities, such as war, peace, hunting, and ceremonial. But there was no centralized leadership and no formal political offices. Power relations cut across various dimensions of society including lineage or clan groupings, gender, and age categories (Cobb and Nassaney 1995). In some tribes, a village council of elders would make decisions after a process of public debate leading to consensus (Lewellen 1983:26).

Power is manifest in the concept of "general will" in places where men and women are relatively equal (Bonhage-Freund and Kurland 1994:297, 301; Cobb 1993:50–52; Trigger 1990; Upham 1990:11) and involved in "holding to" ways of being and relating through traditions (Bender 1990). William H. Marquardt (1992:106) states that power and authority may be available to all individuals to influence events or achieve desired goals. Thus, ultimate power is vested in each individual, as choice maker, seeking to fulfill personal aspirations and perceived needs. People act on their desires, with knowledge of what they want to achieve and a firm belief about how to achieve their goals. Their actions may often be for the benefit of the group as a collective without any thought of self (altruistic behavior) or, sometimes, be based on purely selfish motives (Sober and Wilson 1998). Attempts to dominate at the expense of one's neighbor are usually thwarted by pressure from other members of the group and a set of social norms that define the dos and don'ts of the society. Decisions are shared among members of any given group so that each member will be in the same boat with respect to survival and reproduction.

Permanent positions of status and leadership based on ascription are absent in tribal societies. Instead, leadership is gained through certain personal qualities: charisma, strength, generosity, oratorical skills, hard work, valor, fair-mindedness, capabilities (a leader's strategy set and information about the strategies of followers), wisdom, and the right granted in a dream (Rosman and Rubel 1995:40, 166–167; Skinner 1914:482–484, 507; Tooker 1964:47). This concept is expressed in the anthropologist John N. B. Hewitt's (1911:263) definition for *chief:*

Among the North American Indians a chief may be generally defined as a political officer whose distinctive functions are to execute the ascertained will of a definite group of persons united by the possession of a common territory or range and of certain exclusive rights, immunities, and obligations, and to conserve their customs, traditions, and religion. He exercises legislative, judicative, and executive powers delegated to him in accordance with custom for the conservation and promotion of the common weal.

According to the ethnologist/linguist Horatio Hale (1963:68):

In general, among nearly all the tribes, the rank of chief was personal. It was gained by the character and achievements of the individual, and it died with him. Hence their government and policy, so far as they can be said to have had any, were always uncertain and fluctuating.

A leader's strength does not necessarily refer to aggressiveness or physical strength, like being a great warrior or hunter. The importance of dream experiences cannot be overemphasized as a source of "real" power or strength among Native American societies (Darnell 1988:77). Leadership has no secular sanctions. Referring to dreams, the anthropologist A. Irving Hallowell (1934:398) states that, among the Northern Ojibway, "A man would be practically helpless without them, particularly if he aspires to leadership in certain ceremonies, conjuring, curing or to special prowess in hunting." Hallowell (1947:554) also points out that among Native American peoples:

Human beings are conceived as being in constant need of help from birth to death. So essential is such help that no performance of any kind is interpreted as due to an individual's own abilities or efforts. Leadership, too, always is the result of bestowed blessings. Furthermore, in neither myth, tale nor tradition is there evidence of a human being who left his mark upon the world, who made any discovery, or who invented anything.

In terms of generosity, nineteenth-century tribal leaders of the Plains were noted for redistributing most of their own products and labor for the common good so they were left with prestige alone. For example, extreme generosity was a common attribute among leaders of the Plains Ojibway (Skinner 1914:482), the Plains Cree (Skinner 1914:518), and the Ioway (Skinner 1915:684). The early ethnographers joked that identifying a chief in some Indian villages was easy: they just looked for the poorest person (Ember and Ember 1990:282, 394).

Tribal leadership roles have often been described as positions of negotiation, because of their importance in initiating and maintaining external alliances and trade relations as well as in mediating disputes between self-interested individuals for the economic and social well-being of the community (Bianco and Bates 1990; Bonhage-Freund and Kurland 1994; Tooker 1964:47). These concerns were essential for maintaining a balance of power among entire villages (Lewellen 1983). In addition to these duties, Native American leaders performed a variety of other tasks. They organized feasts and subsistence activities, hosted guests, contributed to decisions regarding warfare, supervised community chores, sponsored ceremonies, coordinated migration movements of the tribe, and stored information concerning territorial boundaries and genealogical histories (Feinman and Neitzel 1984; Langdon 1992:15).

SEXUAL DIVISION OF LABOR: SEPARATE BUT EQUAL

Sexual division of labor is practiced by all tribal societies (Driver 1961:179; Ember and Ember 1990:272; Lewellen 1983:25; Wing and Brown 1979:12), although there can be some degree of flexibility. In a sexually segregated task system, both male and female actors may have access to knowledge and materials unavailable to the opposite sex (Spector 1998:156). The story of Native American gender roles of power, influence, and authority can be largely perceived as "separate but equal," where different roles are expected of men and women by social norms yet neither men's roles nor women's roles can be considered superior. Complementarity, or gender interdependence, would be necessary to achieve social goals. Hence, there is a theme of balanced reciprocity creating harmony in society (Benn 1995; Klein and Ackerman 1995:14). For example, Horatio Hale (1963:65) reported that among the Iroquois "the work of the community and the cares of the family are fairly divided."

Although there is no "methodological breakthrough" for precise gender attribution in division of labor and relations of production in the archaeological record, two primary types of data used by archaeologists include ethnographic analogy (i.e., using data on contemporary tribal societies to make inferences about aspects of prehistoric societies) and the ethnohistoric records compiled by traders, explorers, and missionaries (see Costin 1996:116–121). Perhaps most underused by researchers is the cross-cultural data from the Human Relations Area Files compiled by George Murdock and Caterina Provost (1973), which scored fifty activities by gender participation among a sample of 185 societies worldwide to indicate whether activities were best characterized as "masculine" or "feminine." Their results indicated a strong sexual division of labor, especially among tribal societies.

Among Oneota peoples, we can infer that men did most of the hunting and fishing, butchering, quarrying, metalworking, land clearing, raiding, boatbuilding, housebuilding, and work in bone, horn, shell, and wood. Women were engaged in such activities as pottery production, cooking, gardening, shellfishing, hideworking, preservation of meat and fish, burying the dead, child care, and producing everyday items such as clothing from common raw materials (Benn 1995). The assignment of these tasks by gender appear to be supported by eastern North American ethnohistoric sources (see Blair 1912:212–213, 217; Callender 1978:637–638; Densmore 1928:306; Hale 1963:65; Kinietz 1940:171, 173, 236–237, 283, 407; Neill 1884; Pond 1986; Radin 1923:113, 177; Spindler 1967:604; Swanton 1979:710, 715, 717; Tooker 1964:58–59; Trigger 1969:30; Turner 1894:203, 205; Vehik 1977:171). The archaeologist Mary Whelan (1993:247) makes a very important point regarding past Western ethnocentric attitudes toward Native American gender roles in agricultural activities: "Individuals initiate action and respond to others based on culturally learned expectations for normal interactions. For example, Euro-Americans in Minnesota frequently tried to get Dakota men to take up agriculture, an attempt that met with only mixed success in part because farming was gendered female in Dakota culture."

There are instances of "swing roles," or activities done by both men and women in tribal societies. Although formal political offices were usually held by men, there is evidence that women held formal leadership roles among the Miami and Shawnee (Callender 1978:617). Also, although a shaman (a healer, medicine person, or interpreter of dreams) is commonly thought of as male, women also became shamans, as among the Omaha (Dorsey 1883:274), the Huron (Kinietz 1940:132), and other small-scale societies (Rosman and Rubel 1995:203). According to Roland B. Dixon (1908:2), "The position of shaman may equally well be obtained as a result of individual initiative [versus inheritance], the man or woman seeking to acquire the gift, the position being regarded as open to all."

Women appear to have exerted "real" power in the community through their management of household activities. According to Thomas Forsyth (quoted in Blair 1912:218), "It is a maxim among the Indians that every thing belong to the woman or women except the Indian's hunting and war implements, even the game, the Indians bring home on his back. As soon as it enters the lodge, the man ceases to have anything to say in its disposal." Horatio Hale (1963:65) stated that, among the Iroquois, "The household goods belonged to the woman. On her death, her relatives, and not her husband, claimed them. The children were also hers; they belonged to her clan, and in case of separation they went with her. She was really the head of the household." Citing the missionary Samuel W. Pond's work among the Dakota (or Sioux) in Minnesota in 1834, Mary Whelan (1993:247) also noted this power: "Dakota women's ownership of 'family' tipis and the onerous nature of many of their tasks puzzled Euro-Americans because it challenged their Western gender system." In the household context, one can assume that women were also powerful advisors (Griffin 1992:57; Underhill 1971:91).

The gender activities in Fisher and Langford societies were probably similar and so could be viewed as "separate but equal" work. Each task required numerous individual decisions concerning natural resource management and use, and interaction with others was necessary for cultural reproduction and the balance of the world.

COSMOLOGY: EXPERIENCING A WORLD IN BALANCE

Native North Americans have had a clear conception of the cosmos (referring to the way people view themselves and their surrounding world in cultural terms), the interrelationship of humans and "other beings," the nature of spirit and power, and of life and death, which has developed (with cultural variation) over thousands of years of living, dreaming, and thinking about the natural world and their place *within* it (Berlo and Phillips 1998:21; Furst and Furst 1982). Nature and the supernatural constitute a single intricate system of entities that humans cannot fully confront or have "power over." There is a pervading attitude that an individual must work with nonhuman nature, not against it (Darnell 1988; Feest 1986:7; Hallowell 1934:399; James 1927:341; Johnston 1995; Jones 1905; Redfield 1952). To Native American peoples, the cosmos consisted of animals, plants, rocks, physical objects, fire, and other phenomena thought to have life and to be inhabited by a supernatural spirit (mystery, essence, substance, invisible reality, sacred universal power). The spirit or impersonal power was known by different names among the historic groups: *manitowi (manitou, manito)* by the Algonquian, *orenda* by the Iroquoian, *pokunt* by the Shoshonean, and *wakanda, waka^n, mahopa,* or *xube* by the Siouan tribes, *sulia* by the Salish, *naualak* by the Kwakiutl, *tamanoas* by the Chinook, and *shai* by the Zuni (Boas 1910a:366; Gill and Sullivan 1992:227; Hewitt 1902:37; James 1927; Underhill 1957:128; Wallace 1966:61). Each spirit- or life-giving power was fully capable of helping or hurting people (Riggs 1883; Spence 1911:503–504; Wright 1987:3), often appearing in dreams and vision quests to give special power or protection. Thus, humans were required to maintain proper conduct toward the environment in order to ward off evil forces, to seek assistance, and to keep the cosmos in balance. In the writings of Luther Standing Bear (1868–1939), a Lakota chief, was the uncertainty of nature: "Nature dealt vigorously with the Lakota. . . . The mental reaction of the Lakota was one of unity with these tremendous forces" (DeMallie 1988:8).

Native American tribal society activities may be perceived as scenes and acts in a drama where tension, uncertainty, and ambiguity occur in dichotomous relationships such as culture/nature, tradition/change, good/bad, pure/contaminated, visible/invisible, human/nonhuman, order/chaos, and life/death. With the recognition that humans are mortal and death imminent, religion was born to deny death and to establish a mediating bridge (exercised by shamans or through transcendent beings) between "this world" of humans and the "other world," where omnipotent "other beings" exist. Ritual practices built on human experience, thought, and action provided a means of sociocultural integration, appropriation, or transformation. They were structured around the resolution of such dualistic contrasts as those listed above (Bell 1992:16, 226), providing moments of reunion and reconnection of things, beings, and spheres of existence. Ritual performance is an expression of the principle of reciprocity (to receive benefits one has to give) (Leach 1976:83) between the individual and the supernatural, and thus it provides a share of sacred power. For example, Plains and Eastern Woodlands peoples offered sacrifices so that they could obtain a dream or vision experience, which mediated a sense of transcendent power (Harrod 1987:22–23).

A common feature of Native American worldviews within any given community is the way they "map" space. Each individual strives to attain and maintain a place at the center of an ordered universe of meaningful relations—a vertical, three-tiered cosmos with a middleworld (the world of human existence) suspended below an upperworld (sky world) and above an underworld (see Barbeau 1914:289–290; Bean 1992; Curtis 1952:177; Gillespie 1993; Pauketat and Emerson 1991:926; Penney 1985:180; Sampson 1988; Sullivan 1988; Taylor 1991:67–68). The upperworld and underworld compose the "otherworld," which is beyond daily (mundane) experience and so functions as a realm of supernatural forces, inhabited by distinctive, immensely powerful "sacred beings" (Bean 1992:27; Leach 1976:71). This "complementary dualism" of other- and middle-world systems is typical of most Eastern Woodlands and Plains societies (Penney 1985:180, 183). They are separate but equal spiritual domains where ultimate power resides.

There are many versions of the vertically stratified universe theme found throughout North America. For example, the Menominee believed in a universe divided into three regions: the upperworld, inhabited by the Powers Above, or "benevolent" spirits under the domination of the Great Spirit, Matc Hawatuk (which was probably the Sun until missionary influence), whose main servants were the mythical celestial birds, the thunderbirds, and the Sun and Morning Star; the underworld, inhabited by the Powers Below, or "malevolent" spirits under the domination of the Great White Bear, whose main servants were the giant Underground Panther, the White Deer, and the Horned Hairy Serpent; and "this earth" of humans, where good and bad forces struggle for domination (Skinner 1913:73–85, 1921:29–33). Also, the Mascoutens, or Prairie Potawatomi (Skinner 1924:46–47), along with the Sac (Skinner 1923:34–35), recognized an upperworld associated with the Sun (the Great Spirit) and the thunderbird; an underworld associated with a monstrous, horned-creature, the Underwater Panther; and the earth of humans sometimes personified as an old woman, "Our Grandmother."

Southeastern Native American societies acknowledged the three-tiered cosmos: the upperworld was an orderly and secure place where Sun and Moon deities existed; the underworld where disorder, monsters, and anxiety rule; and the central world where humans live, a place somewhere between complete order and chaos (Hudson 1976:122). The perpetual struggle or state of war existing between "sacred beings" of the upperworld and underworld will be discussed in greater detail in chapter 8.

Among the Plains and Woodland groups, the earthly space of human beings was often conceived as a flat, two-dimensional circle (within a sphere) that was divided into quadrants identified with the four cardinal directions of north, south, east, and west (or sometimes semicardinal directions) and with winds that blow from these directions bringing seasonal changes. They also included zenith (as upperworld), nadir (as underworld), and center to designate meaningful correlations (Berlo and Phillips 1998:22; Furst and Furst 1982:16; Gill and Sullivan 1992:68; Nagy 1994; Powers 1981). For example, the Berens River Ojibway of Manitoba and northwestern Ontario quartered their world through the identification of the four cardinal directions with the winds (Hallowell 1934:391) and identified a sky world on the basis of the movements of the sun and directional orientation of the North Star (Hallowell 1992:74). Alanson Skinner (1926:220) notes that the Ioway also divided the earth into the cardinal directions while adding the zenith, a sky world where Wa-kan-da (God or thunder) exists in heaven, and the nadir, an underworld that was the home of Mother Earth.

Throughout North America, the three worlds of sky, earth, and underworld were linked by a central, vertical axis that provided a path or access to other cosmic realms of being (Berlo and Phillips 1998:22). In other words, it served to connect one to the energy and power of the supernatural upper and underworlds, which ultimately could make them of one mind. The axis is a mediator and unites the visible and invisible worlds, or ordinary and nonordinary reality, providing a sense of order by placing the individual and the community in a specific time-space frame in relation to the very center of the universe. Several forms are used to symbolize this central, vertical axis, including a giant tree (cosmic tree of life), an offering pole often made of cedar or cottonwood (exemplified by the center pole of the nineteenth-century Sun Dance circular ground found among Plains and Plateau tribes), or a ritual plume of smoke wafting upward from a hearth near a human burial or a central location in the community, or from a sacred pipe (Berlo and Phillips 1998:22; Furst and Furst 1982:17; Lincoln 1994; Mansfield 1981; Ridington and Ridington 1970; Sullivan 1988). These concepts of unity or "oneness" with the cosmos were reflected in Native American ritual activity, especially dream and vision experiences and mortuary ritual.

DREAMS AND VISIONS AS ACCESS TO SUPERNATURAL POWER

In Native American tribal societies, dream and vision experiences were common ways of gaining access to the powers of the supernatural world and were viewed as important experiences in the individual's life by providing both a guardian spirit and the determining factors in the individual's role in community life (Berlo and Phillips 1998:25; Boas 1910a:368; Densmore 1950; DeMallie 1988; Feest 1986:12–16; Gill and Sullivan 1992:73; Levinson 1996:55–58). Theirs was an art of *making use of dreams* to experience insights into the universe and a unity with all things. Many Plains and Eastern Woodlands groups engaged in the well-known vision or dream quest, a solitary fasting ritual done often as a puberty rite (as entrance to maturity) in the quest for wisdom, strength, good fortune, and power. The person was asking for help in finding a future path or solving a major unresolved emotional problem. The quest required preparation by the elders and incubation of visions by food, water, and sleep deprivation or sometimes bodily mutilation (self-torture) and mild hallucinogens. During the vision, a supernatural being would visit to act as a guardian spirit or helper, which sometimes came in the form of a powerful animal (e.g., bear, eagle, falcon, raven, panther, or bison) (Rosman and Rubel 1995:198). The interpretation of such important dreams took place in the normal waking state before community members because it was a socially significant act (Hartmann 1998; Levinson 1996:57; Sullivan 1986).

Visions and sleep dreaming could reveal the unconscious wishes or desires of the dreamer as well as of the supernatural beings that appeared in the individual's dream (Wallace 1958). Importantly, they could give each individual psychological and spiritual guidance, creative inspiration, and responsibilities necessary for conducting oneself across those difficult thresholds of transformation (e.g., death of a loved one) that demand a change in the patterns of conscious and unconscious life, thus giving one's life cohesion and meaning (see Densmore 1950; Hartmann 1998:234–235; Piotrowski and Biele 1986; Stewart 1997). Simply put, the dream can pull together available material from a person's past experiences, likes, dislikes, wishes, and fears (the dreamer's emotional concerns) and come up with an image or series of pictures that may help make sense of the problems one encounters each day (Hartmann 1998:235). Most psychoanalysts agree that dreams offer each individual the freedom to define, to explain to others, and to clarify personal or community problems.

The power bestowed by supernatural beings could be for good or bad. Power could arrive in dreams in the form of ideas for decorating pottery vessels or other objects, songs, dances, shamanistic techniques, success in battle or the hunt, or "career opportunities." For example, dreams provided the inspiration for creative ritual performances of song and dance in the well-known Calumet, or Pipe of Peace Dance, found in various forms among the Arikara, Dakota, Kansa, Omaha, Osage, Oto, Pawnee, Plains Cree, and Wichita (Hall 1987, 1997; Skinner 1915:706–709) as well as the Ghost Dance and Sun Dance ceremonies performed in various forms by nineteenth-century Plains and Plateau tribes (Gill and Sullivan 1992:100–101, 291–292; Lienhardt 1968:444; Lincoln 1994; Underhill 1971). The religious performances were held in the common belief that they would "bring an ideal world into being." Dreams also provided the inspiration for the manufacture of richly decorated sacred medicine bundles as found among the Ioway (Skinner 1915:692–693), Sac and Fox (Harrington 1914:132–133), and Kansa (Skinner 1915:753). On the dark side, the significance of the dream for the individual could be judged bad, unfavorable, or impure by its content and, partially, by its effects on the dreamer. Dreams may connect frustration, illness, or bad luck to angered or offended supernatural beings who appeared during dream life.

The topic of dreams and visions in Native American tribes is presented in a large body of literature encompassing tremendous diversity in ethnic, geographic, and historical backgrounds (see Beauchamp 1895; Benedict 1922; Black Elk and Lyon 1991; Brinton 1868:279–280; Bunzel 1982; Callender 1978a:639, 643; Densmore 1929:78–86; Dorsey 1894:395, 510; Driver 1961:470–472; Dugan 1985; Hallowell 1992:84–87; Hewitt 1895; Hultkrantz 1986; Johnston 1995; Jones 1905:187; Kelsey 1992; La Flesche 1889; Lame Deer and Erdoes 1972; Neihardt 1979; Rosman and Rubel 1995:197–198; Skinner 1913:47; Spindler 1967:601; Steltenkamp 1993; Sullivan 1988; Trigger 1969:119–120; Turner 1894:272; Wallace 1958, 1972; White 1949:179–181; Whitten 1985:134–136; Yarrow 1881:95). Such studies prove that this widespread practice was not an irrational superstition. The central importance of dream and vision experiences in Eastern Woodlands and Plains societies is clearly reflected in the following studies of the Ojibway, Seneca, Mandan, and Menominee. Francis Densmore (1929:78) quotes an elderly Ojibway informant:

> In the old days our people had no education. They could not learn from books nor from teachers. All their wisdom and knowledge came to them in dreams. They tested their dreams, and in that way learned their own strength. . . . Try to dream and to remember what you dream.

In a case study of the Northern Ojibway, A. Irving Hallowell (1967:228) states:

> Dream experiences function integrally with other recalled memory images in so far as these, too, enter the field of self-awareness. When we think autobiographically we only include events that happened to us when awake;

the Ojibwa include remembered events that have occurred in dreams. And, far from being of subordinate importance, such experiences are for them often of more vital importance than the events of daily waking life. Why is this so? Because it is in dreams that the individual comes into direct communication with the *atiso'kanak,* the powerful "persons" of the other-than-human class.

Anthony F. C. Wallace (1958:245) reports that among the seventeenth-century Seneca:

> dreams showed powerful supernatural beings who usually spoke personally to the dreamer, giving him a message of importance for himself and often also for the whole community. . . . Dreams are not to brood over, to analyze, and to prompt lonely and independent action; they are to be told, or at least hinted at, and it is for other people to be active. The community rallies round the dreamer with gifts and ritual. The dreamer is fed; he is danced over; he is rubbed with ashes; he is sung to; he is given valuable presents.

For the Mandan, according to the Reverend James Owen Dorsey (1894:510):

> Dreams afford the motives for many of their actions, even for the penances which they impose on themselves. . . . In many cases the guardian spirit is revealed to the fasting youth in a dream. If the Lord of Life makes him dream of a piece of cherry wood or of an animal, it is a good omen. The young men who follow such a dreamer to the battle have great confidence in his guardian spirit.

Among the Menominee, Alanson Skinner (1921:34) notes:

> The matter of getting into communication with the deities, or some of them, was the private concern of every individual of the tribe, male or female, and was accomplished by fasting, and thus "incubating," or artificially inducing, dream-revelations when at the age of puberty. In this way were the war and hunting bundles obtained, as well as personal charms, fetishes, and the rituals of various loosely organized cults.

Sleep dream and vision experiences were a vital, institutionalized aspect of Native American tribal societies that provided a source of empowerment for the individual as well as the entire community. They served to connect ordinary daily activities with a spirit realm, giving an individual's life a greater significance in the cosmic view of things (Tanner 1979). Dream and vision experiences were the primary means of communication between humans and the supernatural world. Certainly, they would have given each person the "power to" do something as well as the directions for how to exercise that power (Tooker 1979:87), which were shaped by cultural or religious tradition (White 1949:180; Whitten 1985:134).

OVERVIEW OF EARLY ONEOTA CULTURE: THE POWER OF CONSENSUS

Early Oneota peoples possessed the "power to" do certain things by consensus or social regulation. This is expressed in the general uniformity of early Oneota material culture, settlement-subsistence patterns, reciprocal exchange systems, mortuary ritual practices, and warfare. The rich and varied artifact assemblages include diagnostic tools, ornaments, and ritual paraphernalia made from ceramic, bone, antler, shell, chert, and copper materials. Settlement-subsistence patterns suggest common interaction of Oneota populations with an environment consisting of a mosaic of forest, prairie, and aquatic/wetland habitats. Mortuary rituals intimate that individuals were relatively equal regardless of age or sex and highlight the power of the collective in creating performance by the living for the living. Oneota exchange systems stressed the importance of reciprocity, while raiding warfare was apparently infrequent within the early societies. This section will provide an overview of the similarities and differences that exist between Fisher and Langford cultures of northern Illinois and other Oneota cultures, particularly the Wisconsin Oneota cultures of the Emergent and Developmental horizons as described by the archaeologist David Overstreet (1997).

Material Culture

Archaeological research has often focused on the material culture traits that define the constituent units of Oneota and readily differentiates it from antecedent or contemporary Late Woodland and other Mississippian societies. As noted earlier, Oneota is often regarded as a "pottery culture" by archaeologists. Like all cultural behavior, the behavior used in the production and decoration of pottery vessels is structured, and the way that the attributes (whether technological or decorative) are patterned on a particular vessel *shape* carries culturally meaningful information (Arnold 1988:5; Shepard 1975:351). Apparently, Oneota vessels were carrying very similar messages. More on this subject will be discussed in chapters 4 and 8.

The typical Oneota vessel is a squat, globular cooking/storage jar often exhibiting a wide mouth, straight or everted rim, rounded to subangular shoulders, and a round base. The prevalence of jars represents a continuation of a Late Woodland tradition of a restricted range of vessel forms. Other vessels that may be present in an Oneota assemblage include bowls, bottles, pinch pots (a small crudely shaped vessel), and palettes. The vessels are usually tempered with shell (Fisher phase), but in such localities as the Wisconsin Door Peninsula (the Mero complex) (Brose 1978:572; Mason 1981:357; Overstreet 1997:257) and the northern Illinois region (Langford tradition) (Jeske 1990:225), grit tempering was also popular. Dale Henning (1995:74) has also noted the importance of grog tempering in Oneota assemblages of the Mississippi Alluvial Plain, southeast Iowa. During the Emergent Oneota horizon (ca. A.D. 1000–1150), the jar shoulder may be decorated with geometric designs consisting of broad curvilinear trailed lines or nested chevrons with punctate border designs. A slight change takes place during the Developmental horizon (A.D. 1150–1400) when jar shoulder decoration may include dot or punctate borders above and/or below nested chevrons, meandering trailed lines, or panels of horizontal or oblique tool trails that are separated by vertical tool trails (Overstreet 1997). Concentric circles, or "targets," may be associated with these motifs (Boszhardt 1994). The lip and rim area may also be decorated with finger or tool impressions (Emerson and Brown 1992; Henning 1995; Staeck 1995; Tiffany 1982). Loop or strap handles are occasionally found.

The Oneota material culture inventory consists of a variety of worked bone, antler, shell, and lithic artifacts. Typical bone and antler tools found on many Oneota sites include deer ulna perforators, beamers made from the metapodial bones of deer or elk, harpoon points, conical antler projectile points, hafted hoe blades often made of deer, elk, or bison scapulae, beaver-incisor chisels, fishhooks, antler picks, needles, and deer mandible sickles. Ornaments (e.g., tubular beads, pendants, ear spools) and gaming pieces (dice or "counters") were also made. Worked freshwater mussel shell occurs mainly as utilitarian artifacts such as fish effigy lures, spoons, hoes, and celtlike scrapers. Ornamental shell objects include disk beads and pendants (Bareis 1965; Brown et al. 1967; Fenner 1963; Griffin 1946).

Chipped stone tools common to Oneota include small, unnotched triangular and hafted projectile points, humpbacked bifaces, planoconvex endscrapers, bifacial drills, and bipolar anvils and cores *(piece esquilles)* (Brown and O'Brien 1990; Gibbon 1986:326–330; Mason 1981:355–359; Santure and Esarey 1990). Functional ground, pecked, and battered stone tools, such as celts, hammerstones, pitted stones, axes, and abraders, have also been recovered from Oneota sites. Jeske (1989:109) states that the lithic assemblages of Langford and Oneota groups are virtually identical. The only difference is that single grooved rectangular abraders and stone discoidals are viewed as strictly diagnostic of the Fisher culture and other Oneota assemblages (Brown 1961:74; Griffin 1946:129). Copper ceremonial paraphernalia and tools also have been recovered in Oneota contexts, such as sheet-copper headdress plates, ear ornaments, rolled tubular beads, pendants, conical projectile points, and double-pointed perforators (Gibbon 1986; Henning 1995; Sampson and Esarey 1993).

Diverse Subsistence Practices

A vital part of Oneota emergence and persistence was the efficient exploitation of a mosaic of forests, prairies, and wetlands and areas conducive to seed-plant horticulture. This diverse strategy was implemented by Fisher and Langford peoples as well as Wisconsin Emergent and Developmental horizon Oneota cultures. Their hunting, gathering, and fishing economy was supplemented by horticultural strategies combining cultivation of C3 plants occupying cool, moist conditions, such as squash and small-seeded starchy or oily annuals, with limited maize horticulture (Brown 1982, 1990; Faulkner 1972). The maintenance of a diverse subsistence base was a continuation of earlier Late Woodland seasonal cyclical patterns. This dependence on nutritional variety may represent a strategy of resistance to the heavy reliance on indigenous or tropical plant food production that was characteristic of Mississippian societies of the Southeast rather than a systemic and unconscious adaptation to the environment. After all, this is an area of the northern Midwest currently considered a major part of the American Corn Belt with its very productive Alfisols (forest soils) and Mollisols (prairie soils) (Oberlander and Muller 1987:312) and so was *not* an agriculturally marginal area. The nonintensive, flexible nature of environmental resource exploitation is viewed as being a highly successful strategy (Brown 1982). It led to flexibility in group size, enabling fissioning of populations at times of social conflict or resource stress, and also served to lessen the power of Oneota leaders, because of the economic self-sufficiency of villagers (Kreisa 1993:48).

Animal procurement (hunting and fishing) was geared to the exploitation of a wide variety of species. Large terrestrial species, such as white-tailed deer and elk, have been viewed as representing important components in the Oneota economy (Gibbon 1986:332), with bison becoming a common occurrence in Classic horizon assemblages (often occurring as bison scapula hoes). Exactly when bison moved east of the Mississippi River is unclear but is probably associated with the droughty conditions of the Pacific climatic episode (A.D. 1150–1450) as will be discussed further in chapter 3. In Wisconsin, aquatic resources provided an important source of protein based on the number of fish and freshwater mussel remains found in refuse pits or midden contexts (Overstreet 1997). Among Oneota in general, small mammals (e.g., squirrel, beaver, and muskrat) as well as birds, amphibians, reptiles, fishes, and freshwater mussels were likely as important as upland game such as deer and elk (Emerson and Brown 1992; Jeske 1990).

In terms of plant food remains, Oneota sites reflect relatively diverse plant exploitation with three distinct components: wild-plant gathering, nut collecting, and plant cultivation (Gibbon 1986:333). Gathered wild plants, such as wild fruits and American lotus, were collected from a variety of environmental contexts (woodland, wetland, and disturbed habitats) and may represent an important secondary food resource. Nut collecting is evident by the remains of hickory, walnut, and hazel derived from Langford features (Jeske 1990), which indicate a heavy reliance on fall nut masts throughout the Langford tradition (Craig and Galloy 1995). It also appears to have been an important activity at the Wisconsin Oneota sites of Walker-Hooper, Bornick, Carcajou Point, and Lasley's Point (Gibbon 1986). The remains of cultivated plants, such as corn, squash, and little barley, have also been recovered at Oneota sites.

Maize production involved cultivating eight-rowed Northern Flint varieties that were drought resistant and required a shorter growing season than twelve- and fourteen-rowed varieties grown in the Central Mississippi Valley (Hall 1991:25, 1993:57; Watson and Kennedy 1991:266). The grain could be eaten green, fresh, parched, boiled, baked, steamed, and roasted. Notably, early Oneota maize cultivation is viewed as providing only a small supplement to the diet (Benn 1989; Brown 1982; Jeske 1990), although its relative importance is problematic (Gibbon 1986:332; Hart 1990). Its importance is all too often explained in terms of a series of optimizing responses to increasing population density, increases in energetic needs, resource competition, depletion of local resources, production risk, and demand for capital investment in technology (Johnson and Earle 1987; Pollack and Henderson 1992; Webster 1983) rather than individual choices that occur within the constraints of traditions (Cobb and Garrow 1996; Schurr and Schoeninger 1995). It should also be cautioned that few ethnobotanical analyses have been conducted on samples from excavated Oneota sites, and there is a lack of analyses conducted on human skeletal stable carbon-isotope ratios. As a result, some interpretations are little more than speculation. Modeling subsistence patterns requires detailed analyses, especially those that entail measures of faunal and floral taxonomic diversity. Although more research is needed to understand the importance of maize horticulture in Mississippian societies, such work is beyond the scope of this study.

Settlement Patterns

The Oneota settlement pattern on the Prairie Peninsula is characterized by discontinuous clusters of permanent or semipermanent villages, seasonal or specialized extraction locations, and bivouacs (Benn 1989; Markman 1991a). There is no evidence for a highly integrated site-size hierarchy typical of many Middle Mississippian polities of the Southeast, and it appears that most Oneota villages had access to similar resources (Kreisa 1993:46). Village sites are often associated with elevated terraces along major streams and their tributaries that afforded easy access to nearby prairie-forest ecotones, aquatic-wetland resources, and arable soils (Birmingham 1975; Hart and Jeske 1991; McGimsey et al. 1985). It appears that upland springs, bogs, and depressions were also vital in habitation selection (Hart and Jeske 1991; Markman 1991a). Most village sites were reoccupied over a long time span and functioned as bases from which hunting and collecting forays were initiated. The broad-spectrum subsistence strategies often involved settlement movements in response to wide seasonal fluctuations in the availability of foodstuffs and the unpredictable annual variations in the apparent migration patterns of important game species, like the elk and the bison.

The general Oneota settlement-subsistence system is probably similar to the interpretive model posited for Langford populations in northeastern Illinois by Jeske (1990:224) in which there are two distinct phases of an annual seasonal cycle: relatively large, semipermanent horticultural villages (or base camps), which were usually in riverine settings and were occupied from spring through late fall or early winter, and outlying hunting camps, found in upland settings, which were occupied by nuclear family units during the winter (probably to exploit marsh or spring resources). However, Hart and Jeske (1991:4) and Markman (1991a: 188–189) point out that current settlement-subsistence modeling efforts are restricted in value because of numerous theoretical and methodological limitations. For example, ethnohistoric data widely used in interpretive modeling should be viewed as useful in a general sense only. The process of village fission-fusion of early historic Native American groups is probably more complex than originally conceived (Markman 1991a). Also, modeling efforts have been adversely affected by the use of site-only data, nonsystematically surveyed sites, univariate statistical techniques, and coarse measures of environmental variables (Hart and Jeske 1991). There are many other reasons for site placement besides subsistence strategies, including access to chert resources, trade, exotic materials, defense, esoteric knowledge, and mates. Often overlooked is the importance of the festival, which is discussed in chapter 8.

Mortuary Ritual Practices

The early Oneota mortuary data reflect a kin-based sociopolitical organization stressing relative equality among the populations. The social status of the deceased is not expressed in burial types and locations or in the quality and quantity of grave goods. Thus, no "big men" or "great men" as powerful leaders have ever been found. Although mortuary offerings and methods of interment were somewhat variable over time and space, there are some meaningful patterns; and it is archaeologists' responsibility to identify the plausible meanings to gain insight into important historical factors or processes. The grave goods and the ritual context of the burial in time and space clearly must reflect the Native American's view of reality (see Brown et al. 1967; Costin 1996:119; Kreisa 1993).

Information regarding mortuary ritual in Fisher and Langford societies is limited, but it suggests meaningful patterns with other Oneota groups as well as continuity with Late Woodland cultures. Fisher phase mortuary data are restricted to the Fisher site of the Des Plaines Valley, while information on Langford tradition mortuary practices comes from the Fisher (Langford 1927; Griffin 1946), Gentleman Farm (Brown et al. 1967:41–43), Material Service Quarry (Bareis 1965), Oakwood Mound (Skinner 1953), Plum Island (Fenner 1963), Reeves (Craig and Galloy 1995), Robinson Reserve (Fowler 1952), and Zimmerman (Brown 1961) sites. Funeral customs included interment of individuals in pits scattered throughout a habitation area. But usually individuals of all ages and both genders were buried in mounds, with single interments often placed in a fully extended or flexed position, indicating that the deceased were fully articulated when buried. The burial mounds may be characterized as either accretional mounds or superimposed mounded cemeteries. The first type was constructed by the amalgamation of small burial mounds and inclusive burials within a restricted area to form, through accretion, a larger mound. The other type involved the construction of a mound over an existing cemetery to form a platform for a second cemetery (Brown et al. 1967; Emerson and Brown 1992).

Oneota mounds have been reported at various locations and times. In Wisconsin, Emergent horizon Silvernale phase sites in the Lake Pepin area are flanked by large mound groups; mounded burials are also associated with the Developmental horizon Grand River phase site of Walker-Hooper, located southwest of Lake Winnebago (ca. A.D. 1100–1300) (Overstreet 1997). Burial mounds were constructed at Lasley's Point of the Fox River drainage system that may be assigned to the McKern phase (ca. A.D. 1000–1200) or perhaps the Classic horizon Winnebago phase (Kreisa 1993). In Illinois, the Oneota Bold Counselor phase cemetery at Norris Farms 36 (ca. A.D. 1300) is a low mound located on the western bluff line of the Central Illinois Valley (Santure et al. 1990). The mounds appear to be a continuation of mortuary mound building from Late Woodland cultures, particularly the Effigy Mound culture (ca. A.D. 750–1200/1250) of southern Wisconsin and adjacent areas of Iowa, Illinois, and Minnesota. It is a tradition that may have extended into historic times as indicated by burial mounds constructed by the Potawatomi (Hewitt 1910:291).

Grave goods were often associated with human burials and generally consist of common artifacts of Fisher phase and Langford tradition material cultures, such as shell spoons with complete ceramic vessels. For example, burial data compiled for the Langford tradition Gentleman Farm site revealed that domestic tools, specifically pottery vessels and freshwater mussel shell spoons, occurred with individuals of all ages and both genders. This pattern is repeated at the Bold Counselor phase Oneota cemetery at Norris Farms 36 (Santure 1990) and other Classic horizon sites in Wisconsin (Kreisa 1993:43). The association of shell spoons with complete ceramic vessels indicates that pots were filled with food at the time of burial (Brown et al. 1967:16–17; Fowler 1952:57; Holmes 1883:43; Lapham 1973:29) and so has ritual meaning as part of a performance by the living for the living.

Another meaningful pattern common to Langford and Bold Counselor Oneota is the presence of burned areas or hearths near some graves, which have been documented at the Gentleman Farm and Norris Farms 36 sites. They apparently represent the remains of graveside fires that aided the spirit of the deceased on its perilous journey to the otherworld, similar to those ethnographically recorded for many historical midwestern groups (e.g., Ojibway, Kansa, Oto, Missouri, and Menominee) (Brown et al. 1967:4; Santure 1990). Women were usually obligated to keep the mortuary fires burning for four consecutive days. A more detailed discussion of patterns relating to burial goods and funerary fire is presented in chapter 8.

By the beginning of the Oneota Classic horizon, there is a temporal shift from mound to cemetery burial, the dominance of extended (supine) burial treatment, a reduction in the quantities of grave goods especially among adult females and subadults (although one may perceive this as a preservation problem with women's textiles and baskets subject to destruction), and burials that may be placed under dwelling floors. However, the data still show a poorly defined marking of individual status (Benn 1989:235; Brown and Sasso 1992:21–22; Kreisa 1993).

Exchange Systems

Reciprocity is the predominant mode of economic exchange in tribal societies, as was probably the case among the Oneota. It involves giving, receiving, and returning goods and services with values defined by tradition. Reciprocity exists without a market system, without money, without a law of supply and demand, and without outside intervention. It is a simple process in which the acceptance of something offered constitutes the assumption of an obligation to return—the recipients placing themselves in a state of "indebtedness" to the giver. Reciprocity creates links or relationships between two individuals or two groups that are usually positive, since it could maintain crosscurrents of obligations within friendship relations (i.e., alliances) (Ember and Ember 1990; Rosman and Rubel 1995:139). It is not only socially cohesive but an expression of a mutual feeling that *both parties belong to the same social system* (Leach 1976:6). This is evident in Fisher and Langford relations with the occurrence of Langford ceramics at Fisher sites, like the Griesmer site of the Kankakee Valley in northwestern Indiana (Faulkner 1972:58) and the Lawrence site of the Middle Rock River valley in northern Illinois (Berres 1998), strongly indicating the exchange of trade vessels among these groups. Similarly, a probable Fisher phase vessel found with a human burial (Burial Feature 31) at the Langford tradition Gentleman Farm site (Brown et al. 1967:10, Figure 7b) and a small quantity of Fisher shell-tempered ceramics at the Langford tradition Reeves site on the Du Page River, northeastern Illinois, suggests reciprocal trade (Craig and Galloy 1995). This behavior stresses equality of status among members of the same social system.

Food is one of the most significant items of exchange in tribal societies, with its display during feasts or festivals representing the political strength of the group and giving aesthetic pleasure. Such exchange feasts were essential for a community to dispose of goods it had in abundance and to store "social credit" for times of scarcity. Thus, participation in feasts by villages equalized the consumption of desirable foods over a widespread area (Ember and Ember 1990:280–281; Gabaccia 1998:16; Gluckman 1968:463; Spielmann 1991:4). Feasts are encountered in virtually all human cultures and are particularly well known in Melanesian pig feasts, Northwest Coast potlatches (Piddocke 1968), and central California Pomo Indian trade feasts, as well as the Busk (green corn dance) festival (Chamberlain 1907; Fletcher 1904:161, 333; Witthoft 1949), Bear feast (Berres et al. 1999), and the Feast of the Dead (Beauchamp 1893; Tooker 1964:130) of the Eastern Woodlands. The communal and ceremonial nature of the festival in midcontinental Native American tribal societies will be discussed at length in chapter 8.

Early Oneota interregional exchange networks appear to have been very loosely organized, sporadic, and unstable primarily because of the lack of well-developed horticultural economies and associated underdevelopment of surplus production necessary to support expansionist prestige economies. Utilitarian goods such as ceramics and lithics were commonly exchanged over short distances, typically between cultural or physiographic regions (Faulkner 1972:58). Excavations at the Langford tradition Reeves site indicate that there may have been limited trade in exotic cherts used for tools, as exemplified by the presence of Dongola/Cobden from Union County in southern Illinois and Burlington from outcrops along the Mississippi Valley south of the confluence of the Mississippi and Rock rivers (Craig and Galloy 1995). However, the chert materials could have been obtained either in local glacial tills or as discarded artifacts from earlier occupants to the area (Herold et al. 1990:63). Personal ornaments manufactured of copper (e.g., rolled tubes or beads) indicate trade in native copper from the Lake Superior region, although this raw material may also have been obtained in local glacial till deposits. Many perishable substances like salt, meat, hides, feathers, and textiles were undoubtedly exchanged, but there is little direct archaeological evidence for this. Salt served an important physiological need created by increasing maize horticulture practices. Fisher and Langford peoples may have exploited saline springs in the Upper Illinois

Valley near Starved Rock, where brine water emanates under hydrostatic pressure from the St. Peter sandstone formation (Payne 1942). The ethnographic literature is also replete with information regarding the exchange of mates and esoteric knowledge within nonhierarchical societies, which likely occurred among the Oneota.

The most conspicuous examples of long-distance exchange are elaborate copper artifacts, such as sheet-copper headdress plates, copper-covered earspools, and pendants that entered the Illinois Valley and elsewhere in the Prairie Peninsula (Brown and Sasso 1992:30; Hall 1962:116–117, Plate 81). The Edwards falcon plate reported at the Langford tradition Material Service Quarry site, La Salle County, Illinois, is similar to other Southern Cult, or Southeastern Ceremonial complex, bird headdresses from the Midcontinent, like the Malden and Spiro falcon plates from southeastern Missouri and eastern Oklahoma, respectively (Sampson and Esarey 1993). As such, these ritual items express powerful themes related to the thunderbird, the mythological upperworld creature prevalent among prairie cultures (Benn 1989; Hall 1991) and throughout most of North America. Overstreet (1995:53) interprets these items as a vital part of the long-term, shared, symbolic system inherent in both emergent Oneota and Mississippian developments. A close connection between Langford and distant sources of finished Mississippian copper artifacts is equally evident in an earspool facing with a spider motif recovered from the Gentleman Farm site. Spider motifs are consistently associated with female aspects of Mississippian symbolism and are a stylistic anomaly for the Upper Illinois Valley (Sampson and Esarey 1993:470). The spider appears as a woman in many Native American mythologies and is responsible for teaching weaving to human beings (Gill and Sullivan 1992:282).

The Classic horizon ushers in some major changes in the long-distance exchange of goods in the Prairie Peninsula and other areas of the Midcontinent. Disc bowl smoking pipes sometimes made of catlinite quarried in southwestern Minnesota were traded throughout much of Wisconsin and northern Illinois and at least as far south as the Lower and Central Ohio Valley (Brown and Sasso 1992). Exotic raw materials known to have been exchanged among Oneota groups include copper, marine shell, Hixton silicified sandstone, Knife River flint, galena, bison scapulae, and finished goods such as shell gorgets, Marginella beads, and trade pottery from the Lower Mississippi Valley. The raw materials apparently moved through intergroup alliances, and production into finished forms and utilization occurred at the household level. No evidence exists for specialization in craft production (Benn 1989). Dale Henning (1995:83) notes that Oneota exchange centers developed about A.D. 1300 and included sites in the La Crosse locality of Wisconsin, the Utz site in north-central Missouri, and the Leary complex in southeastern Nebraska.

Warfare

The emergence of Oneota is correlated with increased competition and social pressures on surplus food production. Reciprocal exchanges, related to such internal activities as feasts and ceremonies or such external activities as gathering or hunting, promotes competition and cooperation between self-interested individuals from different groups and between individuals within those groups. Such reciprocal cooperative endeavors between approximate peers, however, can lead to a cycle of feuding or raiding when socially induced obligations (debt) are not met by surplus products (Benn 1989). This encompasses negative reciprocity when there are attempts at deceitful bargaining, theft, or other varieties of seizure (Ember and Ember 1990:280). Although revenge may be the primary motive for war, conflicts in small-scale societies could also be for defense, religious obligation, or social advancement as well as attempts to acquire land or control trade routes (Milner 1999:108; Swanton 1943:9–17).

Raiding warfare was a feature of tribal-level societies that varied in frequency or intensity over time and space (Hadlock 1947; Milner et al. 1991:595). The subject, however, is poorly understood by anthropologists for prehistoric times in the Midwest primarily because of the small number of osteological warfare studies that have been conducted. Available evidence indicates that warfare was not significant until A.D. 1300 to 1400, but thereafter it continued as an important fact of life into historic times (Brown and Sasso 1992:40; Kullen 1994:12).

Fisher and Langford peoples of A.D. 1000 to 1300 lived during a relatively peaceful time in northern Illinois, as indicated by the absence of palisaded villages occupying easily defensible positions. For example, Bird (1997:89, Table 2) and Emerson (1999:30, Figure 4) have shown that Langford sites of the Middle Rock River and its tributaries favor prairie habitats on the floodplain, easy for an enemy to locate and clearly exposed to any type of attack. Palisades, identified by lines of postmolds, embankments, or ditches were absent at such village sites as Lawrence and Keeshin Farm as well as other sites within the region. The near absence of fortified Oneota strongholds also have been reported during the Wisconsin Emergent horizon, except for Carcajou Point in the Lake Koshkonong locality, and Developmental horizon, except for palisades reported for Walker-Hooper in the Middle Fox River passageway locality (Overstreet 1997).

Specific evidence showing peaceful relations of Langford peoples with Middle Mississippian folk comes from the Noble-Wieting site, a Langford village (dating to A.D. 1200) located near Heyworth, Illinois, at the junction of Kickapoo Creek and Little Kickapoo Creek. The site's "backwoods" location shows that prehistoric peoples were not confined to defended territories as a wild animal within its home range, and its ceramics consisting of both Middle Mississippian and Langford types show the importance of peaceful interaction between two different groups of people (Schilt 1977). Intergroup warfare is perhaps the exception rather than the rule among Native Americans at this time. Arlene Schilt (1977:191–193) states, "A small amount of Middle Mississippian-influenced pottery is consistently found at other Langford Tradition sites (Brown et al. 1967:37), but seldom in the quantity it occurs here [at Noble-Weiting] (23.5% of the total). . . . Many communities with a variety of cultural traditions (Table 20) were co-existing and interacting in the Midwest ca. A.D. 1200." Perhaps there were mutualistic relations between Middle Mississippian groups with their horticultural commitment and Oneota groups with their mixed hunting, gathering, and horticultural activity similar to that experienced in the Plains bison hunter–Pueblo corn farmer food exchange in the American Southwest (see Speth 1991). Mutualistic exchange benefits all participants in the interaction while emphasizing separation between populations. In the case of Plains-Pueblo interaction, food exchange most likely occurred between late fall and early spring when Plains hunter-gatherer groups (with their excess of meat in storage but little corn) could exchange the meat, fat, and hides of large animals like bison for corn grown by Pueblo farmers (with their surplus of starchy calories in storage but little meat).

Incidents of violent deaths have been rarely reported in Langford human osteological assemblages. Emerson (1999:38) reports that the only Langford skeletons with signs of intentional trauma include scalped crania and other head wounds at the Material Service Quarry site and scalped crania and projectile point and axe wounds at the Fisher site. Also, noticeably absent from Langford tradition adult male burials from the Gentleman Farm site are projectile points used for hunting and warfare. Thus, assumptions of *frequent* conflict and warfare are at best equivocal or unproven for northern Illinois during early Mississippi times. This condition would radically change during the fourteenth century, when warfare evolved into a life-and-death struggle between various tribes and bands.

A long period of chronic warfare occurred during late prehistoric times throughout the Midcontinent, which characterizes the Oneota Classic horizon. Power is most vividly seen in resistance to domination. The dynamic social landscape saw shifting cooperative alliances forming for mutual defense, villages located on easily defended ridgetops with stout log palisades, earthen embankments (and ditches built around them), and pressures to maintain larger villages for defense. Where raiding was especially common, areas were completely depopulated to escape vicious fighting by large numbers of well-organized warriors, sometimes becoming "no-man's-lands," or buffer zones, between hostile groups. Lasley's Point in eastern Wisconsin and the Valley View site of the La Crosse locality represent Classic horizon palisaded settlements (Overstreet 1997; Stevenson 1985). Several Huber phase palisaded enclosures have been reported in the Chicago area. Although they have been interpreted as ceremonial rather than defensive, like the Higgin-botham/Comstock Trace site near Joliet (Kullen 1994), their location in easily defensible positions would suggest otherwise (Brown and Sasso 1992:32–34). Many of the Wolf (ca. A.D. 1300–1400) and Fort Meigs (ca. A.D. 1400–1550) phase sites of the western Lake Erie region also consisted of large, palisaded villages, which were located on bluffs over-looking wide floodplain areas for defensive purposes (Stothers and Pratt 1980; Stothers and Graves 1983:119–120; Stothers et al. 1984).

Finally, mortuary data from a Bold Counselor phase Oneota cemetery in west-central Illinois, Norris Farms 36, demonstrates the results of in-ternecine warfare in the form of malnutrition, nutrition-related disease, and warfare-related trauma such as cut marks from scalping and projec-tile points embedded in bone (Milner 1990; Milner et al. 1991; Santure 1990). About 300 individuals were buried in this cemetery, with 50 showing evidence of violent death. The violent deaths were probably the result of intermittent raids upon the associated Oneota village that left the dead mutilated for status-enhancing trophies (Brown and Sasso 1992; Hall 1997:142; Milner et al. 1991:594).

Notably, there is a problem in focusing too much attention on the "dark side" of Native American cultures, as is the recent trend in archaeol-ogy (see Darling 1999:537), especially regarding the act of scalping. Why perpetuate a negative stereotype of Native Americans that was used as pro-paganda by the early European colonial powers (see Underhill 1971:73; Weatherford 1991:167–170)? The modern Western culture's view of scalping (a modified form of head hunting) as simply a pathological or bar-baric act ignores the importance of ritual and religious beliefs in small-scale societies. In historic Native American religious beliefs, the scalp preserved an identity with the scalped person, sometimes achieving the same status of the deceased in the cult of the dead (Hultkrantz 1981:98). Traditionally, they were infrequently gathered from their slain enemies for use in reli-gious ceremonies (Underhill 1971:125, 234). A credible witness to scalp-ing during historic times was George Catlin (1973:238–239):

> The scalp, then, is a patch of the skin taken from the head of an enemy killed in battle, and preserved and highly appreciated as the record of a death produced by the hand of the individual who possesses it. . . . The scalp must be from the head of *an enemy* also, or it subjects its possessor to disgrace and infamy who carries it.
>
> One of the principal denunciations against the custom of taking the scalp, is on account of its alleged *cruelty*, which it certainly has not; as the cruelty would be in the killing, and not in the act of cutting the skin from a man's head after he is dead. To say the most of it, it is a disgusting cus-tom, and I wish I could be quite sure that the civilized and Christian world (who kill hundreds, to where the poor Indians kill one), do not often treat their *enemies dead,* in equally as indecent and disgusting manner, as the In-dian does by taking the scalp.

- The Oneota tribal world appears to have been well structured, involving balanced and opposed but equal forces and resources. Using ethnohistoric records and ethnographic analogy of contemporary tribal societies, we know that relations of power functioned within the concept of "consensus" where men and women were relatively equal. They were engaged in "separate but equal" work activities that expressed complementarity, although there also could be some degree of flexibility in gender roles. Women probably had crucial roles in household activities and may have served as political and ritual leaders. The Oneota peoples' vertically stratified universe consisted of separate but equal supernatural domains of the upperworld and underworld. Both worlds were occupied by immensely powerful beings that, as we shall see in chapter 7, were in constant conflict in this world of human beings. In order to maintain the human world in balance in the midst of uncertainty, it would be vital that each individual communicate with powerful supernatural beings through dreams and visions, and as a collective unit through ritual performances. For example, mortuary ritual involving mound construction, feeding the dead, and graveside fires indicates that the early Oneota peoples were in constant need of world renewal (a transformation from chaos and death to order and life).

The general uniformity of early Oneota (Emergent and Developmental horizons) material culture, settlement-subsistence strategies, mortuary rituals, reciprocal exchange systems, and limited warfare can be best explained in terms of extensive interaction among ethnically and linguistically diverse nonhierarchical societies as well as by people's interacting with the environment (i.e., Prairie Peninsula and environs) in similar ways during the Mississippian period. The power of reciprocity between individuals and communities or villages was widespread judging by the similarities in material culture throughout the Prairie Peninsula. Such interdependence may have equalized the consumption of food and other basic material resources during relatively peaceful times. Villages linked by networks of kin-based relations involving reciprocity also would lessen the power of leaders within Oneota society (Kreisa 1993). Finally, evidence does not support the idea of a "peaceful primitive" past, neither does it support a Hobbesian depiction of Langford peoples on the periphery (referring to the communities located along the Middle Rock River) engaged in constant conflict and warfare with Middle Mississippian chiefdoms and Oneota tribal groups. The location of exposed, nonpalisaded villages in prairie habitats along the Rock River and its tributaries, the highly mixed Middle Mississippian and Langford ceramic assemblage at the Noble-Wieting site, and few instances of violent trauma in human skeletal remains indicate that *power* during Langford times may be viewed in its transformative capacity rather than as a dominating force.

CHAPTER THREE

The Prairie Peninsula Country

The Prairie Peninsula has been widely recognized as an important cultural-biogeographical region (Brown 1965, 1991; Geis and Boggess 1968; Gibbon 1974; Green 1987; Hall 1991; Parsons 1985; Sale 1985; Wright 1968). It consisted of a rich environment of prairie, forest, and aquatic/wetland resources that was subjected to the dynamic processes of changing climatic conditions. Here, long-term reciprocal cultural interaction often occurred within the context of villages occupying highly circumscribed areas along river valleys. In the search for an understanding of Oneota in general, the Middle Rock River region represents a small research area used in attempts to understand Fisher and Langford peoples' interaction with one another, nature, and the supernatural.

THE PRAIRIE PENINSULA AREA

The Prairie Peninsula is distinctive, once consisting of a wedge of grassland extending from the dry central Great Plains into the moist deciduous forests of eastern North America (Figure 3). Prior to Euro-American settlement, it occupied much of Illinois, Iowa, eastern Kansas, northern and western Missouri, southern Minnesota, the southern edge of Wisconsin, and northwestern Indiana, with many disjunct relics of grassland biota found in southern Michigan and western Ohio. Prairie grasses dominated the landscape, with belts of gallery forest along the stream valleys and isolated deciduous forest groves present within the continuous upland prairie (Daubenmire

1978; Geis and Boggess 1968; Transeau 1935). The Prairie Peninsula is distinguished from adjacent regions by its characteristic climate, physiography and geology, hydrology, vegetation, and animal life.

Climate: Characteristics, Variability, and Temporal Change

The existence and extent of the Prairie Peninsula is primarily attributable to the climatic variables of temperature and precipitation. Because the Prairie Peninsula is situated in the middle latitudes of the interior Northern Hemisphere, it experiences a continental climate with extreme seasonal temperature and moisture ranges (i.e., characterized by cold, relatively dry winters and warm, wet summers). These conditions result from the frequency with which three air masses dominate the area during the year as well as the amount of solar radiation received at the ground surface. The air masses are (1) a dry continental air mass originating over the Pacific Ocean; (2) a warm, moist air mass originating over the Gulf of Mexico; and (3) a cold, dry air mass emanating from Canada (Neely and Heister 1987). The amount and distribution of precipitation over the Prairie Peninsula, and the continental United States as a whole, is largely due to the Pacific air mass. Moist air from the Pacific releases most of its precipitation on the windward side of the Rocky Mountains, and the prevailing westerlies carry warm, dry air across the Great Plains. When the westerly wave pattern is predominantly zonal (contained within particular latitudes), the dry leeward Pacific air forms a wedge between the polar air masses to the north and the tropical air masses to the south. Consequently, the pattern of mean annual precipitation displays some broad regularities with precipitation rates decreasing westward from the Prairie Peninsula (from a high of about 40 inches [100 cm] in the east to a low of 12 inches [30 cm] adjacent to the Rocky Mountains) (Bryson 1966; Gist et al. 1950; Trewartha 1968). At times, the westerlies exhibit considerable amplitude in which cold air masses surge southward and warm air streams northward. Where contrasting air masses collide, cyclones often develop that are then swept along by the westerlies.

The winter season (December–February) is characterized by cold temperatures, low precipitation rates, and low values of solar radiation, although the former two are subject to extreme fluctuation. In the Middle Rock River region, the minimum mean temperatures in winter range from about 16 to 20 degrees Fahrenheit (F) and mean maximum temperatures range from about 30 to 38 degrees F (Fehrenbacher et al. 1967). The Prairie Peninsula is relatively dry in winter because of the influx of cold, dry air from the Canadian Arctic. As with temperature, precipitation varies temporally and spatially. This variation is associated with the mean position of the winter storm tracks that follow the edge of the moist tropical air mass from the Gulf of Mexico (Borchert 1950).

The summer season (June–August) is predominantly one of warm

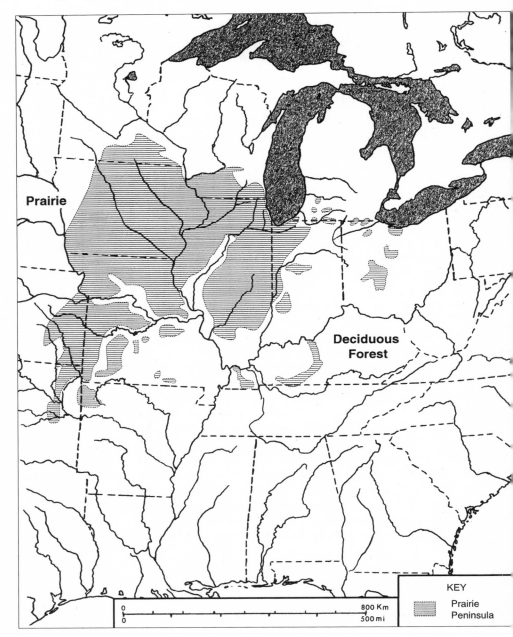

Figure 3 Location of the Prairie Peninsula area (from Transeau 1935).

temperatures and high precipitation rates, with both being extremely variable in magnitude and duration. In the Middle Rock River region, the minimum mean temperature in summer ranges from about 60 to 62 degrees F and maximum mean temperature from about 84 to 86 degrees F (Fehrenbacher et al. 1967). Precipitation over most areas is greater because moisture-laden tropical air masses dominate with a weakening of the westerlies. Thunderstorms are primarily warm season phenomena, with an average of about 38 to 44 occurring per year. They account for nearly 70 percent of the annual precipitation (Neely and Heister 1987) and can generate lightning and tornadoes that threaten lives and damage property. Intense thunderstorms can lead to high flood magnitudes, which usually occur during the March–April spring snowmelt season and during the early summer (June–July) (Knox 1988). Atmospheric and oceanic circulation anomalies, however, may suppress the normal passage of moisture-bearing weather systems, leading to drought development.

Droughts are lengthy periods of extreme moisture deficits caused by less-than-normal precipitation and high evapotranspiration rates associated with high temperatures (Goudie 1992). They often occur as part of natural variations in the climatic system, exhibiting strong variability on interannual and interdecadel time scales (Trenberth et al. 1988). Droughts occur when midlatitude westerlies exhibit an extreme meridional flow pattern that leads to a low- or high-pressure area, preventing the usual west-to-east progression of weather systems (i.e., a blocking system is developed). The typical circulation pattern associated with Midwest droughts during the summer involves development beneath a huge, stationary, warm high-pressure system (high-level anticyclone) centered in either the southwestern United States or the nation's midsection, with the continental high often accompanied by the northward displacement of the belt of strongest westerlies to southern Canada or the northern border states, an abnormally strong ridge in the east-central Pacific, and abnormally deep troughs over both the west and east coasts (Huff and Changnon 1963; Moran and Morgan 1995). Droughts are more severe in the Prairie Peninsula, as measured by high temperatures and below-normal precipitation, than in the forested areas bordering the prairies (Borchert 1950; Britton and Messenger 1969). Studies indicate that the Middle Rock River region experiences a six-month total precipitation of only 60–64 percent of the norm once every 5 years, and a more intense drought occurs throughout Illinois once in 50 years in which precipitation is reduced to 36 to 44 percent of the normal level (Neely and Heister 1987:127).

Oneota social reproduction and variability should be understood within the context of continual spatiotemporal fluctuations in climatic conditions. After all, climatic changes documented throughout the late Holocene (COHMAP 1988; Goudie 1992; Wedel 1986; Wendland 1978, 1983) were important influences affecting vegetation (Bernabo

1981; Gajewski 1988; King 1984) and thus critical determinants of animal biogeography (Purdue and Styles 1987; Semken 1983) and human adaptation (Anderson et al. 1995; Penman 1988). One must be careful, however, not to take an extreme position, arguing either that the natural environment totally determines (environmental determinism) or, conversely, is irrelevant to processes of sociopolitical development (environmental possibilism) (Plog 1990). There is growing scientific evidence that climatic changes were probably abrupt and caused by changes in the world's air mass locations and frequencies (Fischman 1996; Wendland and Bryson 1974). In the Midwest, domination by one of three atmospheric circulation systems produces important vegetational and hydrogeomorphic adjustments that correlate with specific climatic episodes. The epochs, providing the driving force of environmental change, correspond with some midwestern cultural changes through time indicating effects on human subsistence and other aspects of culture.

The origin and development of Oneota in the Prairie Peninsula (Emergent horizon) correlates with the Neo-Atlantic climatic episode of A.D. 650 to 1200–1250 (Wendland 1978). This episode coincides with the "Little Optimum" or "medieval warm epoch" of Europe, marked by glacial retreat (Goudie 1992). A global warming trend was marked in the Prairie Peninsula by the domination of a warm, moist air mass originating over the Gulf of Mexico, bringing mild winters and sufficient summer rainfall to permit the expansion of horticulture (particularly maize) northward and westward beyond the limits of some earlier and later centuries (Hall 1991; Wedel 1986). It also produced cyclonic storms responsible for large paleofloods with magnitudes about 10 to 15 percent higher than recorded for recent floods. For example, floodplain geomorphic evidence from the Upper Mississippi Valley appears to indicate brief periods of large floods between A.D. 750 and 1150 (Knox 1983, 1984, 1985).

A significant climatic shift characterized by more frequent and severe drought conditions appears to have occurred between about A.D. 1200 and 1250, when the Pacific climatic episode (extending to about A.D. 1550) was established (Wendland 1978). During this period, a dry continental air mass descending from the Rocky Mountains, the midlatitude westerlies, dominated the Great Plains and Prairie Peninsula, bringing lower temperatures and decreased precipitation (Wedel 1986). The severity of drought conditions caused by changes in the summer atmospheric circulation system has been estimated to have resulted in a reduction of expected summer precipitation between about 25 and 50 percent in parts of central North America (Bryson 1978; Bryson et al. 1970). Bryson (1978:322) contends that a 200-year drought occurred between about A.D. 1120 and 1350. Such conditions would have had disastrous results for the Middle Mississippian economic system, which was dependent on the availability of horticultural food reserves (Hall 1991). In contrast, impact on the cyclical social reproduction among late prehistoric societies throughout the Prairie Peninsula appears to have been minimal. In fact, what is striking about the Oneota tradition is its durability throughout these climatic changes, which may be attributable to a nonstratified sociopolitical system and semisedentary lifeway, revealing the active role of cultural tradition in resisting and promoting change.

Importantly, the climate "episodes" suggesting long-term (century and millennial) uniform conditions obscure the fact that there were dramatic fluctuations spatially (at the regional and local level) and temporally (decadel and interannual) (Cook et al. 1992; Gordon et al. 1992; Goudie 1993). Recent tree-ring chronologies documented for the southeastern United States have demonstrated the dramatic temporal variability in precipitation extremes occurring on decadel and interannual levels since A.D. 1005 (Anderson et al. 1995; Stahle and Cleaveland 1992). Such climatic variation likely was present throughout the late Holocene in the Prairie Peninsula.

Physiography and Geology

The Prairie Peninsula is situated within one of the larger physiographic provinces in North America, the Central Lowland. This province is a vast plain that covers the central United States, extending eastward from the Great Plains to the Appalachian Highlands and southward from the Great Lakes to the Ozark Plateau (Hunt 1977). The subsurface lithology of the Central Lowland is dominated by broadly warped Pennsylvanian and Mississippian sedimentary rock formations. In general, the age of the bedrock becomes progressively older northward through the area, with the northern margin underlaid by Devonian, Silurian, and Ordovician strata. Bedrock control on landforms is negligible over most of the province, because many of the strata are overlaid by glacial deposits. There are, however, bedrock outcrops along many valley slopes, and some divisions (e.g., Rock River Hill Country) display greater topographic relief because of the deposition of only one till sheet (Leighton et al. 1948).

The Central Lowland was almost entirely glaciated, and its sections are characterized primarily by this continental glacier impact. Two major sections, the Till Plain Section and the Dissected Plain Section, make up most of the Prairie Peninsula. The former is located within Illinois, Indiana, and western Ohio. The broad, relatively uneroded till plain characterizing this section reflects at least two recent episodes of continent-wide oscillation of Pleistocene glaciations from northern latitudes (i.e., Illinoian and Wisconsinan). Glacial deposits are moderate to thick and almost completely conceal the underlying bedrock. They consist of unconsolidated materials such as glacial till, lake-bed silts and sands, windblown silt (loess), and outwash sands and gravels (Leighton et al. 1945; Schuberth 1986).

The topographic relief is slight to moderate over the Till Plain Section, with Illinois having the lowest mean elevation of about 600 feet (183 m) above sea level, compared to such elevations as 700 feet (213 m) for Indiana, 800 feet (244 m) for Missouri, and 1100 feet (335 m) for Iowa. Relief is provided by river valleys that have steep sides and broad floodplains. Also, moraines of Illinoian and/or Wisconsinan till interrupt the flatness of the terrain (Schuberth 1986). The Dissected Till Plain Section occurs west of the Mississippi River, where Kansan till forms a rolling plain interspersed with areas of uniformly level upland divides and level alluvial bottomlands. The uplands are more rounded and the valleys more closely spaced than they are east of the Mississippi River (Hunt 1977).

Most of the Prairie Peninsula was glaciated during the Pleistocene. This process resulted in glacial deposits concealing bedrock virtually throughout the region, with the exception of major river valleys. The mean thickness of the drift deposits is about 100 feet (30 m) (Willman and Frye 1970). The underlying bedrock consists primarily of undeformed, horizontal layers of sedimentary rock. Two of the most extensive formations of this region are the Pennsylvanian and Mississippian systems. Pennsylvanian system strata, containing deposits of coal, limestone, chert, clay, shale, and in places oil and gas, cover about two-thirds of Illinois. The Mississippian system underlies the Pennsylvanian and consists of dolomite, shale, limestone, chert, sandstone, lead, and zinc. These rocks are exposed along the Mississippi River valley in eastern Missouri, southern Iowa, and western Illinois (Neely and Heister 1987).

Hydrology

The Prairie Peninsula is situated almost entirely within the Upper Mississippi River drainage basin, with small segments occupied by the Missouri and Wabash watersheds. The Upper Mississippi River system consists of a watershed of 189,000 square miles (489,510 km²) extending from its headwaters in north-central Minnesota to the confluence of the Ohio River. It includes 14 major river basins exemplified by the Des Moines, Illinois, Wisconsin, and Rock rivers (Becker and Neitzel 1992).

The hydrology has been significantly influenced by Pleistocene glacial events (Knox 1988). The area underlaid by late Wisconsinan glacial deposits (also termed the "Woodfordian Northeast" by Douglas [1976]) is characterized by rivers with a medium to high gradient and rapid flow, while the landscape underlaid by older Pleistocene glacial deposits exhibits rivers with a low gradient and increased dimensions of meandering (wavelength and amplitude). The older river channels, exemplified by the lower segments of the Illinois and Rock rivers, are associated with wide bottomlands containing backwater lakes, sloughs, and marshes. In ecological terms, the rivers are high-energy environments, with most biomass composed of worms, snails, bivalves, and fishes (Hynes 1970).

Numerous inland lakes and ponds, situated away from the major river valleys, complete the surface-water network of the area. These bodies of standing water may be fed by streams, runoff, or groundwater. Most of the natural glacial lakes and ponds (e.g., upland kettle lakes) occur in northeastern Illinois (Neely and Heister 1987). Also, in northern Illinois the geology and topography combine to create aquifers in Silurian Niagara Dolomite rock formations, which feed regional springs (Zeizel et al. 1962). Springs are special habitats that may discharge directly into the channel of the spring stream or into a small basin or pond that overflows into the channel. The uniform conditions of springs, not affected by seasonal cycles, provide ideal habitats for relict floral and faunal species (Hynes 1970).

Soils

In the soil taxonomy for the United States, there are nine soil orders that are correlated with specific ecosystem types. Five orders are present in the Prairie Peninsula, including Mollisols, Alfisols, Histosols, Entisols, and Inceptisols, of which Mollisols and Alfisols are dominant (Fehrenbacher et al. 1967). The relatively flat topography and soils rich in nutrients (nitrogen, phosphorous, and potassium) provide a favorable environment for plant growth.

Mollisols develop under midlatitude grasslands and are derived from alluvium, glacial deposits, and loess. They are closely associated with precipitation and evaporation patterns (P.E. index) and the persistence of prairie (the P.E. index for grasslands is 23 to 63; the eastern forest region's index is 64 to 128 or more) (Ruhe 1983). The upland soils have dark, humus-rich A horizons (mollic epipedons) with high base saturation. They are very productive agriculturally, although the extremely dense mass of roots made it difficult to cultivate without utilizing the steel plow. Alfisols are primarily confined to the drier morainic landforms or to the more rolling, better drained areas bordering stream valleys. The thin surface layers are usually developed under forest vegetation (Fehrenbacher et al. 1967; Ruhe 1983). Alfisols are somewhat less productive but easier to till than the Mollisols. Histosols are organic soils, peats and mucks, represented in wetlands. They occupy only a small portion of the Prairie Peninsula and are located primarily in northeastern Illinois and northwestern Indiana. Entisols and Inceptisols are very young soils that exhibit little or no evidence of having developed pedogenic horizons. They occur infrequently, often near bottomland alluvial deposits (Fahrenbacher et al. 1967).

Prairie, Forest, and Aquatic/Wetland Habitats

The native plant communities of the Prairie Peninsula and the Middle Rock River region are identified with three major habitats: prairie, forest, and aquatic/wetland. Extensive upland grassland (prairie) communities dominated this area. They are considered to have been relatively unproductive for plant foods (King 1984; Styles 1981:66), because resources were seasonally variable and widely scattered. Eastern broadleaf deciduous forest species were restricted to valley bottomlands (e.g., gallery forests), steeper uplands bordering streams, moraines, and isolated groves within the prairie (Geis and Boggess 1968). These forests are characterized by high productivity. Other productive habitats for plant and animal life include rivers, streams, lakes, and ponds along with lacustrine, riverine, and palustrine (marshy) wetland areas. All provided a seasonally variable, patchy distribution of abundant food resources for the Native American inhabitants.

Faunal communities indigenous to both the eastern deciduous forest and the Great Plains grassland contributed significantly to aspect and biomass of the Prairie Peninsula. The distribution and availability of animal resources were strongly associated with particular habitats although varying in response to fluctuations in climatic/environmental conditions (e.g., seasonal cycles) (Shelford 1963). Thus, animal resources would not have been available uniformly across the mosaic of prairie, forest, and aquatic/wetland habitats. For example, stable, predictable, and abundant resources were highly concentrated within river valleys, whereas outside these areas resources would have been characterized as patchy, unpredictable, and scarce to moderately abundant in space and time. Ecotones also existed on the landscape and were inherently variable with changing conditions. An ecotone is defined here as a dynamic zone of transition between two specific biological communities with a relatively high biological diversity and high productivity (Naiman and Decamps 1990). Such a conceptualization is particularly appropriate for a zone between forest and grassland, often called the forest edge. Information concerning the distribution of major plant and animal species found in prairie, forest, and aquatic/wetland habitats are discussed below.

Prairie   A prairie is a midlatitude grassland supporting less than one tree per acre (0.4 hectares). The North American prairie was dominated by grasses (Gramineae), containing about 7,500 plant species from about 600 genera. This genetic diversity is related to abiotic gradients, especially climate, that exist over wide geographical areas (Sims 1988). Grass heights can be divided into tall, medium, and short and are correlated with the east-west precipitation gradient (Sims 1988; Weaver 1954). Tall grasses (canopy height greater than or equal to 5 feet) were common in the Prairie Peninsula, dominated by the sod-forming big bluestem, Indian grass, switch grass, and slough grass. These grasses require abundant moisture, which is found in deep ravines and lowlands throughout the region. Medium-stature grasses (canopy height between 2 to 5 feet) include little bluestem, needlegrass, side-oats grama, blue-bunch wheatgrass, and prairie dropseed. They occur in drier climates or where soil moisture conditions are not enhanced by runoff. Short grasses (canopy height less than 2 feet) dominate drier habitats ranging from a large contiguous expanse of vegetation east of the Rocky Mountains to scattered stands in high topographic positions in the Prairie Peninsula (e.g., ridges that are subjected to high soil-moisture loss through runoff and wind). Dominant shortgrasses include blue grama, hairy grama, and buffalo grass (Bamforth 1988; Weaver 1954).

The upland prairies provided a limited variety of edible plants for human and wildlife consumption. For humans, they contained about 56 edible plant species from three general categories: grasses (e.g., Junegrass, panic grass, little barley, eastern grama grass, maygrass), forbs (e.g., prairie turnip, goosefoot, marsh-elder, sunflower, giant ragweed, Jerusalem artichoke), and woody shrubs (e.g., hazelnut, chokecherry, dewberry, elderberry, smooth sumac). They were collected seasonally as a dietary supplement, providing essential vitamins, minerals, and starches (Kindscher 1987).

Animals associated with the grasslands include the bison, elk, gray wolf, coyote, badger, thirteen-lined ground squirrel, prairie dog, plains pocket gopher, and greater prairie chicken (Hoffmeister 1989; Shelford 1963). Of the limited species diversity available, the large herbivore populations offered the greatest biomass density for human exploitation during the late Holocene, although the precise location of the large herds was unpredictable in space and time.

The American bison (*Bison bison*) was present in portions of the Prairie Peninsula during late prehistoric and protohistoric times (Colburn 1989:26; Shay 1978; Tankersley 1986). A very large herbivore, these highly gregarious grazers favored prairies, forest edges and openings, and dry marshes. Bison are "opportunistic" ruminants displaying a dual migration/nonmigration strategy that enables quick and widespread geographic dispersal. Four major reasons account for their movements: to search for nutritious forage and water, to search for other members of the same species, to avoid human predation and settlement (Bamforth 1987:3), and to search for salt licks. There was an apparent influx of bison herds into the area during the droughty conditions of the Pacific climatic episode (A.D. 1200–1450/1550), which corresponded with increased prairie habitat in the east (Colburn 1989:26; Shay 1978) and greater human predation and settlement of the river valleys on the northern plains. C. Thomas Shay's (1978) study of the frequency of bison remains at sampled sites in southern Wisconsin, northern and central Illinois, and northwestern Indiana showed that less than 5 percent of the sites dating between 1500 B.C. and A.D. 900 contained bison compared with almost 60 percent after A.D. 1000. Based on more recent evidence, most zooarchaeologists would agree that bison migrated east of the Mississippi River during the latter portion of the Pacific climatic episode: Bonnie Styles (1994:36) suggests that bison occurred in Illinois sometime after A.D. 1400, while Kenneth Tankersley (1986) has demonstrated that bison were exploited locally by Fort Ancient people in the Central Ohio Valley at least by A.D. 1450. The increase in bison throughout the Prairie Peninsula during the Pacific episode has been termed an "explosion," with Shay (1978:197, 209) noting that bison effectively expanded their range twelvefold within 500 years. They were extirpated east of the Mississippi River by the 1820s (Hoffmeister 1989).

The wapiti, or elk (*Cervus elaphus*), of the American continent are also large herbivores that were apparently abundant during the late Holocene. Elk were formerly distributed in a variety of habitats including prairies, forest edges and openings, oak barrens, and marshes. As gregarious grazers and browsers, their diet was probably highly variable with the season. The specific habits of the eastern elk are not well known because they were extirpated in the eastern United States by the mid-nineteenth century from overhunting and habitat destruction (Hoffmeister 1989; Jackson 1961; Whitaker and Hamilton 1998:521–525).

Three large carnivores occupied the grassland landscape: gray wolves, coyote, and badgers. The gray wolf, or timber wolf, was found in a variety of habitats including prairie, forest, and forest edge. It was originally abundant throughout the area but was extirpated during the late nineteenth century (Hoffmeister 1989). The coyote, or prairie wolf, is abundant and still occurs throughout the region, primarily in prairies, open woodlands, and brushy areas. The badger was formerly common in the Prairie Peninsula but now is restricted to the extreme northern portion. Badgers live in open sandy fields and grasslands, and sometimes in brushy areas (Hoffmeister 1989; Jackson 1961).

Forest   A forest is commonly defined as an area of closely spaced trees, with at least 50 percent of the acreage under tree canopy (Hart and Jeske 1987). The natural tree growth of the Prairie Peninsula represents relicts within the oak-hickory and maple-basswood forest associations (Greller 1988). It consists almost entirely of broad-leaved species, notably oaks (*Quercus* species), hickories (*Carya* species), maples (*Acer* species), ashes (*Fraxinus* species), elms (*Ulmus* species), black walnut, and basswood (Curtis 1959; Daubenmire 1978). The deciduous forest habitats contain productive stands of nut- and fruit-bearing trees as well as edible forb and woody shrub species situated primarily in ecotone areas. These resources vary in their distribution, density, and productivity.

Nuts from a variety of forest trees (e.g., black walnut and hickory) were an integral part of Native American economic systems in the Prairie

Peninsula. Nut trees were readily available in various densities within the gallery forests (Daubenmire 1978) and upland prairie groves. Brown (1965:60) and Cremin (1978:95) stress the unpredictability in interannual mast production of canopy-level trees, which is strongly related to climatic factors and natural cycles. Tree productivity is affected by the same factors that impact fruit trees, including late springs, hard winters, early and hard frosts, exposure to sunlight, and age. The variation in nut production per tree and/or unit area would have necessitated changes in the adaptation of indigenous populations and wildlife.

Fruit-bearing trees present in the Prairie Peninsula include such species as black cherry, hawthorn, hackberry, and American plum. They are predictable producers, with ripened fruits available between August and October. Each favor different habitats, with black cherry preferring rich, moist, or sandy soils, hawthorn growing well in clearings and stream banks, and hackberry found in mixed hardwood forest and swamp forest areas (Keene 1981). Thickets of American plum are common in drier areas (King 1984).

Numerous herbaceous plant species would have been widely available. Seeds of knotweed, goosefoot, and marsh-elder are available during the fall in the floodplain forest and along lakes, rivers, and valley slopes (Zawacki and Hausfater 1969). They would have provided an important source of carbohydrates for human populations.

Berry-producing woody shrubs exhibit a wide range of habitat preferences and tolerances and were common in forest edges and openings. Most species are shade intolerant, although some, like the common elder, mayapple, and grape, are more prolific in shady areas. Berries provide a reliable and abundant crop annually, unlike nut-bearing trees (Keene 1981). Grapes would have been available in the late summer and early fall, pawpaws in September, and blackberries or dewberries and elderberries in the summer (Zawacki and Hausfater 1969).

The dominant fauna of the forest community include white-tailed deer, black bear, wolves, bobcats, gray fox, tree squirrels, raccoon, opossum, and striped skunk. A number of birds, most notably turkey and passerines, were also available. These species would be most abundant near the forest edges and openings (Shelford 1963).

White-tailed deer have adapted to a variety of habitats, including forests, oak barrens, and swamps, but prefer forest edges. They are essentially browsers that feed on grasses, herbaceous plants, twigs of shrubs and trees, nuts, and bush fruit. Deer density is determined primarily by availability of mast and degree of predation. Deer have small home ranges, and their movements are predictable. The archaeological record clearly shows that deer was the most prominent game species through time, important for food, clothing, and a variety of household tools and utensils made from bone, antler, skin, and sinew (Hoffmeister 1989; Jackson 1961; Keene 1981).

Small mammals that could be easily procured from the forest include squirrels and raccoon. The eastern gray squirrel and eastern fox squirrel are found in areas that are productive for nut gathering. Grays prefer heavily wooded areas, and fox squirrels occur in more open areas such as forest edges and clearings. They maintain small home ranges and would have been available year-round. Raccoon occupy a variety of habitats but prefer wooded areas, particularly along streams and lakes. As opportunistic feeders, they generally subsist on fruits, insects, crayfish, frogs, and a variety of seeds, nuts, and berries. Raccoon occupy relatively small home ranges and would have provided an abundant, dense resource on a year-round basis (Hoffmeister 1989; Keene 1981).

Aquatic/Wetland   This habitat is associated with the open waters of slow-moving, low-gradient and fast-moving, high-gradient streams and rivers, along with marshy wetland areas (marshes, swamps, lakes, ponds, springs, and sloughs). The plant communities of such habitats are generally characterized by a high primary production rate (Niering 1989), although production varies significantly on a seasonal basis, primarily because of fluctuations in the intensity of solar radiation (Goldman and Horne 1983). The dominant potential plant foods of marshy wetland communities often include a mosaic of emergents (e.g., cattails, arrowheads, bulrushes) common in shallow areas (less than six inches deep), and floating and submerged aquatics (e.g., pond lilies, American lotus) present in deeper marshes (Kindscher 1987; King 1984; Niering 1989). Although limited in diversity, the marsh plant communities would have provided a dense, predictable resource base for fall harvests. Riverine systems are not nearly as productive in plant foods as marshes because of the energy flow of rushing water.

A great abundance and diversity of fauna, highly concentrated on a spatiotemporal scale, are available in aquatic/wetland habitats, including mammals, birds, fish, turtles, and freshwater mussels. In the Upper Mississippi River basin, as with other river basins, species richness tends to increase from headwater streams to larger channels downstream as moving water increases in volume or discharge and there are more areas of reduced flow velocity (e.g., increased channel width and meandering) (Moss 1980; Wootton 1990). The wetlands characteristic of downstream areas are especially productive because of an influx or pulse of nutrient-rich main channel water by seasonal flooding, which also keeps the system oxygenated (Niering 1989).

Several semiaquatic mammal species occupy wetlands bordering water bodies (lentic ecotones) and riverine riparian ecotones, including muskrat, beaver, river otter, and mink. They represent a year-round, patchy resource. The muskrat is a productive game species whose prevalence varies with vegetation conditions, with peak densities present in prime marsh areas. The beaver represents another productive game species, with peak densities associated with select areas of the floodplain (i.e., supporting stands of willow, white birch, cottonwood, maple, ash, hawthorn, and herbaceous pond vegetation). River otter and mink, comparable with other Mustelidae, are characterized by low density and high mobility and are subject to cyclical fluctuations in population size (Keene 1981; Reidhead 1981).

The Mississippi Flyway is a major migration corridor that bisects the Prairie Peninsula, extending from the southern Canadian provinces (breeding grounds) to as far south as the Gulf of Mexico and central Mexico (wintering grounds). It supports a variety of waterfowl (ducks, geese, swans) and wading birds (bitterns, egrets, herons, cranes, rails, gallinules) on a seasonal basis. Peak densities in the area occur during the early spring and late fall migrations (i.e., March–April and October–November). Some species winter and/or summer in the area, including the Canada goose, mallard, black duck, hooded merganser, and loon. Expansive wetlands in the Upper Mississippi basin provide optimum habitats for waterfowl populations (Bellrose 1976; Bohlen 1989).

The Prairie Peninsula possesses an abundant and diverse fish fauna. As part of the zoogeographic Mississippi Province of the Nearctic Region described by Moyle and Cech (1988:327), there are about 244 to 264 native species of freshwater dispersants composed predominantly of minnows (Cyprinidae), perches and darters (Percidae), sunfishes (Centrarchidae), suckers (Catostomidae), and North American catfishes (Ictaluridae). The distribution and abundance of any one stream species is determined by an interaction of physical (e.g., gradient, temperature regime, stream order, and fluctuations in flow), chemical, biological, and zoogeographic factors. Moyle and Cech (1988:364–365) point out the importance of gradient (the number of meters of drop per kilometer of stream) in determining the distribution of stream fishes, with an increase in gradient generally related to a decrease in the number and relative abundance of species as well as overall biomass. Fluctuation in flow is another important variable, with floods essential for the reproduction of many species by providing spawning and feeding areas for parents and progeny. A high-magnitude flood, however, may have a negative effect on many fish species by washing away developing embryos or larvae.

Freshwater turtles are available throughout the Upper Mississippi drainage basin. The species found in this area include the soft-shelled turtle, common snapping turtle, musk turtles, common map turtle, Blanding's turtle, red-eared turtle, false map turtle, and painted turtle. With the exception of Blanding's turtle, all are abundant today (Niering 1989; Smith 1961; Styles 1981).

The composition of freshwater mussels in the Upper Mississippi River basin includes at least 51 species from 4 genera. Mussels are an important animal group in the benthic community and provide a food source for many animals including muskrats, fishes (e.g., channel catfish), otters, minks, and some birds (Cummings and Mayer 1992). Species richness varies throughout the area depending on substrate characteristics (e.g., silt, sand, gravel, mud) and water flow velocity. High density and diversity occurs in the most stable habitats of the large river systems, particularly a stable sand and gravel substrate with a moderate to strong water flow (Theler 1983). Species richness is extremely low in silt substrate habitats such as backwater lakes (Styles 1981). Freshwater mussels represent a predictable resource that was probably procured by Native Americans during late summer and early fall when water levels tend to be lowest (Reidhead 1981:141).

MIDDLE ROCK RIVER REGION:
LAWRENCE AND KEESHIN FARM LOCALITIES

The Rock River is one of the principal tributaries of the Mississippi River. Of particular concern to this study is a segment extending from its confluence with the Kishwaukee River at Rockford to where it eventually joins Elkhorn Creek near Sterling, Illinois, which is referred here as the Middle Rock River region (Figure 4). The valley axis runs from northeast to southwest and is about 46 miles (74 km) long. It traverses portions of four counties in northwestern Illinois: Winnebago, Ogle, Lee, and Whiteside. The focus of prehistoric horticultural societies was the resource-rich bottomlands of the Prairie Peninsula, and it is this association that helps explain the Oneota settlement-subsistence pattern observed in the Middle Rock River region. The summary below of the environmental and resource characteristics of this region and the Lawrence and Keeshin Farm site localities includes data on physiography and geology, hydrology, soils, plants, and animals.

A consideration of each site locality provides a useful framework for assessing subsistence activities at each archaeological site in relation to the resource potential of the surrounding area, which can then be used in assessing potential resource differences between sites. For this study, a locality is an unbounded arbitrary territory around a site. It is essentially equivalent to an area regularly exploited by the site inhabitants (Willey and Phillips 1958:18). Unlike a site catchment analysis, there will be no attempt in this study to provide a full inventory of a site's contents and resources potentially available to the prehistoric occupants. It is acknowledged that there are social factors that affect the spatial organization of settlements over a landscape, so that resource structure (availability, predictability, and abundance of resources) is only a single dimension of a regional settlement-subsistence system (Root 1983). The Lawrence and Keeshin Farm sites had similar natural environments at the time of occupation, being located near prairie, forest, and aquatic/wetland habitats.

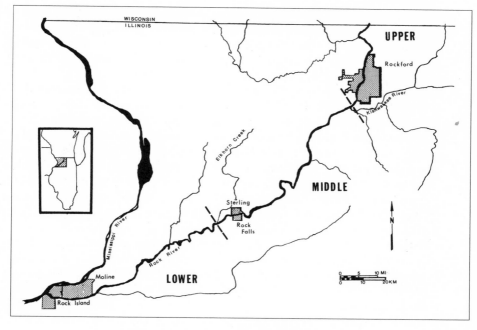

Figure 4 Location of the Middle Rock River region.

Physiography and Geology

The Middle Rock River region and both site localities are located within the geographic or natural region of Illinois known as the Rock River Hill Country Division of the Till Plain Section. It can be distinguished from the other 13 natural divisions in Illinois by its topography, glacial history, bedrock, soils, and distribution of plants and animals (Schwegman 1973).

The basin topography is characterized by nearly level to moderately undulating uplands and bluffs bordering numerous narrow stream valleys. In the uplands, the landscape is underlaid with a thin layer of Illinoian and/or Wisconsinan age glacial till, which are covered with relatively thick loess deposits. The area of pre-Wisconsin Pleistocene glaciation, west of the valley, is characterized by higher relief, steeper slopes, and higher drainage densities in comparison with the region of Wisconsin drifts. The Middle Rock River flows through an extremely narrow bedrock valley, with uplands often bordering the river channel and floodplains with widths rarely exceeding 1 mile (1.6 km) (Anderson and Masters 1985; Schwegman 1973).

The bedrock of the Middle Rock River basin is primarily Ordovician and Silurian limestone and dolomite (Schwegman 1973; Willman et al.

1975). The dolomites of both systems outcrop over a broad area, particularly along the streams. Within the Ordovician System, St. Peter sandstone is exposed in the central portion of the Rock Valley. Cherts occur in the Ordovician Galena and Platteville groups (Morrow 1994), which are found sporadically over the region.

The Lawrence site locality is situated in a portion of the Freeport section of the Rock River Hill Country of Illinois, an area characterized by level to gently rolling topography that is drained by the Rock River. The site lies along the west bank of the Rock River on a very low terrace that is about 20 feet (6 m) above the present floodplain. The wide floodplain is topographically varied and includes terraces, ridges, swales, sloughs, meander scars, and a variety of other fluvially developed landforms. Thus, it is poorly drained and susceptible to spring floods, with high water most common from February through June (Sabata 1995). This area has a thin mantle of Illinoian glacial drift covered with relatively thick loess deposits. Beneath the glacial drift are layers of bedrock consisting primarily of Ordovician and Silurian dolomite and limestone, with sparse and poor-quality chert (Schwegman 1973:10–11). The closest exposure of Ordovician material is more than 4.3 miles (7 km) to the northeast (Willman et al. 1975).

The Keeshin Farm site locality is situated in the same section of the Rock River Hill Country Division (Schwegman 1973), with this area characterized by broad, rolling topography that is bisected by the Kishwaukee River. The rolling uplands rise about 66 feet (20 m) above the valley bottom in the western portion of the locality and have a very thin mantle of Wisconsinan glacial drift covered with a thin layer of loess (Grantham 1980). The site lies along the east bank of the Kishwaukee River on a very low terrace that is about 10 feet (3 m) above the present floodplain. This locale and other "islands" of low terrace appear as gentle rises above the bottomland. Flanking the low-floodplain complex in the vicinity of the Keeshin Farm site is a higher terrace with a distinct scarp that rises nearly 10 to 20 feet (3–6 m) above the surrounding sand and gravel landforms. This terrace is known as the Lake Mills Terrace, consisting primarily of sand and gravel. The underlying bedrock of the area consists of sedimentary material of the Ordovician system. The Platteville and Galena groups are major rock-stratigraphic units of this system, consisting primarily of dolomite and limestone formations, that outcrop along the slopes of the Kishwaukee Valley and Rock Valley bluffs (Willman and Kolata 1978). Chert nodules are occasionally present in the strata. The valley bottom is underlaid by St. Peter sandstone that occurs at the base of the Ordovician system (Salisbury and Barrows 1918).

Hydrology

The Rock River is a large Mississippi River tributary draining an 11,000 square mile (28,490 km²) area in south-central Wisconsin and northwestern Illinois (Baker 1927; Neely and Heister 1987:23). It flows in a south and southwesterly direction for about 175 miles (282 km) before emptying into the Mississippi River at Rock Island, Illinois. The upper and middle river course traverses a landscape underlaid primarily by Wisconsinan glacial deposits, and the lower reaches flow through Illinoian till. Thus, the substrate is generally very coarse throughout the river's length and is usually composed of sand and gravel. The Rock River is a typical warmwater stream with substantial flow and temperature variation, high productivity, and shallow channels. The middle sector of the basin is subject to discussion below.

Early travelers saw the Middle Rock River as shallow, swift, and sometimes rock obstructed (Thwaites 1976). It is fast moving apparently due to a moderate-gradient longitudinal profile. In contrast, reaches downstream exhibit a meandering channel system with a low gradient and a broad shallow floodplain containing marshes and small backwater lakes (Birmingham 1975). The Middle Rock River has the characteristics of a youthful stream in an area exposed to erosion after the retreat of Late Wisconsin ice sheets (Baker 1927). The relatively straight channel, with a width of about 820 feet (250 m), exhibits low sinuosity and high stability. This reach has undergone modification with the construction of three mainstream storage reservoirs at Oregon, Dixon, and Sterling–Rock Falls. Dams at these locales tend to decrease water velocity, limit the movement of sediment downstream, and influence fish migration and species composition.

The river's maximum streamflow generally occurs between March and June. Normally, the basin floods annually, caused by heavy rainfall or sudden winter or spring thaws with resultant snowmelt runoff from the large tributary areas (Illinois Technical Advisory Committee on Water Resources 1967). Minimum water levels are usually between August and February.

Springs are known to occur locally, especially in the sandstone areas of the central portion of the region (Schwegman 1973). According to long-time local residents, springs and the streams leading from them provide very uniform conditions, where animals are protected from cold winters or warm summers.

Within the Middle Rock River basin, the two principal tributaries are the Kishwaukee River and Elkhorn Creek. An eastern tributary, the Kishwaukee River drains an area of about 1,667 square miles (4318 km²). The linear length of the river is about 57 miles (92 km), with riffles, runs, and pools that are especially rich in mussel species. At its juncture with the Rock River near Rockford, Illinois (located about 2,460 feet [750 m] northwest of the Keeshin Farm site), the stream is filled with deep glacial outwash deposits (Kempton et al. 1985), which are responsible for the irregular, meandering, braided channel. The shallowness of the channel has created significant problems in the high frequency and magnitude of floods. Also, wide fluctuations in stream discharge and unstable channels have led to bank collapse and channel wandering within the locality. A northern tributary, Elkhorn Creek flows a linear distance of 48 miles (77 km) to join the Rock River near Sterling–Rock Falls, Illinois. Its basin encompasses 249 square miles (645 km²) (Mitchell 1948). The extensive floodplain of the lower reaches of Elkhorn Creek is similar to the Lower Rock River. Elkhorn Creek lies only 1.2 miles (2 km) west of the Lawrence site.

Soils

The soils in the region have developed primarily from late Pleistocene loess and glacial outwash, with scattered areas of soils developed from alluvium. The uplands are covered by extensive loess deposits that developed under nearly level to rolling prairie vegetation. Transitional loess soils formed under deciduous forest and mixed prairie grasses are also found on the uplands, occurring in a narrow band bordering the western portion of the river valley. The bottomland terraces consist of soils developed primarily from glacial outwash under the influence of prairie and deciduous forest vegetation. There are also sandy to clayey alluvial sediments that border the main channel in the bottomland (Fehrenbacher et al. 1967). Modern soils and United States General Land Office (GLO) survey notes have been used to effectively model general late prehistoric vegetative types and will be used to assess vegetation distributions in the localities surrounding the Lawrence and Keeshin Farm sites.

Most of the Lawrence site locality north and west of the Rock River, including the terrace location of the site, is mapped as the Richwood-Elburn-Drummer soil complex, with nearly level to moderately sloping silty soils that formed in loess and in the underlying loamy, stratified sediments. The native vegetation was primarily a mixture of prairie, marsh, and sedge meadow communities, although patches of floodplain forests were also present. The immediate site area was probably covered by elm and hackberry, with an oak-hickory canopy present immediately to the west, as indicated by Richwood and Lamont soils, classified as Alfisols (Sabata 1995).

The Ambraw–Zumbro–Du Page soil unit is restricted to the floodplain adjacent to the Rock River. This unit consists of nearly level to gently sloping loamy and silty soils that formed in loamy or sandy alluvium (Sabata 1995). The native vegetation was primarily a mixture of prairie, marsh, and sedge meadow communities, although gallery forest and floodplain forest canopy on Rock River islands apparently were present. A gently rolling prairie was noted immediately east and south of the Lawrence site and Rock River by GLO surveyors. They also noted a wet prairie along the Rock River in the extreme northern and southern portions of the locality, and on a large island about 0.6 miles (1 km) to the northeast they recorded a forest consisting of elm, ash, walnut, hickory, hackberry, bur oak, and red oak trees. The wet prairie probably consisted of big bluestem, bluejoint grass, and cord grass (Schwegman 1973).

The extreme eastern portion of the locality is dominated by the Dickinson-Lawler soil complex, made up of nearly level and gently sloping loamy soils that formed in wind- or water-deposited sandy and loamy sediments or in loamy sediments over sandy outwash (Sabata 1995). The native vegetation consisted of mesic prairie communities, the dominant grasses being big bluestem, Indian grass, and prairie dropseed (Schwegman 1973). The GLO records indicate that this area was level prairie.

Small bodies of open water (ponds and streams) associated with old meander scar sloughs are situated in the southeastern portion of the locality, which were possibly active during the Lawrence occupation. Spring Slough exemplifies one paleochannel of the Rock River. It still maintains a shallow watertable, with channel fill deposits consisting of Houghton muck, Ambraw clay loam, Calco silty clay loam, and Marshan loam. The soils and flora probably provided a good habitat for wetland wildlife in late prehistoric times.

Soils of the Keeshin Farm locality were formed in alluvial and outwash sediment on stream terraces and floodplains as well as in loess and glacial deposits on uplands. The soils compose three major map units: Comfrey-Selma, Flagler-Warsaw-Hononegah, and Griswold-Winnebago. The low-terrace/floodplain complex is dominated by the Comfrey-Selma unit: deep, poorly drained, nearly level soils that formed in recent alluvium or in outwash sediment. The native vegetation of the terrace east of the Kishwaukee River probably consisted predominantly of wet prairie, containing bulrushes, sedges, and tall grasses like big bluestem, bluejoint grass, cord grass, Indian grass, and switch grass. Wetland gallery forests and island groves were probably dominated by red oak, Hill's oak, cottonwood, quaking aspen, silver maple, black willow, American elm, and ash trees (Fell 1955; Schwegman 1973). Comfrey loam soil occurs in two ponded locales in the southeastern portion of the locality. This soil is typically covered by water one to five feet deep. Wetlands often consist of wild rice, water plantains, cattails, sedges, bulrushes, and other water-tolerant grasses, trees, and weeds. Native seed-bearing, water-tolerant plants provide food and cover for wetland wildlife, including ducks, geese, muskrats, mink, and wading birds (Grantham 1980).

The Flagler-Warsaw-Hononegah soil unit is present in the northeastern portion of the locality. It occurs on high stream terraces, like the Lake Mills Terrace, and consists of nearly level to sloping soils that formed in loamy and sandy sediment underlaid by sandy and gravely sediment (Grantham 1980). The native vegetation consisted almost entirely of sandy prairie of mesic and dry grassland communities (Fell 1955; Fell and Fell 1956). Flora species probably included prairie dropseed, side-oats grama, witchgrass, sandbur, big bluestem, little bluestem, June grass, and Indian grass (Fell 1955; Schwegman 1973). Small prairie groves consisted almost entirely of bur oak (Fell 1955).

The extreme western portion of the locality, west of the Kishwaukee River, is dominated by the Griswold-Winnebago soil complex. It occurs on uplands and is characterized by deep, well-drained, gently sloping to strongly sloping soils that formed in glacial till or in thin loess and the underlying glacial drift (Grantham 1980). The soils are formed under the dominant influence of deciduous forests, a mixed growth of black, burr, red, and white oak along with hickory, hard maple, and walnut (Fell 1955).

Habitats with Associated Plant and Animal Communities

The Middle Rock River region supports abundant and diverse plant and animal communities that are closely associated with the landscape. The Illinois Department of Natural Resource's Division of Energy and Environmental Assessment (1996:3) lists 950 plant taxa, or botanical types, along with 285 species of vertebrates (animals with backbones), including 39 native mammal, 122 native bird, 78 native freshwater fish, 13 amphibian, and 33 reptile species. They also report 33 native mussel and 10 native crustacean species here. Their abundance and distribution, however, have been significantly modified since Euro-American settlement by modern land clearing, urban development, agricultural practices, pollution, river control, and the introduction of alien species. Only remnants of the bottomland forests and upland prairies and groves remain, and upland oak barrens have been destroyed (Fell 1955; Wade and Wade 1977). Therefore, community distributions existing before Euro-American settlement have been reconstructed from botanical and soil surveys and from the United States General Land Office survey records of the 1830s. The following summary of the Rock River Hill Country Division plant and animal communities applies to most of the region (Fell 1955; Schwegman 1973).

Prairie   Extensive prairies existed on the uplands of the Rock River Hill Country. The vegetation was primarily of long-lived perennials that included dry-, mesic-, or wet-adapted species. The dry upland prairies contained species of the northern Great Plains such as pasque flower, plains buttercup, June grass, and Wilcox's panic grass along with the dominant little bluestem and side-oats grama (Schwegman 1973). The grasses consisted primarily of warm-season, medium-stature species. Dry prairies occurred on sandy, gravely, or limestone (dolomite) sites exemplified by steep slopes along the Rock River and some of its tributaries, moraines, and terraces (Fell 1955; Wade and Wade 1977). Mesic communities were the most prevalent in the upland prairie, with big bluestem, Indian grass, and prairie dropseed dominant. Important associated species were leadplant, prairie dock, switch grass, and compass plant. The wet sites contained an abundance of tall grasses such as big bluestem, switch grass, cord grass, and bluejoint grass (Fell 1955; Schwegman 1973).

Fauna associated with upland prairies include the white-tailed deer, bison, elk, coyote, gray wolf, badger, cottontail rabbits, thirteen-lined ground squirrel, pocket gopher, and greater prairie chicken. Dry upland prairies are often considered to have been relatively resource-poor for human purposes, except when bison and elk herds were present (Kind and Goldstein 1982; Springer 1984; Styles 1981). In contrast, wet prairie habitats apparently had greater productivity levels with high potential yields of migratory waterfowl and resident birds available, particularly in the spring and fall (Green 1987; Springer 1984).

Forest Deciduous forests occurred in the uplands, bluffs, ravines, and floodplains. Stands on the rolling dry upland were dominated by black oak, white oak, bur oak, and wild cherry. More mesophytic mixed hardwood stands, dominated by sugar maple, slippery elm, basswood, and red oak, occurred on gentle slopes, on low morainic ridges, and in isolated prairie groves (Geis and Boggess 1968; Schwegman 1973). Gallery forests of the Middle Rock Valley were dominated by silver maple, black willow, cottonwood, American elm, bur oak, white oak, and basswood trees (Bebb 1860; Fell and Fell 1958; Schwegman 1973).

The forests would have supported white-tailed deer, gray wolf, lynx, bobcat, black bear, tree squirrels, raccoon, fox, striped skunk, and mink (Bent 1877; Springer 1984). A number of birds, most notably turkey, bobwhite, passenger pigeon, and passerines, would also have been available. Most species would have been abundant near the forest edges, especially along stream and river margins, and openings. Several species were extirpated from the region in the nineteenth century, including the black bear, gray wolf, lynx, and passenger pigeon (Bohlen 1989; Hoffmeister 1989).

Aquatic/Wetland Of the resource-area types, the most important to the inhabitants was probably the aquatic/wetland habitat. Aquatic/wetland plant communities were dominated by the arrowhead, yellow pond lily, plantains, cattail, bulrush, sedge, and, occasionally, common reed. These communities occurred along stream margins, sloughs, and marshes (Fell 1955; Schwegman 1973).

Aquatic/wetland fauna provided abundant, patchy, and easily procured resources. Fish, mussels, turtles, birds, and migratory waterfowl were found in marshes, ponds, and streams. In addition, deer, raccoon, frogs, and turtles would have been readily accessible along marsh and stream edges. The seasonal potential for this habitat would have varied considerably. Regionally available fish species of importance for human exploitation included bullheads and catfishes (Ictaluridae), bass (*Micropterus* species), sunfishes (Centrarchidae), darters and perches (Percidae), suckers (Catostomidae), drum (*Aplodinotus grunniens*), pikes (Esocidae), gars (Lepisosteidae), sturgeons (Aciponseridae), and paddlefish (Polyodontidae) (Bent 1877; Fago 1982; Smith 1979). A number of freshwater mussels were also available, with the distribution varying from 19 species present in the upper part of the system to 33 species present in the lower portion (Baker 1927; IDNR/EEA 1996). Many species of waterfowl and wading birds were available seasonally or year-round (Bohlen 1989). Beaver, muskrat, and mink often frequented the open water too.

• The Lawrence and Keeshin Farm localities would have provided the late prehistoric inhabitants immediate access to a wide variety of animal habitats that supported various aquatic, terrestrial, and avian species of potential economic importance. The Prairie Peninsula as a whole, and the Middle Rock River region and site localities in particular, consisted of an environmental mosaic of prairie, forest, and aquatic/wetland habitats, a vast biogeographical area distinctive for its environmental redundancy. Situated in the middle latitudes of North America, with a continental climate, the freshwater environments of streams, lakes, and wetlands contain the same major groups of organisms, including viruses, bacteria, fungi and fungi-like organisms, green plants (algae and macrophytes), protozoans, rotifers, crustaceans, aquatic insects, worms, mollusks, fish, amphibians, reptiles, birds, and semiaquatic mammals (Goldman and Horne 1983:165–195; Needham and Needham 1962; Niering 1989). Also, since these aquatic/wetland systems are situated in the Prairie Peninsula, prairie and forest habitats are located nearby. This environmental redundancy has important implications for understanding relations of power during late prehistoric times and how Native American inhabitants viewed their cosmos.

Oneota villages had access to similar resources, making them relatively self-sufficient, which may explain, in part, the limited power of leaders. Villages were located on elevated terraces within proximity of extremely productive aquatic/wetland environments and prairie-forest ecotones as well as highly fertile horticultural soils (Alfisols) that could be easily worked with a digging stick or hoe. The village inhabitants had access to local chert sources (for tools) exposed as glacial cobbles in stream beds or present in beds of dolomite and limestone formations outcropping along the valley bluffs. Salt sources near Starved Rock, Illinois, were also locally available to Fisher and Langford peoples. This near self-sufficiency meant that populations would be less amenable to control by a leader (Kreisa 1993).

Oneota inhabitants of the Prairie Peninsula had to live with risk and uncertainty. Just when and how large would the bison herds be as they moved through the area on their way to better forage, salt licks, or water sources? How large would the nut mast production be this year? Would violent thunderstorms during the late spring and summer generate tornadoes and lightning to threaten lives and damage homes, or devastate crops by hail, high winds, or flooding? Is there a possibility of a severe drought causing stress on animal life and crops (which would have been prevalent during the Pacific climatic episode)? How could they *make use of their dreams* to provide insights into these problems and create unity with all things again?

Archaeology of the Middle Rock River

Little research has been conducted on Oneota cultures in the Middle Rock River region. Our understanding of the late prehistoric period is largely predicated upon nonrandom surface survey data and limited test excavations of large sites, with few radiocarbon dates, biased subsistence data, and little knowledge of variability in site types or locations. Additionally, much of the research performed is unpublished and remains accessible only as in-house reports, delivered papers, and photocopied (or dittoed) manuscripts. Such research has not been conducted within a long-term regional or topical framework. To date, the research designs have followed the culture ecology perspective regarding human-environment interactions.

OF RESEARCH FOR THE
MIDDLE ROCK RIVER REGION

The concern with contextual-functional approaches during the 1940s through early 1960s (Willey and Sabloff 1974) is reflected in previous investigations by professional archaeologists in the region. Archaeological projects were directed to the goals of chronology building, descriptive creation of the role of environment in prehistoric settlement-subsistence patterns, and site-specific research often conducted in advance of site destruction through urban development. Fieldwork in the Middle Rock Valley consisted of pedestrian surveys of selected areas, salvage excavations, and educationally oriented projects designed to involve nonprofessionals in supervised field projects.

The first archaeological survey of the area was conducted in 1961 by Elaine Bluhm Herold through the Department of Anthropology at the University of Illinois, Urbana-Champaign. The survey universe extended from the confluence of Mississippi and Rock rivers to Sterling–Rock Falls, Illinois. Information was obtained regarding the range and distribution of archaeological sites in the river valley (Bluhm et al. 1961). Some unpublished survey, testing, and salvage work was also done in the Sterling–Rock Falls area by the University of Illinois in association with the Illinois Archaeological Survey and highway salvage program (Benson 1972). Most important was the salvage excavation conducted at the Lawrence site in 1963, which demonstrated the existence of a Fisher phase occupation in the region.

A limited number of surveys and excavations were conducted in the Rockford area in the mid-twentieth century. For example, in 1954 the Keeshin Farm site was investigated as part of an educationally oriented project. The fieldwork was conducted under the direction of J. Joseph Bauxar, Rockford College anthropologist, and Milton Mahlberg, former director of the Rockford Natural History Museum, with the assistance of museum personnel and volunteers. The work was significant in the history of the Middle Rock Valley archaeology by providing insights on Langford and early historic Native American groups (Winnebago or later Potawatomi) inhabiting the area (J. Joe Bauxar, letter to the author, 1999).

During the early 1970s, portions of the Middle Rock Valley were surveyed in connection with the Historic Sites Survey program sponsored by the Illinois Archaeological Survey in conjunction with the Illinois Department of Conservation and the National Park Service (Fowler and Birmingham 1974, 1975; Fowler and Peters 1972). The surveys were designed to provide baseline data on changing regional settlement distributions. Sites were located through collector-informant interviews and reconnaissance of selected locations, while site information pertaining to spatiotemporal placement, artifact inventory, and cultural resource impact were recorded. The archaeological findings of these ecologically oriented projects were used to construct predictive models of late prehistoric regional settlement patterns and cultural-materialist histories (Birmingham 1975; Benchley and Birmingham 1978; Benchley et al. 1981). Economic symbiosis provided the basis for explaining the major cultural transformations. Hence, the cluster of Langford sites in the Sterling–Rock Falls area was perceived as indicative of the efficient exploitation of multiple ecozones in riverine settings. The Fisher phase Lawrence site location within this midst was viewed as an anomaly.

Within the last three decades, numerous Cultural Resource Management projects have been conducted in the Middle Rock Valley as a response to the National Historic Preservation Act of 1966, with extensive research conducted under the auspices of the Illinois Department of Transportation (IDOT) (e.g., Mehrer 1991; Studenmund 1988; Wolforth et al. 1995). Although lacking a specific problem orientation, this research, involving systematic survey and site-testing activities, has provided information regarding late prehistoric settlement patterns. The main problem shared by these investigations is that they are too site-specific, and investigations often involve small test excavations within the proposed right-of-way. Therefore, only limited data have been obtained pertaining to the structure and function of sites.

SITE DESCRIPTIONS AND EXCAVATION PROCEDURES

The data for this study is derived from excavated pits at the Lawrence site (11WT40) in Whiteside County, Illinois, and the Keeshin Farm site (11WO23) in Winnebago County, Illinois. Both sites represent late prehistoric villages situated on low terraces overlooking major fluvial channels. Archaeological investigations at these sites documented well-preserved feature deposits. These materials, coupled with chronometric dates, document Oneota occupations occurring sometime between A.D. 1040 and 1270.

Lawrence Site

Lawrence is a Fisher phase village encompassing approximately 0.74 acres (0.3 ha). This site is situated on a low, east-facing terrace overlooking the Rock River at an elevation of 630 feet (192 m) above sea level. It is situated about 1.9 miles (3 km) west of the Sterling–Rock Falls metropolitan area, extending along the eastern outskirts of Como, Illinois. The site has been destroyed by construction activities.

The Lawrence site was in the process of being destroyed by construction of a new housing subdivision in the spring of 1963 when the impact was communicated to University of Illinois archaeologists by John Washburn of Sterling, currently IDOT's Chief of Geological Assessment. Salvage excavations began immediately in April through the cooperation of a Rock Falls contractor, V. H. Lawrence & Sons. The crew consisted of University of Illinois students and members of the Council of Illinois Archaeologists from the Chicago area under the direction of Elaine Bluhm (later Elaine Bluhm Herold) and Charles J. Bareis (then a research associate and a former resident of Nachusa and Dixon). At that point, heavy machine scraping had destroyed cultural features along the river bank and removed the plow zone and upper portions of features in other construction areas.

The brief 1963 salvage investigations, lasting five days, initially required delineating features against the lighter clay subsoil. Pit features were then cross-sectioned, the profiles mapped, and the second halves removed, with each feature excavated by hand troweling. Feature fill was not dry-sieved, and no flotation samples were collected because this recovery technique was not employed in midwestern archaeology until the late 1960s. Although the excavations were very hurried, small-artifact recovery was high because of excellent preservation and a diligent field crew.

A total of 73 features were exposed during heavy machine operations, of which 65 pit features were completely excavated and fully recorded along with numerous postmolds. The pit features include two human burials, with the remaining either hearths or storage facilities that were reused as refuse dumps. The majority of the pits were round or oval in plan view and basin-shaped, bell-shaped, or cylindrical in profile view. All were very shallow due to the grading of upper portions. The artifacts appeared to be primarily Fisher phase Oneota; there were also materials affiliated with a minor Langford component, however (Birmingham 1975:17). The median values of four uncalibrated radiocarbon dates obtained for four features range between A.D. 1160 and 1270 (Table 2). The median values of the calibrated dates range between A.D. 1261 and 1294, making it contemporary with Langford tradition occupations of the Fisher, Zimmerman, and Washington Irving sites in the Upper Illinois Valley (Boszhardt et al. 1994; Markman 1991b:134).

Keeshin Farm Site

Keeshin Farm is a Langford tradition village site encompassing 4.9 acres (2.0 ha). Early Woodland and early-nineteenth-century historic Native American components are also present. It occupies a low, west-facing terrace overlooking the Kishwaukee River at an elevation of 690 feet (210 m) above sea level and is located about 2.5 miles (4 km) southwest of the Rockford metropolitan area. Limited field investigations were conducted here by Rockford area archaeologists in 1953 (Clift 1953) and 1954, and again by University of Illinois archaeologists in 1993 and 1994.

Before the most recent research, controlled surface collections and limited excavations were conducted in the summer of 1954 by J. Joe Bauxar and Milton Mahlburg. During this field season, a five-foot grid oriented upon magnetic north, and paralleling a fenceline, was laid out on a high area along the eastern portion of the site (north of the 1994 excavation block) because it was thought to be a refuse mound (J. Joseph Bauxar, letter to the author, 1999). Twenty excavation units measuring approximately five square feet were opened. Five pit features were exposed at the base of the plow zone in four of the excavation units and were subsequently excavated. The ceramic and lithic materials recovered from these features are curated at the Burpee Museum of Natural History in Rockford and have been analyzed by M. Catherine Bird and Rochelle Lurie of Midwest Archaeological Research Services,

Table 2.

Radiocarbon dates from the Lawrence and Keeshin Farm sites.

		UNCALIBRATED DATES			CALIBRATED DATES	
Site Name	Feature	Before Present	s	A.D.	Dates A.D.	Sample No.
Lawrence	59	790	110	1160	1261	M-1593
	27	780	110	1170	1263, 1273, 1275	M-1592
	16	690	110	1260	1292	M-1594
	39	680	110	1270	1294	M-1595
Keeshin Farm	32	860	70	1090	1210	CI-131
	3	910	70	1040	1160	CI-132

Note: Calibrated dates A.D. obtained from intercepts (Method A: two-sigma level)
(Stuiver and Reimer 1993).

Inc., Harvard, Illinois. The materials are diagnostic of Langford and early historic Native American occupations.

IDOT-sponsored archaeological investigations of the site were conducted in 1993 and 1994 by the Illinois Transportation Archaeological Research Program at the University of Illinois. The archaeological investigations were part of a cultural-resource survey and subsurface testing for the proposed expansion of the Greater Rockford Airport. An initial pedestrian survey in October 1993 was designed to relocate the site and define its boundaries. A sample of material included one Early Woodland Kramer preform and a projectile point, along with nine grit-tempered Langford sherds. Although the Greater Rockford Airport expansion plans were tentative at this time, it was recommended that additional archaeological investigations should be conducted to evaluate the impact of agricultural activity and possible future construction.

Additional archaeological investigations were conducted in the fall of 1994, which focused on evaluating the extent and integrity of prehistoric deposits. The site survey involved a controlled surface collection in which a metric grid was established over the recently plowed site. Artifacts were collected in 10-x-10-meter squares plotted systematically over a low- to moderate-density artifact scatter. Topographic contours, landmarks, field boundaries, and controlled surface collection reference points were mapped using a transit.

Subsequent to the controlled surface collection, a total area of 0.43 acres (0.17 hectares) was exposed by machine scraping along the southern site perimeter, which represents about 9 percent of the total surface scatter of the site. The area was shovel scraped to reveal the presence or absence of cultural features during plow-zone removal. These investigations resulted in the identification of 41 features. Thirty-one features were actually excavated; the remainder were left for the subsequent field season because of poor winter conditions. Feature 1 as well as Features 4 through 8, immediately north of the excavation block and within the plow zone, were excavated . All features within the block excavation were hand-excavated in cultural zones when possible. Each pit feature was cross-sectioned, the profile mapped, and then the second half removed. Feature fill was dry-sieved through 1/4-inch (6.4 mm) mesh hardware cloth and at least one 2.2-gallon (10-liter) sediment sample was collected for flotation from each cultural zone in the second half.

The Langford occupation of the site apparently occurred during the eleventh century A.D. Recent uncalibrated radiocarbon dates obtained from two features (3 and 32) have median values ranging between A.D. 1040 and 1090. The median values of the two calibrated dates range between A.D. 1156 and 1210. As such, the settlement would have been roughly contemporaneous with the Mississippian occupations of Aztalan in the Crawfish–Rock River valley (Richards 1992) and Lundy in the Apple River valley (Emerson 1991a) as well as the Langford occupations of Cooke, Material Service Quarry, Robinson Reserve, and Zimmerman sites in the Upper Illinois River basin (Markman 1991b:134) and the Fisher occupations of the Lawrence site in the Middle Rock River region and the Moccasin Bluff site in the St. Joseph River valley in Michigan (Bettarel and Smith 1973).

CHAPTER FIVE

Animal Exploitation and Consumption

Human exploitation and consumption of food resources are determined by cultural rules or customs that may vary among societies (Abrahams 1984:21; Armelagos 1994:235; Rosman and Rubel 1995:60, 156–158; Vialles 1994:4–5, 128). There are rules for both common and festival meals that remind one of what is to be consumed, with what food preparation and cooking techniques, what kinds of utensils are used, who will be eating, where they will sit, and in what order foods are to be served (Abrahams 1984:28; Rosman and Rubel 1995:60–61; Wing and Brown 1979:14–16). There are also rules on how the remains are to be disposed. Distinctions of food/non-food categories of cultural groups involve sets of contrasts such as acceptance/avoidance, attraction/repulsion, pure/dirty, raw/cooked, cooked/rotten, and celebration/rejection. Thus, the adage "you are what you eat" is applicable to every human group. Food is nutritionally invaluable to human survival by providing essential calories, protein, fats, minerals, and carbohydrates. Equally important, food is recognized as a mode of communication and symbol of *power* within and between cultures, providing markers for subcultural or regional group identity (Abrahams 1984:22; Jolley 1983:71; Lee 1957; McIntosh 1996:17–19; Styles 1993:267; Wing and Brown 1979:16) and explicit expressions of power by transforming bountiful seasonal harvests into occasions for pleasurable feasts where the kind of food and drink involved are never random (Gabaccia 1998:16; Leach 1976:60; Malinowski 1968:28–29; Trigger 1969:93–96; Wallace 1966:63). Generations pass on cuisine traditions (organized in patterned sets of food behavior) that are learned early and internalized through persistent peer and institutional pressures. Such customs and traditions are considered vital to the welfare of the family and the community so that the supply of food is not jeopardized (Wing and Brown 1979). Also, they permit members of each group to embrace their ancestry and meaningful cultural distinctions, which is important in the construction of one's identity. Food choice, preparation, and cuisine are as expressive as they are technical (Salvador 1967:245–246).

As animal consumers deeply familiar with their natural environments, Native Americans fostered different definitions of "good taste" and preferences that can be linked to varied culinary and secondary uses of only a fraction of the mammalian species available for human consumption (Armelagos 1994:235; Gabaccia 1998:14–15). Because meat is what sustains life, it remains a very exalted food among cultures. However, the importance of wild animals was more than just providing "red" meat or protein-rich butcher's meat to the community, which has been the focus of much zooarchaeological research. Undervalued in many studies are animal fats and greases (especially black bear grease) that contributed to the palatability and flavor of staples in the Eastern Woodlands and Plains (Gabaccia 1998:15; Neill 1884:250; Wallace 1949:38). Dietary fat is the most concentrated source of energy of all the nutrients, providing nine kilocalories per gram, about twice that contributed by either protein or carbohydrate (Mead et al. 1986:459). The fatty meat of bear, muskrat, and beaver could have been particularly important during winter and early spring when only lean meats were available (Wright 1987). There were many uses for the bones: some elements (especially the humeri and femora of deer, elk, and bison) were cracked for marrow and treated as a highly esteemed food resource, eaten raw or obtained by boiling crushed bones and skimming the floating grease or oil (Jolley 1983:174; Leechman 1951; Peale 1871); and other remains were modified into tools, ornaments, and utensils that often embodied important symbolic meanings (Parmalee 1959). Animal skins and fur were used for clothing, shelter, and accessories.

The restricted use of particular game animals in small-scale societies may be partly attributed to food taboos (Wallace 1966:62). Every religious system has rules of taboo involving certain activities forbidden under the sanction of supernatural punishment (Boas 1910a:368; Ember and Ember 1990:435; Rosman and Rubel 1995:60–61). Taboos surround food not to be eaten and animals not to be killed (untouchable), either permanently or at certain seasons or occasions, to prevent the power within them from injuring the person (Underhill 1957:128). For example, one division of the Omaha was forbidden to eat the elk while another was not allowed to eat the shoulder of the bison; the Iroquois could not eat the animal from which their family name was taken; most Athabascan-speaking peoples of northwestern North America associated the river otter with the spirits of the dead and so were forbidden to touch the animal; and the Navaho were forbidden to touch the flesh of the bear (Boas 1910a). There are also social taboos or rules of ethical conduct intended to placate the animal spirits controlling the food supply by showing respect (Underhill 1957:130; Wright 1987:3). For example, dogs were not permitted to gnaw the bones of certain animals, such as the bear, because it was a sign of disrespect for the animal's spirit. Also, the "first fruits" ceremonies for plants and animals were a vital part of the communal religious observances of Native Americans (Boas 1910a:368; Underhill 1957). The sanctity of particular animal species and the special disposal or display of their remains after processing and consumption is of interest to the zooarchaeologist because their presence or absence in the archaeological record may denote the values (culturally defined ideals of what is true, right, and beautiful that underlie cultural patterns) of the human group being studied. As the Canadian archaeologist J. V. Wright (1987:4) states, "Archaeology should be able to test certain hypotheses in an attempt to explain the absence of a species or of parts of an animal from segments of the archaeological record."

This chapter examines early Oneota animal exploitation and utilization in the Middle Rock River region through samples obtained from refuse pits at the Lawrence and Keeshin Farm sites. Both settlements showed similar access to a wide variety of prairie, forest, and aquatic/wetland resources within a one-mile radius (see chapter 3), which may be reflected in animal procurement for food as well as bone and antler technology observed in the archaeological record. If Langford and Fisher peoples represent two different ethnic groups, then their animal consumption and disposal habits may be different. If not, then perhaps an intersite comparison of the assemblages of animal remains may show distinct *patterns* comparable to other Oneota assemblages in the Prairie Peninsula and environs, especially regarding the heavy exploitation and utilization of white-tailed deer and fish, which were mainstays in the late prehistoric diet of Prairie Peninsula inhabitants. Using ethnohistoric data concerning human-human and human-animal interaction among small-scale societies of the Midcontinent, perhaps one can gain insights into these patterns and what they suggest regarding relations of power. What were the symbolic aspects and economic significance of animal species within the assemblages? How can the absence of certain species be explained by taboo? Did gender have a determining role in the procurement, processing, and uses of animals?

Efforts to use faunal data to address such concerns in anthropological archaeology has been accompanied by extensive methodological research. Zooarchaeologists must account for biases in faunal data caused by sampling methods and sample size, ensure precise faunal identifications (which are significant to cultural studies), and address the debates over valid and reliable measures of taxonomic abundance.

Sampling, Identification, and Quantification

The Lawrence and Keeshin Farm animal remains were derived from hand excavation (shoveling and troweling) and dry-sieving and are hereafter referred to as macrofaunal remains (biased toward large animals). The Lawrence remains, associated with the Fisher component, were recovered from 46 of the 66 pits excavated during the 1963 salvage operations. They came from the basal portion of pits because the upper portions had been removed through heavy machine scraping. Notwithstanding, the composition of the assemblage was extensive, which is attributable to the diligence of the field workers and excellent bone preservation in mildly alkaline calcareous clay loam matrix. The Keeshin Farm remains were obtained from 15 of the 31 pits excavated during the 1994 investigations and are identified with the Langford component.

The analysis initially involved identifying and sorting the macrofaunal remains by indeterminate and identifiable classes for each pit feature. Subsequently, identifications were made to the least inclusive taxonomic level possible, subject to limitations imposed by taphonomic processes, similarity between species, extent of the comparative collection, and the researchers' expertise. The taxonomic identifications were made by direct comparison to modern osteological and pelecypod collections maintained by the University of Illinois Laboratory of Anthropology. Limited use was also made of illustrated and descriptive osteological references by Olsen (1960, 1968), Gilbert (1990), and Gilbert et al. (1985) along with pelecypod references by Parmalee (1967) and Cummings and Mayer (1992). Zoological nomenclature of the identified taxa follows Jones et al. (1982) for mammals, the American Ornithologists' Union (1982) for birds, Smith (1979) for fish, Conant (1975) and Conant and Collins (1991) for reptiles, and Cummings and Mayer (1992) for freshwater mussels.

The quantification of remains was accomplished by tabulation of the number of identified specimens (NISP) per taxon (species, genus, family, or higher taxonomic category), which is simply measuring the total number of "specimens" that can be identified. The strengths and weaknesses as well as special applications of this technique have been extensively reviewed (Grayson 1984:16–92; Klein and Cruz-Uribe 1984:24–38; Lyman 1994a, 1994b; Marshall and Pilgram 1993; Ringrose 1993). Commonly perceived weaknesses of NISP focus on the "interdependence" of specimens (the fact that one cannot demonstrate which specimens came from different individuals) and that NISP values may not reflect past human behavior because the measure is greatly affected by postmortem activities such as trampling, food preparation techniques, scavenger activities by animals, redistribution of bones across a site (either by humans or animals), differential effects of preservation, and the recovery technique employed (Brewer 1992; Grayson 1984; Lyman 1994b).

In order to circumvent the problems associated with NISP as a valid ratio-scale measure of taxonomic abundance, which compares the relative numbers of specimens, similarities between faunal components at the two sites were also assessed with an ordinal measurement, which gives an ordering or ranking of cases in terms of the degree to which they have any given characteristic. Whereas ratio scales require that magnitudes between measured items be factual (reflecting actual conditions), ordinal level measurements do not (See Brewer 1986, 1992). Spearman's rank coefficient was employed to measure the degree of association for taxa at Lawrence and Keeshin Farms. In this study, taxonomically composite classes are also manipulated as units—forest, prairie, and aquatic/wetland—to examine habitat representation patterns.

An intersite comparison will now be made of the assemblages regarding taxonomic/skeletal composition, examining what they mean in terms of external relations. A discussion of taphonomic processes (i.e., how animals are altered by human and natural phenomena from a living organism to the archaeological record) will follow.

SITE COMPARISONS: THE EMPIRICAL DATA

Animal remains associated with the Lawrence and Keeshin Farm sites indicate that a variety of faunal resources in the Middle Rock River region were exploited. However, the Lawrence assemblage is characterized by greater proportional representation of taxa and species richness. The Lawrence sample consists of 9,842 specimens, with a total vertebrate NISP of 9,150 and freshwater mussel NISP of 692. Vertebrate remains include 5,855 specimens (64%) identifiable below the class level, and the invertebrate fragments include 178 specimens (26%) identifiable below the level of class. A total of 17 mammal, 15 bird, 7 reptile, 0 amphibian, 14 fish, and 12 freshwater mussel species are represented (Table 3). The Keeshin Farm sample contains 6,113 vertebrate specimens and five freshwater mussel (Pelecypoda) fragments. The vertebrate remains include 3,153 specimens (52%) identifiable to order, family, genus, or species. A total of 6 mammal, 1 bird, 1 reptile, and 6 fish species are represented. Most remains were recovered from Features 22, 32, and 34, comprising about 92 percent of the specimens.

Table 4 lists the rank order abundances of these classes based on specimen counts for each assemblage. There is a strong positive correlation ($r_s = +.71$) between the animal classes from the two sites. However, it is not significant at the 5 percent level of significance (α) probably because of the small Keeshin Farm sample size and absence of flotation material that would have increased fish NISP tabulations. (Flotation is an important technique developed to assist in the recovery of animal and plant remains from archaeological deposits and involves suspending feature fill in

Table 3.

Comparison between the Lawrence and Keeshin Farm faunal samples.

TAXON	LAWRENCE NISP	KEESHIN FARM NISP
Mammals		
Homo sapiens (Human)	2	
Scalopus aquaticus (Eastern mole)	5	
Vespertillionidae (Plainnose bats)	1	
Procyon lotor (Raccoon)	51	2
cf. *Procyon lotor*	5	
Mustela frenata (Longtail weasel)	4	
Mustela vison (Mink)	1	
Canis latrans (Coyote)	106	
Canis lupus (Gray wolf)	9	
Canis familiaris (Domestic dog)	1	
Vulpes fulva (Red fox)	7	
Lynx canadensis (Lynx)	2	
cf. *Lynx canadensis*	2	
cf. *Lynx rufus* (Bobcat)	2	
Citellus tridecemlineatus (Thirteen-lined ground squirrel)		3
Sciurus carolinensis (Gray squirrel)	3	
Castor canadensis (Beaver)	46	
Ondatra zibethica (Muskrat)	150	7
cf. *Ondatra zibethica*	3	
Sylvilagus floridanus (Eastern cottontail)		6
Cervidae (Deer)	562	
Cervus elaphus (Elk)	216	6
Odocoileus virginianus (White-tailed deer)	3,457	2,920
cf. *Odocoileus virginianus*	3	
Bison bison (Bison)	2	
Unidentifiable mammal bone	668	274
Subtotal	**5,294**	**3,218**
Birds		
Podicipedidae (Grebes)	1	
Podilymbus podiceps (Pied-billed grebe)	5	
Egretta thula (Snowy egret)	1	
Anatidae (Swans, geese, ducks)	1	
Branta canadensis (Canada goose)	22	
cf. *Branta canadensis*	5	
Anas platyrhyncos (Mallard)	49	
cf. *Anas platyrhyncos*	2	
Anas rubripes (Black duck)	3	

TAXON	LAWRENCE	KEESHIN FARM
	NISP	NISP
Birds *(continued)*		
Anas discors (Blue-winged teal)	8	
Aix sponsa (Wood duck)	24	
cf. *Aix sponsa*	5	
Aythya marila (Greater scaup duck)	1	
Mergus merganser (Common merganser)	3	
cf. *Mergus merganser*	3	
Haliaeetus leucocephalus (Bald eagle)	1	
cf. *Tympanuchus cupido* (Greater prairie chicken)	3	
Meleagris gallopavo (Turkey)	8	10
Fulica americana (American coot)	4	
Strigiformes (Owls)	2	
Strix nebulosa (Great gray owl)	1	
Chordeiles minor (Nighthawk)	2	
Agelaius phoeniceus (Red-winged blackbird)	4	
Passeriformes (Perching birds)	5	
Unidentifiable bird bones	300	354
Subtotal	**463**	**364**
Reptiles		
Chelydra serpentina (Snapping turtle)	36	
Terrapene ornata ornata (Ornate box turtle)	64	
cf. *Terrapene ornata ornata*	1	
Graptemys pseudogeographica (False map turtle)	11	
Graptemys sp. (map turtle)	17	
Trachemys scripta elegans (Red-eared slider)	3	
cf. *Trachemys scripta elegans*	3	
Chrysemys picta (Painted turtle)	11	
Graptemys/Trachemys/Chrysemys	122	63
(Map, sliders, painted turtles)		
Apalone mutica mutica (Midland smooth softshell)	4	
Apalone spinifera spinifera (Eastern spiny softshell)	57	87
cf. *Apalone* sp.	4	
Unidentifiable turtle	18	7
Subtotal	**351**	**157**
Amphibians		
Anura (Toads and frogs)		3
Ranidae (True frogs)	3	
Subtotal	**3**	**3**
Fish		
Acipenseridae (Sturgeons)	15	
Acipenser fulvescens (Lake sturgeon)	65	
Lepisosteidae (Gars)	4	
Lepisosteus sp. (Gar)		1
Esocidae (Pikes)	3	

TAXON	LAWRENCE	KEESHIN FARM
Fish *(continued)*	NISP	NISP
Esox spp. (Pike)		1
Catostomidae (Suckers)	9	1
Ictiobus bubalus (Smallmouth buffalo)	20	
Ictiobus cyprinellus (Bigmouth buffalo)	11	
Ictiobus niger (Black buffalo)	36	
Ictiobus sp. (Buffalo)	5	
cf. *Ictiobus* sp.	1	
Moxostoma anisurum (Silver redhorse)	5	
Moxostoma duquesnei (Black redhorse)	43	9
Moxostoma macrolepidotum (Northern redhorse)	44	
Moxostoma sp. (Redhorse)	21	3
Ictaluridae (Catfishes and bullheads)	13	
Ictalurus furcatus (Blue catfish)	20	
cf. *Ictalurus furcatus*	1	
Ictalurus punctatus (Channel catfish)	292	5
Ictalurus spp. (Catfish/bullhead)	20	11
Centrarchidae (Sunfishes)	1	
Ambloplites rupestris (Rock bass)	3	2
Micropterus dolomieui (Smallmouth bass)	5	
Micropterus salmoides (Largemouth bass)	37	4
Micropterus sp. (Bass)		1
Percidae (Perches and darters)	1	
Stizostedion vitreum (Walleye)	2	2
Aplodinotus grunniens (Freshwater drum)	53	5
Unidentifiable fish bone	2,309	273
Subtotal	**3,039**	**318**
Freshwater Mussel		
Quadrula pustulosa (Pimpleback)	9	
Amblema plicata (Threeridge)	21	
Fusconaia ebena (Ebonyshell)	2	
Cyclonaias tuberculata (Purple wartyback)	7	
Elliptio crassidens (Elephant-ear)	9	
Elliptio dilatata (Spike)	3	
Actinonaias ligamentina (Mucket)	62	
Leptodea leptodon (Scaleshell)	3	
Ligumia recta (Black sandshell)	22	
Venustaconcha ellipsiformis (Ellipse)	8	
Lampsilis siliquoidea (Fatmucket)	4	
Lampsilis cardium (Plain pocketbook)	28	
Unidentifiable mussel	514	5
Subtotal	**692**	**5**
Indeterminate bone		2,053
GRAND TOTAL	**9,842**	**6,118**

water with organic material having a low specific gravity, such as carbonized seeds, floating to the surface while heavier inorganic materials, such as soil and rock, will sink to the bottom.) Still, they are consistent with other Oneota faunal assemblages.

TAXONOMIC/SKELETAL COMPOSITION AND EXTERNAL RELATIONS

Mammals

Mammalia is clearly the most significant class in the assemblages, with bone occurring in most pit features containing fauna. At the Lawrence site, mammals contributed about 54 percent (5,294 NISP) of the total NISP, with seventeen taxa identified to the species level. At Keeshin Farm, mammal specimens accounted for about 53 percent (3,218 NISP) of the total NISP, with six taxa identified to the species level. Their remains were recovered from all features except Feature 35. The dominance of mammals is exactly what we have come to expect from Oneota assemblages, which is largely due to the presence of a single large-mammal taxon, white-tailed deer.

Deer was an economically important species since it served as a source for food, tools, and hides; had a large body size surpassed only by elk and bison; and would have been abundant in a wide variety of habitats including forests, forest edges, and oak barrens throughout the Prairie Peninsula. The domination of their remains in archaeological assemblages has been reported for Langford occupations of the Robinson Reserve (Fowler 1952:51–52), Noble-Wieting (Parmalee and Bogan 1980a:6), and Reeves (Craig and Galloy 1995:9–7) sites along with later Oneota Classic horizon occupations of the Chicago area, including Anker (Bluhm and Liss 1961:112–113), Oak Forest (Bluhm and Fenner 1961:159), Huber (Parmalee 1990:106), and Hoxie Farm (Foss and Parmalee 1990:109) sites. Deer is also dominant at eastern Wisconsin Oneota sites, as exemplified by Carcajou Point, where nearly 90 percent of the sample came from this animal (Gibbon 1986:332).

White-tailed deer is the most abundant and ubiquitous taxon in both assemblages examined here. Their remains comprise about 65 percent (3,460 NISP) of the identified mammal and 59 percent of all identifiable vertebrate specimens at the Lawrence site. Deer is represented in all but three pits containing animal remains (Features 11, 18, and 48), with most found in Features 64 (28%), 9 (10%), 27 (9%), and 45 (8%). In comparison, they comprise about 91 percent (2,920 NISP) of the identified mammal and 48 percent of all identified vertebrate specimens at the Keeshin Farm site. Deer was recovered from 13 features, with most remains (81%) found in Features 32 and 34.

Analyses of white-tailed deer body-part representation at the Lawrence site provides a striking parallel to Keeshin Farm (Table 5).

Table 4.

Rank of abundance for the animal classes.

Class	LAWRENCE			KEESHIN FARM		
	Rank	NISP	Percent	Rank	NISP	Percent
Mammals	1	5,294	53.8	1	3,218	52.6
Birds	4	463	4.7	2	364	5.9
Reptiles	5	351	3.6	4	157	2.6
Amphibians	6	3	.03	6	3	.01
Fish	2	3,039	31.0	3	318	5.2
Freshwater Mussels	3	692	7.0	5	5	.02

$r_s = +.71$

There is a strong positive correlation ($r_s = +.85$) between the deer body-part representation for the two sites, which is significant at the 5 percent level of significance (α). Virtually all skeletal portions are represented in the assemblages, which show a fairly uniform representation. The data suggest that entire carcasses were transported to the village sites for food processing (meat, bone marrow, and bone grease), manufacturing of bone and antler artifacts, and hide processing.

Deer antler, craniofacial, and dental fragments make up 7 percent of the Lawrence and 12 percent of the Keeshin Farm assemblages. In contrast, the axial and proximal appendicular skeletal remains (i.e., vertebrae, ribs, sternum, proximal forequarters and hindquarters) comprise 69 percent of the Lawrence and 62 percent of the Keeshin Farm assemblages. These are the high-utility, or meat-rich, body segments. Also, some of these units (i.e., femur, tibia, humerus, radius, ulna, and vertebrae) have been shown to contain high grease fat yields in ungulates (Bunn 1993; Emerson 1993; Vehik 1977). The distal appendicular or limb elements (i.e., other foot bones, distal forequarters, and hindquarters) comprise 24 percent of the Lawrence and 26 percent of the Keeshin Farm assemblages. The presence of these appendicular elements indicate that factors other than nutritional utility influence skeletal-part compositions of the assemblages. For example, metapodial beamers found at Oneota villages may often represent the byproduct of their removal from carcasses, skinning, and manufacture on-site.

Table 5.

Skeletal portions of white-tailed deer represented in the assemblages.

	LAWRENCE			KEESHIN FARM		
Deer Skeletal Portions	Rank	NISP	(%)	Rank	NISP	(%)
Head						
Antler		36			3	
Cranium		8			5	
Mandible		16			1	
Isolated Teeth		7			7	
Subtotal	7	67	(7)	6	16	(12)
Vertebrae						
Cervical		55			8	
Thoracic		21			1	
Lumbar		80			12	
Sacrum		3			1	
Caudal		-			2	
Subtotal	2	159	(18)	1	24	(18)
Ribs and Sternum						
Ribs		136			20	
Sternum		2			-	
Subtotal	4	138	(15)	2	20	(15)
Proximal Forequarter						
Scapula		25			1	
Humerus		51			9	
Radius		59			6	
Ulna		23			2	
Subtotal	3	158	(18)	5	18	(14)
Distal Forequarter						
Carpal		5			-	
Metacarpal		49			4	
Subtotal	8	54	(6)	8	4	(3)
Proximal Hindquarter						
Innominate		32			5	
Femur		53			8	
Patella		11			-	
Tibia		66			7	
Subtotal	1	162	(18)	2	20	(15)
Distal Hindquarter						
Calcaneum		6			-	
Astragalus		5			2	
Distal Fibula		4			1	
Other Tarsal		16			4	
Metatarsal		48			12	
Subtotal	5	79	(9)	4	19	(15)
Other Foot Bone						
Phalange		75			11	
Sesamoid		3			-	
Subtotal	6	78	(9)	7	11	(8)
Grand Total		895	(100)		132	(100)

$r_s = +.85$

Other large mammals apparently represented a relatively minor component in northern Illinois Fisher and Langford economies in comparison to white-tailed deer. Elk and bison could also have provided food, tool, and hide sources available year-round, and yet both are poorly represented in the assemblages. Elk, or wapiti, comprises only about 4 percent (216 NISP) and 0.2 percent (6 NISP) of the identified mammal remains at Lawrence and Keeshin Farm, respectively. Bison bone is also poorly represented at Lawrence, and it is absent at Keeshin Farm. At Lawrence, two bison specimens were recovered from Features 29 and 57, consisting of a proximal left humerus (humeral head and upper shaft portion, with a deltoid crest more rugose than elk) and a proximal third phalange, respectively.

Bison remains also occur in low frequency in other assemblages east of the Mississippi River during the Oneota Emergent and Developmental horizons (Stevenson 1985:141; Theler 1989:170). In Illinois, for example, only four specimens were found at the Langford tradition Robinson Reserve site in the Chicago area (Fowler 1952:52). There is the distinct possiblity that bison were hunted elsewhere and then the meat as well as the tongue and liver taken from the carcass and transported to the settlement. Thus, bone elements would be rare or absent at the village (J. Joseph Bauxar, letter to the author, 1999; Stevenson 1985:141). On the other hand, the rarity of bison remains may be due to availability, because a substantial influx of bison into the area did not occur until sometime during the Pacific climatic episode, perhaps not until the 1400s (Brown and Sasso 1992; Purdue and Styles 1987; Tankersley 1986). The rapid and widespread dispersal of these "opportunistic" ruminants may have been induced by greater human predation and settlement of alluvial valleys on the Northern Plains (e.g., proto-Mandan along the Middle Missouri River). Perhaps more important, there were changes in forage quality and abundance as the cool, dry Pacific episode may have resulted in patchy or poor-quality forage in the Northern and Central Plains (Bamforth 1988:35; Bozell 1995; Koch 1995) while producing increased forage abundance and quality in the eastern Prairie Peninsula (i.e., abundant big bluestem forage of low nutrient value may have been replaced on particular landform locales by shorter grasses having higher concentrations of nutrients).

Although elk remains were present at both villages, data on skeletal portions in Table 6 show that their representation contrasts sharply. The Lawrence assemblage consists of almost all skeletal elements, suggesting that entire field-butchered carcasses were transported to the village for further processing and consumption. On the other hand, the Keeshin Farm assemblage consists of a few appendicular skeletal portions (i.e., left proximal radius, left proximal/shaft metatarsal, left naviculo-cuboid, left external and middle cuneiform) suggesting that only those portions were transported back to the village. The axial units could have been stripped

Table 6.

Skeletal portions of elk represented in the assemblages.

	LAWRENCE		KEESHIN FARM	
Elk Skeletal Portions	NISP	(%)	NISP	(%)
Head				
Antler	4		-	
Cranium	-		-	
Mandible	4		-	
Isolated Teeth	3		-	
Subtotal	11	(8)	0	(0)
Vertebrae				
Cervical	7		-	
Thoracic	4		-	
Lumbar	8		-	
Sacrum	-		-	
Caudal	-		-	
Subtotal	19	(13)	0	(0)
Ribs and Sternum				
Ribs	20		-	
Sternum	1		-	
Subtotal	21	(15)	0	(0)
Proximal Forequarter				
Scapula	3		-	
Humerus	4		-	
Radius	8		1	
Ulna	1		-	
Subtotal	16	(11)	1	(25)
Distal Forequarter				
Carpal	9	-		
Metacarpal	3	-		
Subtotal	12	(9)	0	(0)
Proximal Hindquarter				
Innominate	6		-	
Femur	8		-	
Patella	-		-	
Tibia	10		-	
Subtotal	24	(17)	0	(0)
Distal Hindquarter				
Calcaneum	2		-	
Astragalus	-		-	
Distal Fibula	-		-	
Other Tarsal	4		2	
Metatarsal	14		1	
Subtotal	20	(14)	3	(75)
Other Foot Bone				
Phalange	16		-	
Sesamoid	2		-	
Subtotal	18	(13)	0	(0)
Grand Total	141	(100)	4	(100)

Table 7.

Skeletal portions of muskrat in Lawrence assemblage.

Skeletal Portions	NISP (%)	Skeletal Portions	NISP (%)
Head	28 (19)	**Forelimbs**	22 (15)
Cranium	7	Scapula	5
Mandible	21	Humerus	7
Vertebrae	29 (19.7)	Radius	5
Cervical	6	Ulna	5
Thoracic	1	**Hindlimbs**	30 (20.4)
Lumbar	13	Femur	15
Caudal	9	Tibia	12
Ribs	1 (0.7)	Calcaneous	3
Other Foot Bones	16 (10.9)	**Innominate**	21 (14.3)
Phalanges	15		
Metapodia	1		

of meat and the associated skeletal elements discarded at the kill site. However, such a simplistic economic assessment based on the "schlepp effect" of Perkins and Daly (1968) may, instead, reflect sample size or human processing and disposal practices.

Muskrat is the second-most abundant mammal species at the Keeshin Farm site, and it ranks third in the Lawrence sample. At Keeshin Farm, it is represented by only seven specimens recovered from Feature 22, with both cranial and postcranial parts noted. The small quantity of remains is surprising given the nearby favorable wetland habitat for these large aquatic rodents. At Lawrence, muskrat is represented by 153 specimens, comprising about 3 percent of the identified mammal remains. Virtually all parts of the skeletal body are represented (Table 7): of the skull and axial skeleton, the mandibles, vertebrae, and innominates are well represented; of the appendicular skeletal units, most elements are well represented with the exception of some foot bones (i.e., carpals and tarsals). This evidence suggests that whole animals were brought to the site for processing.

Coyote is fourth in NISP values at Lawrence, occurring in eight features and concentrated in Feature 38 (64%). Almost all parts of the skeleton are represented (Table 8), providing evidence of yet another mammal species that was transported whole to the habitation site for processing. In skeletal-part representation, ribs clearly dominate (47.2%). Also common are hindlimbs (16%) and forelimbs (13.2%). No skinning,

Table 8.

Skeletal portions of coyote.

Skeletal Portions	NISP (%)	Skeletal Portions	NISP (%)
Head	10 (9.4)	**Forelimbs**	14 (13.2)
Cranium	3	Scapula	4
Mandible	4	Humerus	2
Isolated Teeth	3	Radius	4
Vertebrae	5 (4.7)	Ulna	3
Cervical	1	Carpal	1
Thoracic	1	**Hindlimbs**	17 (16.0)
Lumbar	3	Femur	5
Caudal	-	Tibia	7
Ribs	50 (47.2)	Fibula	3
Other Foot Bones	7 (6.6)	Calcaneous	1
Phalanges	5	Astragalus	1
Metapodial	2	**Innominate**	3 (2.8)

Table 9.

Skeletal portions of raccoon.

Skeletal Portions	NISP (%)	Skeletal Portions	NISP (%)
Head	15 (31)	**Forelimbs**	16 (33)
Cranium	1	Scapula	2
Maxilla	4	Humerus	3
Mandible	9	Radius	5
Isolated Teeth	1	Ulna	6
Vertebrae	0 (0)	Carpal	-
Cervical	-	**Hindlimbs**	7 (14)
Thoracic	-	Femur	1
Lumbar	-	Tibia	2
Caudal	-	Fibula	2
Ribs	8 (16)	Calcaneous	2
Other Foot Bones	3 (6)	Astragalus	-
Phalanges	3	**Innominate**	0 (0)

disarticulation, or defleshing cut marks were observed on the canid bones, unlike those noted in Lynn Snyder's (1991) analyses of canid bones from the Great Oasis Packer site in Nebraska. Coyote remains were notably absent in the Keeshin Farm sample, even though the species may have been common to the environment adjoining the site.

The mammal species ranking fifth in abundance at Lawrence is raccoon, with 56 specimens found in 14 pit features. Of the skull and axial skeleton, both mandibular and maxillary portions are well represented (Table 9). Of the appendicular skeletal units, the scapula, humerus, radius, ulna, femur, tibia, fibula, and calcaneous are present. Raccoon remains were rare in the Keeshin Farm assemblage, with only two specimens (canine tooth and humerus) recovered.

Beaver is sixth in abundance at Lawrence, which held 46 identifiable specimens whose distribution was relatively uniform among 14 separate features. Vertebrae, innominate, and upper hindlimb portions (femur, tibia) contributed 39 percent (18 NISP). Cranial parts and dentition contributed 33 percent (15 NISP) of the site total, while forelimb portions (scapula, humerus, radius, ulna) are represented by 24 percent (11 NISP). Noteworthy is the absence of beaver in the Keeshin Farm assemblage even though wetland habitats were within the immediate vicinity of the site.

The remaining mammals in the Keeshin Farm assemblage include eastern cottontail and thirteen-lined ground squirrel, each accounting for less than one percent of the identified mammal remains. The eastern cottontail remains consist of bones from the lower back leg (tibia and fibula), foot bones (calcaneous and phalange), and an incisor tooth. Three ground squirrel specimens were recovered from Feature 19 and probably are intrusive. It is unlikely that the Langford inhabitants consumed or otherwise utilized such small rodents. Both species are absent in the Lawrence assemblage. The remaining 11 species in the Lawrence assemblage each contribute 0.2 percent or less of the sample. In descending order of relative abundance, they are gray wolf, red fox, eastern mole, longtail weasel, lynx, gray squirrel, human, bobcat, bison, mink, and domestic dog. Also present in the assemblage was a specimen of the plainnose bat family (Vespertilionidae).

Birds

Avian remains occur in low frequency at both sites. It is the fourth-most frequent class at Lawrence, with 463 NISP, or 4.7 percent of all fauna, recovered from 25 pit features. The Keeshin Farm assemblage contains 364 bird specimens, comprising only 5.9 percent of the total NISP, recovered from Features 3, 22, and 32. Turkey was the only species identified. The absence of waterfowl (swans, geese, and ducks) and wading birds (e.g., grebes and coot) at the Keeshin Farm site was unexpected given the nearby wetland habitats.

Fifteen taxa were identified to the species level in the Lawrence assemblage. Mallard remains are the most commonly identified, accounting for 10.6 percent (49 NISP) of the identified bird remains. The specimens were recovered from 11 pits, with most found in Feature 41. The mallard is a common dabbling duck of the Mississippi Flyway and is found in a variety of aquatic/wetland habitats (Bohlen 1989:26). The second-most abundant bird species is another dabbling duck, the wood duck, which made up 6.3 percent (29 NISP) of all identified birds. The remains were recovered from 13 pits and were relatively uniform in distribution. These river ducks are a common migrant and summer resident in northern Illinois and would have been present in the Middle Rock Valley from late February through late September to November (Bohlen 1989:24). Slightly less common than the wood duck is the Canada goose, comprising 5.8 percent (27 NISP) of all bird NISP, followed by blue-winged teal, turkey, and pied-billed grebe. Next in abundance are nine species, each contributing less than 1 percent of the sample. In descending order of relative abundance, they are red-winged blackbird, American coot, greater prairie chicken, black duck, nighthawk, snowy egret, greater scaup duck, bald eagle, and great gray owl. Also present in the assemblage were grebes (family Podicipedidae), swans, geese, and ducks (family Anatidae), owls (order Strigiformes), and perching birds (order Passeriformes).

The small quantity of bird remains at these two sites is not surprising, since similar findings have been documented at most Oneota sites including those in the Des Moines Valley in Iowa (Kelly 1990:399), the La Crosse, Wisconsin, area (Scott 1994; Theler 1989, 1994:387), the Middle Illinois River valley (Styles and King 1990:60), the Chicago area (Foss and Parmalee 1990:109; Fowler 1952; Michalik 1982:34; Neusius 1990:271; Parmalee 1990:105), the American Bottom of the Middle Mississippi Valley (Kelly 1992:500), and the St. Joseph River (Bettarel and Smith 1973:132) and Kalamazoo River (Barr 1979; Higgins 1980) valleys in southwestern Michigan. They also occur in low frequency in historic contexts at the Sac and Fox Crawford Farm site in the Lower Rock River valley of northwestern Illinois (Parmalee 1964), the Potawatomi Windrose site in the Kankakee River valley of northeastern Illinois (Martin 1996:479), the Michigamea and Kaskaskia Waterman site in the American Bottom (Parmalee and Bogan 1980b), and the Kickapoo Rhoads site in central Illinois (Parmalee and Klippel 1983).

This widespread scarcity suggests individual choice, constrained by tradition, in procurement and final burial practices rather than in preservation or seasonal exploitation factors. Regarding taphonomic factors, some bird skeletal parts apparently have a high survivability rate under fire (i.e., coracoid, long bone shafts, ribs, vertebrae) and so would be preserved in the archaeological record (Berres 1996:119). In terms of seasonality, most of the sites noted above are located within productive habitats for waterfowl and wading birds and appear to have been occupied during warmer seasons of the year when a variety of avifauna would be present.

Individual choices may have involved ritual deposition of most bird remains away from habitation refuse pits because of the religious significance of birds as sacred creatures of the upperworld. The small sample of raptorial (hawks, owls, eagles) and passerine (perching) birds in the Lawrence assemblage suggests that they provided a source of decorative feathers and body parts (e.g., heads, wings, claws) for personal adornment and ritual objects. Featherwork was found among historic tribes throughout North America. Such work was highly colorful, elaborate, and diverse in style (Gilbert et al. 1985:2–8; Highwater 1983:144–145; Swanton 1979:251–252). The number and variety of passerine birds (e.g., buntings, chickadees, flycatchers, kinglets, and wrens) encountered at the historic Kickapoo site of Rhoads in central Illinois was interpreted by Parmalee and Klippel (1983:272) as exploitation for their colorful plumage in decoration or body adornment. Ubelaker and Wedel (1975) and Parmalee (1977) note that Plains groups used bird remains for dress ornamentation and ceremonial paraphernalia such as head gear, whistles, fans, dance regalia (e.g., wands), and medicine bundles.

Reptiles

Reptiles were relatively uncommon, representing the fifth-most and fourth-most frequent class in the Lawrence and Keeshin Farm assemblages, respectively. The reptile remains reflect an effort at exploiting turtles exclusively. Most were acquired from aquatic/wetland habitats, with the exception of the ornate box turtle. In the Lawrence assemblage, seven taxa were identified to the species level, listed here in descending order of frequency: ornate box turtle, eastern spiny softshell, snapping turtle, false map turtle, painted turtle, red-eared slider, and Midland smooth softshell. Aquatic turtle remains from Keeshin Farm are infrequently represented by softshell and map, slider, or painted turtle. The eastern spiny softshell was the only species identified. The low species diversity here could be attributed to a small sample. Except for softshell turtles, all species could have been harvested during the late spring to early summer when clutches are laid on dry, sandy terrace margins (Theler 1989:186). Thus, they would have provided minor, periodic food supplements. Turtle remains are poorly represented at other Langford sites, including Robinson Reserve (Fowler 1952:51), Noble-Wieting (Parmalee and Bogan 1980a:3), and Reeves (Craig and Galloy 1995:9–25).

Amphibians

Amphibian remains are poorly represented at both sites, ranking last in NISP totals, and are also rare at other late prehistoric sites. Three specimens assigned to the true frog (family Ranidae) are the only elements identified from the amphibian class at Lawrence. The identifiable bone fragments consist of two femora and one tibiofibula, which were recovered from Feature 44. At the Keeshin Farm site, amphibian remains consist of toad or frog (order Anura) bones that were recovered exclusively from Feature 19. Only three indeterminate specimens were identified, none of which were cut or burned. The remains are probably naturally deposited and so do not represent a part of the Fisher and Langford subsistence economies.

Fish

Fish is the second-most important class in the Lawrence faunal assemblage (constituting about 31 percent of the total assemblage) while ranking third at the Keeshin Farm site (contributing 5.2 percent). The slight disparity in their rankings may reflect differing sample sizes (see Grayson 1984:116–130) and, perhaps more important, biases toward large fauna due to the absence of flotation samples in the Keeshin Farm study. Certainly, the richness and abundance of fish species would significantly increase with higher recovery rates associated with flotation (see Styles 1981; McConaughy et al. 1993). A high ranking for fish should not be surprising given each site's proximity to a main river channel. Fish would have been more predictable in their habits (e.g., spawning and nesting patterns), easier to procure, and more abundant than other meat sources. Particularly evident is the ubiquity and abundance of catfish and suckers in the archaeological record, indicative of their significance as important food resources. Individual choices constrained by tradition probably had some effect on Fisher and Langford fishery, which were choices consistent with other Oneota groups.

At Lawrence, 14 taxa were identified to the species level, which were present in 33 pit features. At Keeshin Farm, 6 taxa were identified to the species level, which were recovered from Features 15, 19, 22, 24, 32, and 34, with most remains present in Features 22 (30%) and 32 (68%). Even with the disparity of macrofauna sample sizes and biases in recovery techniques, there are some remarkable similarities in the fish assemblages.

Bullhead catfish (family Ictaluridae) is the most abundant fish group at both sites. At Lawrence, it accounts for about 47 percent (346 NISP) of all remains identified at least to the family level and 11 percent of all identifiable fish bone. Two species are present, including channel catfish and blue catfish. Channel catfish dominates by constituting 84 percent (292 NISP) of all catfish and bullheads. It was found in 19 pit features, with most present in Features 34 (26%) and 38 (20%). Like all bony fish, catfish have many distinctive bones that can be identified with a specific anatomical region (see Cannon 1987:13). Specimens associated with these regions are listed in Table 10 and show that whole fish were brought to the settlement for processing.

The blue catfish bones represent 6 percent (21 NISP) of all catfish and bullheads, with the remains recovered from Features 16, 20, 39, and 41. The elements are presented in descending order of frequency as five quadrate, four dentary, and three ceratohyal-epihyal, along with two each of articular, hyomandibular, and preopercular. Also represented are one each of ceratohyal, cleithrum, and opercular.

Table 10.

Channel catfish skeletal specimens associated with anatomical regions.

Anatomical Region	NISP	Anatomical Region	NISP
Olfactory Region		**Mandibular Arch**	
Ethmoid	1	Palatine	2
Supraethmoid	7	Quadrate	6
Vomer	1	Mesopterygoid	9
Orbital Region		**Hyoid Arch**	
Parasphenoid	3	Hyomandibular	19
Occipital Region		Epihyal	4
Supraoccipital	1	Ceratohyal	6
Basioccipital	2	Ceratohyal-epihyal	2
Otic Region		**Pectoral Girdle**	
Prootic	1	Posttemporal	4
Investing Bones		Cleithrum	52
Frontal	25	Coracoid	31
Supratemporal	1	Pectoral Spine	45
Prefrontal	2	**Pelvic Girdle**	
Lateral Skull Bones		Basipterygium	1
Dentary	20	**Vertebral Column**	
Articular	11	Atlas Vertebra	1
Articular/Dentary	2	Modified Second Vertebra	7
Preopercular	8	Pterygiophore	3
Opercular Series		**Caudal Skeleton**	
Opercular	14	Ultimate Vertebra	1

At Keeshin Farm, bullhead catfish accounts for about 47 percent (16 NISP) of all remains identified at least to the family level and about 5 percent of all fish. Channel catfish was identified from 5 specimens (articular, opercular, ceratohyal, epihyal, and pectoral spine) occurring in Feature 22, with the remaining specimens found in Feature 32. Bullhead catfish is also the most abundant group identified at other Oneota sites in Illinois. For example, it is well represented in the Reeves site assemblage, constituting the second-most important family (Craig and Galloy 1995), and it is the most significant group identified at the Fisher site (Parmalee 1962). Of the catfish group, channel catfish is most common in the assemblages. They may have been harvested while guarding their nests in hollow logs or underwater cavities from early to midsummer (Theler 1989:191). The zooarchaeologist James Theler (1994:388) notes that the procurement of channel catfish is a persistent aspect of Oneota faunal assemblages in western Wisconsin. Fish assemblages from the Central Des Moines River valley also show an Oneota selective process geared toward large catfish as well as adult-sized suckers (Kelly 1990:396).

The sucker (family Catostomidae) is the second-most frequent fish group in both assemblages. It represents 6.4 percent (195 NISP) of all fish remains at the Lawrence site, with the following six species identified: northern redhorse, black redhorse, silver redhorse, black buffalo, bigmouth buffalo, and smallmouth buffalo. The anatomical regions present indicate, once again, that whole fish were brought to the site for processing. Northern redhorse is the most abundant by a slight margin, accounting for 22.6 percent (44 NISP) of all suckers. The remains were found in seven pits, with the majority from Feature 21 (57%). There are nine anatomical regions represented, listed here in descending order of frequency: lateral skull, hyoid arch, orbital region, opercular series, pelvic girdle, branchial arch, pectoral girdle, olfactory region, and vertebral column.

Black redhorse is the second-most abundant of the sucker group, representing 22 percent (43 NISP) of the NISP total. The remains were found in six features but occur predominantly in Features 38 (37%) and 41 (30%). The specimens associated with distinctive anatomical regions are presented in descending order of frequency: opercular series, lateral skull bones, pectoral girdle region, hyoid arch, orbital region, vertebral column, mandibular arch, and caudal skeleton.

The third-most frequent species is black buffalo, accounting for 18.5 percent (36 NISP) of identifiable sucker specimens. The remains were found in eight pit features and are characterized by a relatively uniform distribution. There are 10 anatomical regions represented by this bony fish species: opercular series, lateral skull bones, hyoid arch, pectoral girdle, vertebral column, caudal skeleton, orbital region, occiptial region, mandibular arch, and branchial arch. Smallmouth buffalo represents the fourth-most abundant sucker species (10.3%), followed by bigmouth buffalo (5.6%) and silver redhorse (2.6%).

At Keeshin Farm, suckers account for about 29 percent (13 NISP) of fish bone identified to the family level and 0.2 percent of all fish. The identifiable remains include black redhorse (9 NISP), recovered from Features 22, 24, and 32, and redhorse (3 NISP), recovered from Feature 22. Identifiable specimens of black redhorse include quadrate, dentary, opercular, pharyngeal, and maxilla bones.

Suckers are the most abundant group at the Reeves (Craig and Galloy 1995) and Noble-Wieting (Parmalee and Bogan 1980a) sites and were also second in abundance at the Fisher site (Parmalee 1962). Of the sucker family, redhorse was common at all sites. The species in the genus were probably captured during the spring, as they ascended small and medium-sized rivers to spawn in shallow, swift riffles (Page and Johnston 1990).

Sturgeon (family Acipenseridae) is the third-most frequent fish group at Lawrence and is completely absent in the Keeshin Farm assemblage. It represents about 11 percent (80 NISP) of identifiable remains to the family level and 2.6 percent of the total fish assemblage. One species, lake sturgeon, is represented exclusively by fragments of bony plates. The remains were recovered from four features, with most found in Feature 41 (94%). Other sturgeon remains unidentifiable to species were also recovered. They include 14 bony plates from Feature 16 and 1 bony plate from Feature 29. The lake sturgeon found in the assemblage could have been procured in rocky rapids or shoals in the spring when they aggregate to spawn (Smith 1979:11). Sturgeons were notably absent in the Reeves (Craig and Galloy 1995) and Fisher (Parmalee 1962) assemblages.

Sunfish (family Centrarchidae) is the third-most and fifth-most frequent group in the Keeshin Farm and Lawrence assemblages, respectively. The centrarchid species are comparatively small fish that would have been difficult and time consuming to harvest. It is possible that the fish were caught nonselectively in nets. This fish group was the third-most important family at Reeves (Craig and Galloy 1995) and negligible at the Fisher site (Parmalee 1962). At Lawrence, it constitutes 1.5 percent (46 NISP) of the fish assemblage, with three species identified: largemouth bass, smallmouth bass, and rock bass.

Largemouth bass has the highest frequency of specimens, representing 80.4 percent (37 NISP) of the NISP total. The remains were found in seven pit features, with most present in Feature 41 (57%). There are seven anatomical regions represented, listed here in descending order of frequency: lateral skull bones, opercular series, pectoral girdle, orbital region, mandibular arch, branchial arch, and the olfactory region.

Smallmouth bass is the second-most abundant of the sunfish group, representing 10.9 percent (5 NISP) of the total NISP. The specimens were found in Features 41 and 59. They consist of two interhyal, one

interopercular, one opercular, and one posttemporal. The third-most frequent species is rock bass, accounting for only 6.5 percent (3 NISP) of
the NISP totals. All specimens were recovered from Feature 41 and consist of a cleithrum, an opercular, and a supraoccipital. One sunfish specimen was unidentifiable to the species level. It was recovered from Feature 38 and was noted as a quadrate.

At Keeshin Farm, sunfish account for 0.1 percent (7 NISP) of the fish
assemblage. Identified from this family were rock bass (2 NISP), recovered from Features 22 and 32, along with largemouth bass (4 NISP) and
bass (1 NISP), recovered from Feature 22. Rock bass was represented by
a preopercular and a cleithrum, and largemouth bass specimens include a
dentary, a quadrate, a posttemporal, and a parasphenoid.

Freshwater drum, a monotypic taxon in the central United States
(family Sciaenidae), is the fourth-most important species in both assemblages. At Lawrence, it represents about 7 percent (53 NISP) of all remains identified to the family level and 2 percent of all fish in the assemblage. The remains were recovered from 13 pits, with the highest
frequency found in Features 41 (23%) and 21 (17%). Pharyngeal bones
(23 NISP) and isolated teeth (7 NISP) are dominant, followed by four
maxilla, three premaxilla, three hyomandibular, and two each of cleithrum, otolith, subopercular, and supracleithrum. Also present are one
each of articular, dentary, opercular, parasphenoid, and quadrate.

At Keeshin Farm, drum specimens represent about 11 percent (5
NISP) of all remains identified to the family level and 2 percent of the
entire fish assemblage. The remains were distributed in Features 22,
32, and 34, with pharyngeal bones and a tooth present. This taxon was
absent at Noble-Wieting (Parmalee and Bogan 1980a), infrequent at
Reeves (Craig and Galloy 1995), and was the third-most significant fish
at Fisher (Parmalee 1962), with the variation probably reflecting differences in habitat. Drums typically inhabit turbid water over a mixed
sand and silt bottom in large rivers (Smith 1979:299). Theler
(1984:203) suggests that large drums could have been procured as
they fed at freshwater mussel beds, an optimal time being midsummer
to fall when water levels are often lowest. They could also have been
caught during the early summer when spawning in the shallow waters
of streams (Whelan 1987:131).

Gars (family Lepisosteidae), pikes (family Esocidae), and perches and
darters (family Percidae) are present in both assemblages, but are poorly
represented. The paucity of remains is comparable to other Oneota assemblages. Gars compose the sixth-most abundant fish group at
Lawrence, comprising only 0.13 percent (4 NISP) of the fish NISP. No
species could be identified for this fish taxa. The four specimens found in
Features 27 and 41 consist of two dentary, one maxilla, and one verte-
bra. The remaining two fish groups are equally represented by three
specimens and include pikes and perches and darters. Each represents

only 0.1 percent of the fish NISP totals. Identified with pikes are specimens recovered from Features 16 and 57. The bones consist of three dentary. A species identified with the perches and darters was walleye, with a cleithrum and a maxilla recovered from Feature 57. A dentary unidentifiable to a perches and darters species was recovered from Feature 38. Walleye was also present in the Keeshin Farm assemblage, with a preopercular and an interopercular recovered from Feature 22. The remaining fish identified by one specimen each are gar, represented by a bony plate from Feature 22, and pike, represented by a dentary from Feature 32.

Notably absent in the Lawrence and Keeshin Farm assemblages were bowfin. The absence may be attributable to the fact that bowfin prefer quiet, well-vegetated backwater lake habitats (Smith 1979:23), which are lacking near the two habitation sites. Bowfin was noted at other Oneota sites, like Zimmerman (Parmalee 1961), Fisher (Parmalee 1962), Griesmer (Parmalee 1972a), Fifield (Parmalee 1972b), Huber (Parmalee 1990), Oak Forest (Neusius 1990), and Reeves (Craig and Galloy 1995), where it was available.

Freshwater Mussels

The relative abundance of freshwater mussel fauna varies significantly between the sites. Mussels make up the third-most frequent class at Lawrence, with 692 unmodified valve fragments recovered from 26 pits. But they rank fifth in the Keeshin Farm sample with only five shell fragments recovered from two features, 15 and 19, and all unidentifiable as to species.

Twelve mussel species are represented in the Lawrence assemblage. The most abundant is the mucket, accounting for 9 percent (62 NISP) of the mussel assemblage. It was found in 15 pits, but most were recovered from Features 38 (26%) and 26 (24%). Plain pocketbook is second in abundance with 28 valve fragments. It was closely followed by black sandshell and threeridge. Next in abundance are eight mussel species, each contributing 0.1 percent or less of the sample. In descending order of relative abundance, they are pimpleback, elephant-ear, ellipse, purple wartyback, fatmucket, spike, scaleshell, and ebonyshell.

NATURAL AND CULTURAL MODIFICATION OF BONE

Natural modification by animal gnawing, root etching, and weathering was uncommon, limited to less than 1 percent for each assemblage. At Lawrence, animal gnawing occurs on only 28 specimens in the assemblage, with carnivore and rodent damage noted on 20 and 8 specimens, respectively. Nineteen specimens from deer, elk, beaver, mallard, and muskrat display evidence of root etching in the assemblage. Bone weathering was noted for 39 specimens, which were recovered from 19 pits across the site. At Keeshin Farm, only 4 specimens exhibit gnaw marks, representing less than 1 percent of the assemblage. Evidence of root etching was limited to 3 deer bones recovered from Feature 3. Bone weathering was noted for only 15 specimens, which were recovered from Features 7, 19, 22, 24, 32, 33, and 34. The small quantity of weathered bone at both sites may reflect limited exposure to the elements (air, wind, sun, rain, and temperature) before burial. The overall low-frequency pattern of natural modification suggests that the remains were rapidly buried in the habitation areas, reflecting planned rather than random disposal of animal refuse.

Cultural modification of remains are attributable to butchering, burning, and the manufacture of artifacts. Butchering activities involved hide or skin removal, dismemberment of major skeletal portions, and filleting or removing meat from a bone. Only a small proportion of each assemblage displays butchery marks. Specimens that had been exposed to fire were either calcined or blackened. A clear contrast between the assemblages exists with regard to burning. The percentage of burned bone is much higher for Keeshin Farm (51%) than for Lawrence (8.8%). The higher frequency and variety of bone and antler artifacts found at Lawrence also contrasts with that from Keeshin Farm, which is probably attributable to differences in sample sizes and/or site activity areas.

Butchering

Butchering and transport decisions probably were interdependent and based on cooking and consumption practices at the habitation sites. The data indicate that animal carcasses were transported whole from the kill site to the locus of butchery and consumption, the villages. It is perplexing, however, that butchery-marked bones occur infrequently in the assemblages, making it difficult to discern a "butchery pattern." At the Lawrence site, a total of 37 specimens exhibit this form of human modification, which includes eight species (Table 11). White-tailed deer exhibits the largest proportion of cut marks of any single species, observed on 16 specimens but still comprising only 0.5 percent of all deer bone. Cutmarks were also noted on elk, beaver, muskrat, raccoon, lynx, turkey, and eastern spiny softshell. At Keeshin Farm, butchering marks were present on 6 deer bone specimens recovered from Features 3, 22, 24, and 34 (Table 12). A general pattern for white-tailed deer may have involved the separation of the body along the thoracic cavity and cutting the forequarter into at least three parts (scapula/humerus, radius, and metacarpal), and there was a similar treatment of the hindquarter (femur, tibia, and metatarsal). Attempting to gain insights into butchery activities is untenable with the data available on other animals in the assemblages.

Table 11.

Cut-marked skeletal portions in the Lawrence assemblage.

Taxon	Skeletal Portion	Location	Feature
White-tail deer	Mandible	Ascending and horizontal ramus	42
	Cervical vertebra	Centrum	9
	Cervical vertebra	Axis (C-2) dorsal surface	64
	Rib	Shaft	31
	Rib	Shaft	42
	Humerus	Distal medial epiphysis	64
	Metacarpal	Proximal - medial articular facet	64
	Metacarpal	Proximal anterior shaft	64
	Pelvis	Acetabulum/pubis	9
	Tibia	Anterior shaft	27
	Tibia	Distal - medial malleolus	64
	Naviculo-cuboid	Tarsal anterior surface - right side	9
	Naviculo-cuboid	Tarsal anterior surface - left side	9
	Astragalus	Medial side	37
	Astragalus	Lateral side	41
	First phalange	Lateral side	39
Elk	Cervical vertebra	Axis (C-2) ventral surface	57
	Lumbar vertebra	Ventral surface and prezygapophyses	17
	Radius	Proximal posterior	20
	Femur	Anterior shaft	35
	Naviculo-cuboid	Tarsal lateral and medial surfaces	26
	First phalange	Lateral/ventral/proximal juncture	26
Beaver	Humerus	Supracondylar ridge	59
	Radius	Distal shaft	17
	Radius	Proximal anterior shaft	35
	Pelvis	Inferior to acetabulum on pubis	21
	Pelvis	Inferior to acetabulum on pubis	39
	Tibia	Medial/posterior lower shaft	16
Muskrat	Mandible	Horizontal/ascending ramus juncture	39
	Tibia	Distal medial/anterior surface	57
Raccoon	Ulna	Medial shaft	42
Lynx	Femur	Proximal epiphysis	63
Indeterminate mammal	Rib		20
Turkey	Rib	Proximal	16
Indeterminate bird	Rib		42
	Tibia	Distal posterior surface	42
Eastern spiny softshell	Femur	Proximal	44

Table 12.

Cut-marked skeletal portions of white-tailed deer.

Feature	Skeletal Portion	Location
F. 3	Tibia	Anterior crest
F. 3	Indeterminate long bone	Shaft
F. 3	Metatarsal	Posterior/lateral shaft
F. 22	Metatarsal	Posterior/lateral shaft
F. 24	Rib	Shaft
F. 34	Naviculo-cuboid	Tarsal anterior surface

Burning

Cultural modification attributable to burning was present at each site but in different proportions. At Lawrence, burning occurred on only 9 percent (802 NISP) of the vertebrate remains (Figure 27), with 7 percent (639 NISP) heavily burned (calcined) and 2 percent (163 NISP) blackened. For individual feature assemblages, burned remains were absent from 14 pits. The greatest frequency occurred in Features 30 and 34, with burned material making up 50 percent of the remains. At Keeshin Farm, 51 percent of the faunal remains were burned, with 49 percent (3013 NISP) calcined and 2 percent (163 NISP) blackened. Burned remains were absent in Features 24 and 35 but present in other features across the site. Apparently, there was differential burning of bone by class, with burning accounting for 84 percent of bird, 41 percent of reptile, 29 percent of mammal, 11 percent of fish, and none of the amphibian remains.

Interpretation of burning modification is not fully understood because of the difficulty in distinguishing between naturally and humanly burned bone as well as attempts to correlate burned bone with either cooking or disposal of food waste. Thus, burned bone may not be a good indicator of human behavior until actualistic research explores the variability of burning modification along different dimensions to unravel the taphonomic histories of assemblages (Lyman 1994b:392; Neuseus 1990:271–272; Oliver 1993:219). Although difficult to demonstrate without isotopic analysis and actualistic studies, the discoloration (black staining) along with pulverized and fragmented axial parts (e.g., pre- and postzygapophyses and spine segments of vertebrae) of bone in the assemblages (e.g., Feature 34 at Keeshin Farm) suggest that they were boiled to extract fat or grease, an activity commonly noted in ethnographic and ethnohistoric literature (see Oliver 1993:219; Vehik 1977:172–173).

Bone and Antler Artifacts

Although the amount of macrofaunal remains recovered from the Lawrence site was substantial, only a small quantity of utilitarian and nonutilitarian bone and antler items were present. Forty-one artifacts were found at Lawrence; only six were recovered from the Keeshin Farm site. Such cultural modification was restricted primarily to bone and antler from the deer family (Cervidae). Interestingly, there was a notable absence of modified fish and freshwater mussel remains despite their relative abundance at other Oneota sites. The bone and antler artifacts have been classified according to functional categories using criteria established by the archaeologists Howard Winters (1969) and Lynn Alex (1980:108–111) with the understanding that it is impossible to precisely identify the function of an individual artifact. These categories include skin and hideworking implements, hunting and fishing implements, horticultural implements, toolmaking tools, ornaments, gaming pieces, ceremonial paraphernalia, and miscellaneous worked bone.

Skin and Hideworking Implements Skin and hideworking implements in the Lawrence assemblage include bone awls, an antler scraper, and beamers. Four splinter awls were recovered from Features 31, 35, and 53. All consist of bone splinters, sharpened and smoothed at the working tip with the proximal ends unworked. Two specimens are made of large mammal bone fragments, and the others are made of bird bone. Awls were used to pierce hides and skins before sewing and in basket and mat construction (Alex 1980:108).

A large elk antler scraper was made from a flattened section of beam, which was found in Feature 59. The bit and the edges up the sides are heavily worn, and there are numerous striations perpendicular to the thin, dull bit on one face. The wear pattern indicates that it was used plane-fashion (with an oblique scraping surface) in an activity such as removing unwanted subcutaneous tissue from hides (Jonathan Reyman, personal communication, 1996). These implements have often been identified as knives, celts, spades, or hoes as well as celtlike scrapers (Brown 1961:57, 1965:166–167; Faulkner 1972:102–103). Skinner (1926:291) reports that elkhorn hoe-shaped scrapers of the Plains type (a tool notably absent among Eastern Woodlands groups) were used by the Ioway.

Two broken beamers made from the left metatarsals of elk were present in Feature 59 at Lawrence. One is depicted in Figure 5. This implement was often manufactured by splitting ungulate metapodials (cannon bones) along the axial plane, thus producing two long scraping faces on the modified element. Subsequently, the scraping surfaces were ground to an appropriate bevel. The tool was used to remove unwanted adhering tissues, fat, and hair from large hides (Alex 1980:108; Brown 1965:167; Wright 1987:8–9). Deer and elk metapodials were the common raw material for these tools in the Prairie Peninsula and its environs as well as in the Middle Ohio Valley (Brown 1965; McKern 1945:187) and appear in high frequency in the Fisher and Langford assemblages (Faulkner 1972:102). The implements also have been reported for the Sac (Skinner 1925:134) and the Ioway (Skinner 1926:291).

Another broken beamer produced from a left elk metatarsal occurred in Feature 33 at Keeshin Farm. It consists of the proximal portion of the element that has been broken at the shaft, measuring 13.6 cm in length. The two beveled scraping edges are prominent on the shaft and are set about 2.2 cm apart. The tool was heavily weathered, especially on the base, with split-line cracking and exfoliation visible. Some rodent gnaw marks are also present.

At Keeshin Farm, one pointed tool made of a split bone (mammal rib?) was found in Feature 32. The unperforated specimen consists of two fragments that may represent an unfinished sewing or matting needle. The modified end tapers to a sharp point while the opposite end is blunt and smooth. This slender, curved specimen is 0.3 cm thick, with the distal fragment measuring about 3.2 cm in length and the proximal fragment 5.3 cm in length.

Fishing Implements   Two fishing implement types were identified in the Lawrence assemblage including fishhook and harpoon. One bone fishhook, found in Feature 26, is made from an indeterminate mammal bone that is flattened in cross-section (Figure 6). The point and upper shank are absent, perhaps broken either during use or before it was com-

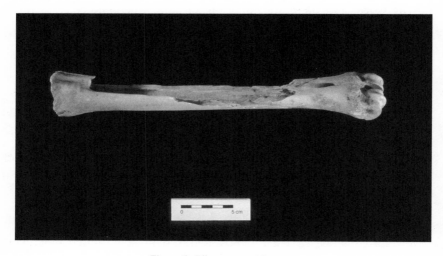

Figure 5   Elk metatarsal beamer.

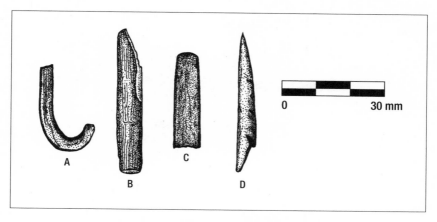

Figure 6 Selected culturally modified bone:
A, fish hook; D, possible needle fragment; B and C, counters.

pleted. This specimen resembles some associated with the Oneota Grand River phase and recovered from the Walker-Hooper site (McKern 1945:129, Plate 24). Fishhooks occur infrequently in Fisher and Langford assemblages, indicating that line fishing was only employed in a marginal way in trot lines. Thus, other means of catching fish, such as netting, gigging, and shooting, were more important.

Three unilaterally barbed spear points (harpoons) occurred in Features 20, 39, and 64. One heavy specimen exhibits a high barb near the distal end, bilateral grooves worn along the entire length of the implement, and a tapering spatulate butt wider than the shaft and the distal end (Figure 7A). It is probably made from a long bone fragment of the deer family (Cervidae). The butt is perforated with an oblong hole measuring about 0.6 cm in length and 0.4 cm in width. This nearly complete specimen measures about 13.8 cm in length, 2.1 cm in width, and 0.9 cm in thickness. Two much smaller harpoon fragments made from indeterminate mammal bone were also recovered. One exhibits low multiple barbs (Figure 7B) while the other has a single, low point barb (Figure 7C). Similar harpoons were found at the Fisher site (Griffin 1946:28), all of which were probably used for fishing (Brown 1965:171). The use of harpoons in large fish procurement has been well documented for the Ioway (Skinner 1926:290), Potawatomi (Clifton 1978:734), and Huron (Trigger 1969:30). They could also have been used to hunt beaver and muskrat during the winter. For example, Reidhead (1981:124–125) notes that the Huron employed harpoons to hunt beaver, and the Potawatomi and Native American groups and whites in Canada employed iron harpoons to capture muskrat (Martin 1996:468–469; Woolworth and Birk 1968:72–73), sometimes spearing them as they swam under thin ice.

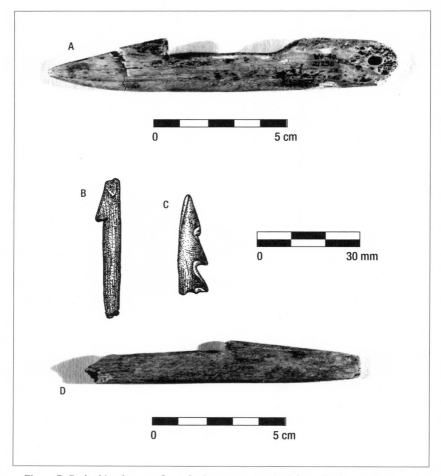

Figure 7 Barbed implements from the Lawrence site: A–C, bone harpoons; D, scraper.

Horticultural Implements Two horticultural implements recovered at Lawrence include an antler pick and scapula celt. The large elk antler pick, found in Feature 59, exhibits polish over most of the tine, including the tip. Picks were apparently used as digging implements (Faulkner 1972:102). They have been reported primarily in Oneota contexts at Norris Farms 36 in west-central Illinois (Santure and Esarey 1990:97), the Howard Goodhue site in central Iowa (Gradwohl 1982:150), and the Bryan and Bartron sites in eastern Minnesota (Gibbon 1979) as well as the Mississippian/Oneota Crable site in Illinois (Smith 1951). A fragment of a right deer scapula, recovered from Feature 63, may have been used as a spatula-like utensil. The vertebral border has been smoothed to a rounded tip, and the spine has been cut or broken. Tools resembling this celt or knife are reported from the Hoxie Farm (Herold et al. 1990:73) and Zimmerman (Brown 1961:57) sites. Ethnographic sources indicate that such blunt-ended knives were used in the cutting and scraping of squash (Alex 1980:109).

Toolmaking Tools Antler pressure flakers and split beaver incisors comprise toolmaking tools found at the Lawrence site. Three small flakers of worked antler tine (Cervidae sp.) were recovered from the Lawrence site, Features 27, 36, and 63. They are complete, consisting of cut bases and rounded tips. The tip of one is pitted. The length of these specimens range from 4.2 to 4.9 cm. Similar artifacts are reported from late prehistoric components in the Prairie Peninsula (Herold et al. 1990:76).

Three longitudinally split beaver incisors, presumably used as woodworking chisels or cutting tools, were recovered from Features 31, 38, and 64. No wear appears along the split broken edges. One fragment exhibits transverse cut marks on the lingual side of the tooth. Modified beaver incisors have been reported at a number of Oneota sites in the Prairie Peninsula, including the Anker (Bluhm and Liss 1961:129), Huber (Herold et al. 1990:80), Norris Farms 36 (Santure and Esarey 1990:95), and Plum Island (Fenner 1963:77) sites. Hall (1962:Plate 16) and Theler (1989:218) report modified beaver incisors from Oneota sites in Wisconsin, and Schilt (1977:103) reports two from the Noble-Wieting Langford component in Illinois.

Ornaments The only ornaments for study are four possible bone tube or bead fragments that were recovered from Features 8, 35, 57, and 63 at Lawrence. Three were made from the polished shafts of hollow bird long bones. The other is a mammal long bone fragment exhibiting cut marks in preparation for making a tube. Similar artifacts have been reported in Oneota contexts (Faulkner 1972:137; Gibbon 1986:326; McKern 1945:129; Santure and Esarey 1990:89).

Gaming Pieces A broken antler "counter," or gaming die, was recovered from Feature 16 at Lawrence (Figure 10C). This specimen is considered a gaming piece because of the absence of percussion scars on the end indicative of a tool used for stone working. It is 0.8 cm wide and 0.4 cm thick. Another possible cylindrical counter was found in Feature 32 at Keeshin Farm (Figure 10D). It is probably made of antler that was burned to a calcined condition prior to deposition. The specimen measures 4.5 cm in length and 0.8 cm in width. Longitudinal striations are visible on the external surface, and it exhibits rounded ends.

Counters are short segments of antler or bone from the deer family (Cervidae) with rounded or squared ends. They are reported at many late prehistoric sites throughout the Prairie Peninsula (Faulkner 1972:104; Gibbon 1986:326; Herold et al. 1990:77–79). Counters are particularly abundant in the Langford assemblage at the Fisher site (Griffin 1946:30) and also have been reported at the Anker (Bluhm and Liss 1961:126), Hoxie Farm (Herold et al. 1990), Noble-Wieting (Schilt 1977:106), Plum Island (Fenner 1963:75), and Zimmerman (Brown 1961:57) sites.

The gaming pieces were probably part of bowl-and-dice games that were ubiquitous throughout much of North America and are thought to have a long tradition in the Eastern Woodlands and Plains (Culin 1907:32, 44–225). Skinner (1924:41–42) reports on this game played by Prairie Potawatomi women. It is also documented for the Huron (Herman 1967:595), Illiniwek (Culin 1907:72), Ioway (Blaine 1979:182), Iroquois (Speck 1955:16, 82–83), Oto (Whitman 1937:13), Ottawa (Kinietz 1940:268), Sac (Skinner 1923:56–57), and Winnebago (Radin 1923:122). This game of chance involved the use of dice usually having two faces, distinguished by color or markings, and the instruments for keeping count. Across North America (130 tribes belonging to 30 linguistic stocks), variation in the game occurred more in terms of the materials employed (wooden staves or blocks, split canes, bone staves, beaver and woodchuck teeth, peach and plum stones, walnut shells, corn kernels, and bone, shell, pottery, or brass discs) rather than in the method or object of play. The game was usually played at fixed seasons during festivals or religious rites (Culin 1907:31; Yarrow 1881:195–197). Both men and women participated, but usually apart. A clear winner emerged when one of the opposing sides guessed the correct number(s) appearing during a throw or series of throws and, consequently, won all that was wagered. The winner could have been an individual or an entire village (Herman 1967:595–596; Kinietz 1940:268; Trigger 1969:100). Such games showed who had the greatest "luck," which was a positive quality or virtue and was necessary for success in life (Lienhardt 1968).

Ceremonial Paraphernalia   Ceremonial paraphernalia of bone were found at Lawrence only. Possible avian regalia were present in Feature 27. The well-preserved left-wing elements (carpometacarpus, first phalanx, and second phalanx) of a turkey suggest the former presence of feathered parts, perhaps used for ornamentation or for fans. The inclusion of a bald eagle talon and great gray owl second phalanx in such contexts tends to support this assumption, since they may reflect procurement of birds of prey for adornment or ritual purposes rather than serving as food items. There are numerous ethnohistoric references pertaining to the ritual importance of turkey feathers for fans, plumes, and blankets (Gilbert et al. 1985; Hall 1991:29) and eagle claws for one of the component parts of a medicine bundle, specifically used in a Hidatsa ceremony governing trapping rights (Wilson 1928). Theler (1994:387–388) provides yet another possible interpretation of the turkey wingtip. This skeletal portion (manus) holds the stout, primary flight feathers that could be used for arrow fletching. The fact that turkey wingtips have been found at other Oneota habitation sites, including Farley, Tremaine, State Road, Midway, Valley View, and Gunderson, may support this interpretation.

One probable needle fragment, presumably a body-tattooing instrument, was found in Feature 35 (Figure 10B). It is made of indeterminate mammal bone and exhibits an extremely sharp point, shallow oblique notches on the superior/lateral edge, a heavily smoothed and polished surface, and a small brown stain that may represent pigment. Scarifying needles were found associated with human burials and pigments at the Oneota Norris Farms 36 cemetery (Santure and Esarey 1990:89–90).

Miscellaneous Worked Bone　Several miscellaneous worked bones were recovered from the Lawrence site. A unilaterally barbed bone scraper was found in Feature 20 (Figure 7D). This implement is made of a flat splinter of indeterminate Cervidae bone. It exhibits a low barb at the shaft midsection and an extremely dull, flat scraping edge at the distal end. A shallow unilateral groove is worn along the entire length of the implement. The artifact surface is highly polished. This nearly complete specimen measures 9.9 cm in length, 1.6 cm in width, and 0.8 cm in thickness.

The inferior portion of the right scapula of an elk was used as tool stock. It was recovered from Feature 35. The block of bone was deeply grooved longitudinally to produce two long blanks that were never separated. Also found were nine small fragments of mammal bone that exhibit modification and are probably portions of larger but indeterminate artifacts. They were recovered from Features 20 (N=3), 27 (N=1), 35 (N=3), and 38 (N=2).

At Keeshin Farm, two unmodified bird bones could not be categorized because of their fragmentary nature. One calcined fragment, recovered from Feature 32, is 2.64 cm in length and still exhibits polish over its entire exterior surface. The other specimen, recovered from Feature 22, is 2.2 cm in length and also exhibits polish on its surface. Both may represent bone tube or bead fragments.

Worked Turtle Plastron　One calcined fragment of worked turtle plastron was found in Feature 32 at Keeshin Farm. It measures 1.2 cm in length by 1 cm in width. The plastron interior shows evidence of scraping in the form of fine incisions. Species identification or function could not be determined.

HABITAT REPRESENTATION

The environment surrounding each site (i.e., the locality) was divided into three general biotic communities—forest, prairie, and aquatic/wetland (these faunal communities were discussed in chapter 3)—to provide insights on how the Lawrence and Keeshin Farm inhabitants utilized various species and their habitats. Fauna NISP values were used to compare the estimated use of available habitats.

Despite each site's proximity to broad expanses of upland prairie, only limited emphasis was placed on the exploitation of prairie fauna. Species characteristic of prairie habitats at Lawrence comprise 4.8 percent (401 NISP) of the identified specimens to the order level. This contribution is made by elk, coyote, ornate box turtle, gray wolf, greater prairie chicken, and bison. Similarly, prairie resources at Keeshin Farm account for 0.3 percent (9 NISP) of the identified specimens to the order level. Elk and thirteen-lined ground squirrel are the only prairie species recognized. The low frequency and absence of bison remains for Lawrence and Keeshin Farm, respectively, was expected given that the incidence of bison bone in archaeological contexts in the eastern Prairie Peninsula remain low until protohistoric times (Colburn 1989; Shay 1978). Also, bison availability appears to correspond with changing climatic/environmental conditions of the Pacific climatic episode, as previously discussed, along with greater human predation of bison herds on the Central Plains during the late Holocene (Koch 1995:56).

A high proportion of species represented by the faunal remains in both assemblages are attributed to forest habitats, although there is a significant bias associated with the abundance of white-tailed deer. Forest fauna at Lawrence comprise 42.9 percent (3561 NISP) of the identified specimens to the order level. This contribution consists of deer, raccoon, turkey, red fox, perching bird, longtail weasel, lynx, eastern mole, gray squirrel, bobcat, owl, nighthawk, bald eagle, and plainnose bat specimens. Forest resources dominate the Keeshin Farm assemblage, accounting for 85.5 percent (2938 NISP) of all identified specimens to the order level. The species composition is limited to deer, turkey, rabbit, and raccoon. Notably, the representation of forest fauna is significantly reduced without the presence of deer remains in the assemblages. Without deer, the proportion of forest fauna falls to 2.1 percent at Lawrence and 3.5 percent at Keeshin Farm.

Aquatic/wetland habitats were important to the occupants of both sites. These fauna at Lawrence comprise 52.3 percent (4343 NISP) of the NISP sample, which includes fish, freshwater mussel, turtle, muskrat, duck, beaver, goose, grebe, coot, red-winged blackbird, amphibian, mink, and snowy egret remains. Local aquatic resources at Keeshin Farm account for 14.3 percent (490 NISP) of all specimens identified to the order level. This contribution is made of fish, turtles, muskrats, freshwater mussels, and amphibians. Excluding deer from the NISP totals significantly increases the importance of these fauna, which then represents 89.6 percent of the NISP at Lawrence and 94.8 percent of the NISP at Keeshin Farm. Fish is the most significant class in this category for both sites, with all species easily accessible from the main river channels. The species composition of freshwater mussels at the Lawrence site is especially informative in regard to local aquatic habitats.

The diverse mussel species represented in the Lawrence samples indicate that this locality, just upstream from the Rock River and Elkhorn Creek confluence, exhibited wadeable shoals, diverse stream habitats, and good water quality. The complex of purple wartyback, mucket, black sandshell, and ellipse dominate the identified taxa (56%). They are characteristic of the high-energy, well-oxygenated riffles or raceways of medium to large rivers. These species have been reported in a mixed sand and gravel substrate (Cummings and Mayer 1992). The complex of pimpleback, threeridge, fatmucket, and plain pocketbook are also well represented in the identified sample (35%). They can be found in a variety of stream sizes and substrates consisting of mud, sand, or gravel. Regarding the other four species in the Lawrence assemblage: ebonyshell typically inhabits large rivers and prefers a substrate of sand and gravel; elephantear commonly occurs in large rivers and tolerates a substrate of mud, sand, or fine gravel; spike is found in mud or gravel in small to large rivers and occasionally in lakes; and scaleshell is most typically found embedded in the mud of large rivers (Cummings and Mayer 1992).

HARVESTING AND PROCESSING ACTIVITIES: COMPLEMENTARITY

The faunal remains from Lawrence and Keeshin Farm show no evidence of differences in social status or ethnicity. Instead, the recovered specimens support the notion of a cooperative, egalitarian Oneota society. The exploitation of resources by men and women required choices, some of which did not involve group maximization of resources through a practical cost/benefit principle. In tribal societies, much of the work involved cooperative effort because individualism was not useful (Underhill 1957:133). Women's activities in the exploitation and utilization processes were deemed complementary to those of men despite probable limited access to formal positions of authority. Women were perceived as having power in household activities based on ethnohistoric accounts (Blair 1912; Whelan 1993:247), as discussed in chapter 2. Therefore, decisions made at the kill site by primarily male hunters may have been correlated with women's decisions (as wife, mother, or sister) in the households concerning the manner of distribution or apportionment of carcasses as well as processing at the habitation site.

Individual or relatively small numbers of animals could have been taken by sufficiently skilled hunters with techniques and devices such as snares, traps, stalking, encounter ambush, and small-scale surrounds. At the kill site, a number of decisions had to be made concerning butchery and transport (Lyman 1994b:299). Diane Gifford-Gonzalez (1993:185) lists several factors, including:

1. size of the animal, relative to that of the human processors;
2. number of animals requiring immediate processing;
3. distance of the animal from the destination of its products;
4. number of persons in carrying party;
5. condition of the carcass at the time encountered;
6. time of day;
7. gear at hand to effect field processing;
8. processing technology available at destination site;
9. ultimate form or forms the animal products will take.

It was argued that culinary processing and the ultimate form of products (nos. 8 and 9) are the factors that actually drive most butchery and transport decisions.

This study has shown that the Fisher hunters decided to transport whole mammal carcasses (e.g., deer, raccoon, muskrat) from the kill site back to the settlement for processing and use. Since women's culinary equipment included ceramic vessels, meat and bone segments could have been boiled together as stews. They also could have been roasted, or baked or steamed in subterranean "ovens," with meat removed after cooking and shared between households as is common among small-scale societies (Gifford-Gonzalez 1993:184; Marshall 1993).

The pulverized condition and discoloration of some unburned mammal bone, white-tailed deer in particular, suggests that after removing the meat from the bone some elements were broken for marrow extraction (marrow being highly esteemed in small-scale societies). They, along with other bones, such as vertebrae, were then crushed and boiled in pots or hide-lined pits to extract fat or grease. This woman's activity is commonly noted in ethnographic (Bunn 1993; Emerson 1993; Oliver 1993; Zierhut 1967) and ethnohistoric accounts (Allen 1876:195; Catlin 1926:131; Densmore 1929; Merriman 1926:82; Paget 1909:78; Peale 1871; Turner 1894:278; Wissler 1910). Also, it has been suggested for other Oneota (Harvey 1979:79; Jans-Langel et al. 1995:66) and historic (Hurlburt 1977) assemblages as well as archaeological assemblages in other parts of the world (Marshall and Pilgram 1991). Using ethnohistoric documents, the zooarchaeologist Susan Vehik (1977:171) noted that bone grease was used commonly by Native Americans with a mixture of lean, dried strips of meat and chokecherries to produce pemmican, which is exactly what its name means (*pemmi*—meat, *kon*—fat). Pemmican was a highly concentrated, well-preserved food for use during the winter months or while traveling long distances. Bone grease also was used comparably as a modern butter or lard, as a condiment for pemmican, and to tan hides. This activity may have implications for understanding the cultural modification of bone and mammal skeletal composition as discussed above (and dramatically affecting NISP and MNI [minimum number of individuals] counts).

Another important domestic activity conducted at the settlement was skin- and hideworking, which met the clothing needs of the people. The methods employed were similar among the northern and western tribes of the United States, with groups of women engaged in a long, arduous process of fleshing, scraping, braining, stripping, graining, and working the hide (Driver 1961:172–175; Harrington 1941; Mooney 1910:591–594). Among the Plains tribes, James Mooney (1910:592) states:

> The fleshing process begins as soon as possible after the hide is stripped from the carcass, while the skin is still soft and moist. The hide is staked out upon the ground, fleshy side up, when two women working together, scrape off the flesh and fat by means of a sort of gouge with serrated edge [or having a beveled edge as in what archaeologists term a beamer]. . . . Next comes the scraping, a very laborious process, the instrument used being a sort of adz, made of wood or elk-horn, with a blade of stone or iron set at a right angle to the handle. Several women worked together. . . . Then comes the braining process, in which the skin is thoroughly annoited with a mixture of cooked brains and liver, grease, and pounded soaproot (yucca), all mixed together and applied with a sponge of soaproot fiber. . . . Next comes the stripping, intended to squeeze out the surplus moisture and the dressing mixture . . . [graining] is done with a globular piece of bone, as large, as can be conveniently held in the hand, cut from the spongy portion of the humerus of a buffalo or other large animal. With this the whole surface of the skin is rubbed as with sandpaper to reduce the hide to uniform thickness and smoothness and to remove any hanging fibers. . . . Then comes the process of working or softening, to render the skin pliable. This is done by drawing the skin for some time in seesaw fashion across a rope of twisted sinew stretched between two trees a few feet apart . . . two women again working together, one at each end of the skin.

Fish procurement in the high-energy environment of the main channels may have involved highly cooperative ventures by men using various types of equipment like simple spears or harpoons, hooks, gorges, and seines. Large river fish, such as sturgeon, redhorse, and buffalo, would have been available in shallow areas during the spring spawning season where they could have been speared, an activity indicated by the presence of bone harpoons in the Lawrence assemblage. Wooden spears may also have been effective for large fish procurement, since they were widely used historically (Higgins 1980:23, Swanton 1979:338). Catfish and freshwater drum may have been caught using gorges or hooks attached on trot lines, a successful technique used by modern commercial fishermen in Illinois (Martin and Masulis 1993). The presence of a fishhook in the Lawrence assemblage may be related to this technique. Large seines or gill nets would have provided an effective mass-catch technique for all fish sizes (Rostlund 1952), although the absence of net sinkers in the assemblages does not support their use by Fisher or Langford fishermen. Perhaps their absence is attributable to limitations imposed by a swift current and a rocky river bottom that would tend to cause the net to snag.

Fish were transported whole from the procurement site to the habitation as indicated by their skeletal representation documented for the Lawrence site. They probably would have been gutted, cooked, preserved by smoking or drying, and stored, although Erhard Rostlund (1952:137–144) points out the variability in such activities among historic Native American groups.

The low diversity and low frequency of mussel shell accumulations found at the Lawrence site suggests very selective, low-intensity harvesting activities. At least 31 species have been reported from the area near the site, but less than half are represented within the sites' assemblage (N=12). Even when one considers the loss of some specimens through attrition (e.g., postdepositional processes), the data suggest that the Fisher inhabitants were selecting certain mussel species. Whether women were involved exclusively in such selective collecting behavior is debatable. Ethnographic accounts indicate that children were also actively involved and that men might occasionally collect them as fishing bait (see Claassen 1991).

Freshwater mussels were utilized in various ways as a source of food, implements (e.g., hoes, fishing lures, scrapers), domestic utensils (e.g., containers, spoons, an aplastic tempering agent in ceramic manufacture), and ornaments (see Herold et al. 1990:82–83; Holmes 1883; Santure and Esarey 1990:98–102). Processing would involve cleaning, cooking (steaming, baking, boiling, or smoking), and removal of meat from the shell (Ford 1989) to be used possibly in stews and soups. Their low ranking in the Lawrence and Keeshin Farm assemblages corroborates Paul Parmalee and Walter Klippel's (1974) contention that mussels served a supplemental role in the prehistoric diet because it was not particularly high in food energy. After their initial use for food, the valves of some species were chosen to serve an important secondary function as tools and utensils. In particular, spoons were commonly fashioned from plain pocketbook mussels, as shown by their prevalence in Fisher (Parmalee 1962:403), Gentleman Farm (Brown et al. 1967:35), Norris Farms 36 (Santure and Esarey 1990:98), and other Mississippian components. The left valve was often chosen because it was most suited to be held by the right hand (Brown et al. 1967:35; Holmes 1883:199). Muckets, a similar species, were also used for tools and are common in the Lawrence assemblage. Their prevalence in the archaeological record may be attributable to a large, thick-shelled structure and to the fact that they are widespread and locally abundant in rivers (Cummings and Mayer 1992). But why implements, utensils, and ornaments were not found in the Lawrence and Keeshin Farm assemblages is questionable, perhaps due to small sample sizes.

CONCLUSIONS

The analysis of the fauna from the Lawrence and Keeshin Farm sites shows the great potential of zooarchaeological data in providing insights into procurement, transport, culinary practices, and food refuse disposal patterns among early Oneota peoples living in northern Illinois. Fisher and Langford peoples were very selective in their animal procurement pursuits. Cultural factors rather than a simple adaptation to the environment played a significant role in animal consumption concerns (see White 1984:190–191). Choices were guided by the availability of animal species, prohibitive customs or taboo systems, well-established gourmet eating habits, and economic reasons such as obtaining food, hides, and furs. Demands for a whole complex of bone, antler, and shell utilitarian and nonutilitarian items also had to be considered. Questions related to consumption choices can be addressed by identifying patterns in the analyzed faunal assemblages and interpreting such patterns by searching the ethnohistoric sources for models of Indian conduct. One must also use comparative faunal data from other Oneota and Mississippian groups in the Midcontinent to explore relationships. The observed patterns may reflect relations of power within and between small-scale societies where power to make decisions is based primarily on religious beliefs and cultural rules rather than force (Turner 1972:270).

Both faunal assemblages are dominated by white-tailed deer remains, which is typical of other Oneota assemblages. The emphasis on deer apparently represents a long tradition extending from prehistoric into historic times. Deer was clearly a favored economic resource among historic Eastern Woodlands cultures (Curtis 1952; Driver 1961:28–29; Parmalee and Bogan 1980b; Parmalee and Klippel 1983:286; Swanton 1979:249). It was one of the few big game animals available, thriving in a wide range of climatic and habitat conditions, quickly adapting to changes and withstanding adversity. Because they would often weigh less than 90 kg (200 lbs) (based on modern harvested deer records), they could be easily transported whole from the kill site to the camp or village for processing and consumption. Deer was used for many different purposes: fresh venison provided energy and a palatable, high-quality protein that could be prepared and served in a variety of ways; the heart, liver, kidneys, and pancreas (sweetbread) were probably consumed as delicacies (Ashbrook 1955:119); limb elements were cracked for sweet-tasting marrow (Hurlburt 1977:16); the brains were used in tanning hides (Peale 1871); deer hides were in demand for capes, coats, gloves, moccasins, blankets, and body cover; tallow was used as a rubbing liniment; antlers were used for awls and projectile points, and foot bones (metapodials) were used as scrapers to remove hair from a hide; ornaments and pendants were made of deer antler and teeth (Blessing 1956; Jackson 1961:420); and the bones could be crushed and boiled in water to obtain grease with soup being a secondary product (Hurlburt 1977:19–21; Vehik 1977). Some of these uses have been identified in the assemblages examined in this study.

Although deer consumption remained high for most Oneota groups through time, data compiled for the Emergent Mississippian and Mississippian groups in the Central Mississippi River valley show that their representation is relatively low (Berres n.d.; Styles 1994:44). Deer also appear in low frequency at the Hardin Village site in the Middle Ohio Valley where Fort Ancient peoples suffered from protein deficiency (perhaps the most widespread nutritional deficiency) (Reidhead 1980:177). This pattern is probably linked to an increased reliance on cultivated starchy seeds, particularly corn, and increased sedentary occupations, creating a high-carbohydrate, low-protein, and low-fat diet (Styles 1994). The strong regional patterning may indicate differences in food choices and cuisine, with their powerful symbolic associations marking regional identity. Corn functioned as food but was also meaningful in the entire religious cycle of ceremonials bound with the growing cycle of corn. Unfortunately for the Mississippian horticulturalists living in the American Bottom and Middle Ohio Valley, dietary choices involving dependence on corn may have led to a high mortality rate, especially among infants who could become easier prey to other diseases (Wing and Brown 1979:34–35).

Sometimes the hunters' choices appear to be based simply on availability. For example, large game mammals such as elk and bison were probably less significant than white-tailed deer during the Emergent and Developmental horizons because of availability: as gregarious, migratory species dependent on grasslands for forage, elk and bison would only become more readily available with changes in prairie vegetation and more intense human predation occurring sometime after the establishment of the Pacific climatic episode (ca. A.D. 1350–1400). Wapiti herds provided an abundance of fresh meat, hides, and other products to the inhabitants of the Prairie Peninsula and its environs. The taste of wapiti, however, may have influenced its exploitation, with historic accounts suggesting that the meat was coarse and the fat of poor quality (sticking to the teeth and roof of the mouth) (Hurlburt 1977:30). An unexplored aspect of Oneota elk utilization concerns regional cultural differences in the manufacture of antler and bone tool types. For example, regional or kin group identification may be communicated to others in stylized patterns of activities like scraping hides with beamer tools from a particular element of Cervidae. Although sample sizes are extremely small, the Lawrence and Keeshin Farm data show that beamers were made from the left metatarsals of elk. In contrast, Fort Ancient peoples apparently made them from right deer metatarsals (Breitburg 1992).

Many other mammal species would have been available near the Lawrence and Keeshin Farm sites, but their harvesting was probably fortuitous rather than systematic. In other words, they were not the focus of a specific hunting strategy. They include such small and medium-sized mammals as beaver, muskrat, raccoon, coyote, fox, squirrel, and eastern cottontail. They also show that animal exploitation was focused primarily on floodplain habitat resources, specifically forest and aquatic/wetland species. At Lawrence, a variety of floodplain fauna are present in small numbers, including carnivores (red fox, lynx, bobcat, raccoon, mink, and longtail weasel) and rodents (beaver, muskrat, and gray squirrel). The faunal assemblage from the Keeshin Farm site is much less diverse (probably owing to small, biased samples), but the species (raccoon, rabbit, and muskrat) are still representative of forest and aquatic/wetland habitats.

Aquatic/wetland resources, particularly fish and freshwater mussels, would have provided abundant, predictable, warm-season resources that were easily procured by inhabitants knowledgeable about their habits. Fish provided excellent sources of digestible proteins and essential minerals, vitamins, and fats (Ashbrook 1955:43). Although a variety of species were available, catfish and often sweet-meated, though bony, suckers were the most popular food fish, which is comparable with other Oneota communities in the Central Des Moines River valley (Kelly 1990:396) and western Wisconsin (Scott 1994:410; Theler 1994). They were particularly vulnerable to spearing or netting while guarding their nests in shallow water. Similarly, more than thirty species of mussels were available to the Lawrence inhabitants, yet the food gatherers commonly chose to exploit the mucket inhabiting gravel or mixed sand and gravel of river beds.

Native American religious beliefs cannot be ignored by the zooarchaeologist, because they have undoubtedly affected the data base (Wright 1987:3). As stated previously, historic Native Americans were concerned with how living animals around them, with their souls or spirits, affected daily life. Nature was active and personal. Although consumed, the animal spirit was considered immortal and wielded such power as to prevent others of its species from being captured by hunters unless appeased by ritual compensation (Boas 1914:405; Grinnell 1893:119; Skinner 1914b:203; Underhill 1957:130). One must retain the good will of the food animals for survival. Strict observance of a great variety of proscriptions were conducted, many combined under the term "taboo," to restore equilibrium and the status quo, thus keeping the world in balance by controlling and channeling human interaction (Boas 1910a:368; Wallace 1966:106). How may this be reflected in the archaeological record?

One of the interesting aspects in this comparative study of animals from the two sites is discovering what animals are absent. The most notable is the black bear. Clearly, bears should have been exploited, because they were abundant in the forested and dense brushland of the Prairie Peninsula (Jackson 1961; Whitaker and Hamilton 1998) and were continuously hunted historically for highly valued meat, fat, hides, fur, and oil (Curtis 1952:182; Hallowell 1926:61–74; Jackson 1961:319–320).

But there is a distinct scarcity or absence of bear remains cross-culturally and through time at aboriginal habitation sites, which appears to reflect their sanctity. The powerful bear spirit was highly revered for continued success in hunting or healing the sick. After a bear had been killed and consumed, there was a fear that, if dogs gnawed or even touched the remains, the bear spirit would be offended. The domestic dog apparently was not a revered animal during Mississippian times in the Midwest (Parmalee 1962:406) and may have been recognized as a dirty, ugly, brooding creature (Abrahams 1984:32) because of being a scavenger of carrion and human leftovers. To keep the bear remains from being contaminated meant disposing them away from the habitation site, as exemplified by the Ojibway's collecting and burying them or the Menominee practice of tossing the remains into a stream (Berres et al. 1999).

Such marks of reverence may also have been given to the river otter, because it is usually absent or rare in Oneota and other Native American faunal assemblages. They also were often ritually tossed back into the water so as not to offend the animal's spirit (Wright 1987:4). The zooarchaeologist Paul W. Parmalee (1959:89) notes the ritual significance of this mustelid at the Fisher site where a nearly complete skull was found on a woman's forehead in the middle level of the Big East Mound EM, possibly having been worn in the form of a headdress. Another river otter skull had been ritually placed with an Oneota human burial at the Anker site, wrapped in sheet copper with copper disks placed in the eye sockets.

Also notable was the paucity of birds in the Oneota assemblages. This can be better explained in terms of reverence for the animal spirit than in economic terms (i.e., maximization of food-resource exploitation) (Kelly 1990:397). As will be shown in chapter 7, Native American peoples maintained a long history of revering birds as supernatural beings of the upperworld in art, ideology, myth, and religious belief. They were probably concerned with how the spirits of the birds would affect their welfare. The sanctity of their remains may have often required final disposal away from the habitation site, which is particularly applicable to raptorial species (see Wright 1987:3–4).

Power permeated human social relationships and practices in Oneota everyday life and would be apparent within the household through certain stereotyped tasks: men hunting mammals, and women in charge of household economic activities. Hunting decisions made by male groups often may have been guided by the ultimate form or forms the animal product would take within the household and the community. Whole animal carcasses were shown to be transported to the village for on-site butchering, skin dressing, bone tool production, and cooking of meat and bone into foods. One can then argue for gender complementarity for creative production, with both men and women actors performing important roles in the society. Gender roles were interdependent to create unity or harmony. The Oneota mortuary record is used to support this assumption. Equality is stressed by the distribution of similar burial goods regardless of gender or age at the Bold Counselor Oneota Norris Farms 36 cemetery (Santure and Esarey 1990:106), the Huber Oneota Hoxie Farm cemetery (Herold et al. 1990:18, 22), and the Langford Gentleman Farm cemetery (Brown et al. 1967). Gender division of labor is expressed at Norris Farms 36 by the inclusion of arrowpoints exclusively with males while weaving equipment was associated with a female. These differences in gender occur among historic tribal societies like the Omaha: "If the deceased be a man, his weapons are then laid by his side; if a woman, her sewing-bag containing her awl, quills, and articles used for embroidery" (La Flesche 1889:9).

Ceramic Vessels

Vehicles of Communication

For Oneota society, household utilitarian pottery and funerary ware conveyed relations of power and acted as vehicles of communication. For archaeologists, the vessels not only have heuristic value in formulating chronologies (e.g., through horizon styles) but express culturally meaningful information (Arnold 1988:5; Benn 1989, 1995; Braun 1991; Hall 1977:501, 1991:29; Link 1995; Pauketat and Emerson 1991; Rosman and Rubel 1995:237–241; Sampson 1988; Willoughby 1897). Like language and art in general, they provide a mode of communication, a way of conveying messages that relate to personal emotions, involving both cultural meaning and a feeling of aesthetic pleasure. The way that the technological and decorative attributes are patterned on a particular vessel *shape* (in the case of Oneota, a globular jar) may reveal the artisans' personal power, through technical skills and inspiration that comes to one in dreams, needed to create beauty and meaning in their ongoing lives. In small-scale Oneota societies, vessels may also reflect the strength of the community, because the artist works within the tradition of one's culture. Thus, a vessel is a product of communal tradition (Rosman and Rubel 1995:241).

In any art composition, "the whole is more important than its parts" to express *meanings* and *ideas* (Nagy 1994:40; Ocvirk et al. 1968:158; Rosman and Rubel 1995:238). The cultural anthropologist Edmund Leach (1976:49) states, "The indices in nonverbal communication systems, like the sound elements in spoken language, do not have meaning as isolates but only as members of sets." Cultural meaning requires transformations from metaphor (symbolic) to metonym (sign) and back again, comparable to the contrasts in music when harmony is distinguished from melody. Thus, the combined attributes (e.g., symbols) on an Oneota globular jar certainly can be viewed as communicating powerful inner meanings (cosmological and religious) across Oneota and other Mississippian and Late Woodland ethnic boundaries, with such meanings often having great antiquity, as will be discussed at length in chapter 7.

The archaeologists James B. Griffin (1943:279) and John W. Griffin (1946:18, 20, 22) noted the close relationship between the Fisher and Langford ceramic traditions, especially in terms of vessel form, rim form, surface finish, appendages, and decoration. Fisher phase ceramic assemblages are characterized by the Fisher ceramic series that have been described and illustrated as Fisher Plain, Fisher Trailed, Fisher Cordmarked, and Fisher Noded (see Allee 1949; Brown 1961; Fenner 1963; Griffin 1943; Griffin 1946, 1948; McKern 1945). The ceramics are almost exclusively shell tempered, which is common in Oneota assemblages. The ceramic types in the Langford series also are well documented and include Langford Plain, Langford Trailed, Langford Cordmarked, Langford Noded, Langford Collared, and Langford Bold (see Allee 1949; Brown et al. 1967; Fenner 1963; Griffin 1943; Griffin 1946, 1948). Angular particles of crushed rock (mafic or quartz grit) were often used as tempering agents and, therefore, are diagnostic for this ware group.

Both ceramic traditions show influences from Mississippian occupations of the American Bottom and/or Illinois River valley, other Oneota societies, and ceramic traditions extending into the Late Woodland period. The strong similarities in art styles (the component elements of art and how they are put together during specific periods of time), with the exception of tempering, means that the Fisher and Langford cultures *belonged to the same social system* within the Oneota cultural tradition and conveyed similar visual messages of power. How may this be reflected in the Lawrence and Keeshin Farm ceramic assemblages? What are the similarities and differences, and how can they be interpreted?

LAWRENCE AND KEESHIN FARM VESSEL TYPE DESCRIPTIONS

A large collection of discrete vessels, represented by rim sherds and associated neck and shoulder areas when present, were collected from individual pit features at the Lawrence and Keeshin Farm sites. Segments of 93 vessels were identified, with 67 reported from the Lawrence site and 26 reported from the Keeshin Farm site. Since both assemblages are dominated by jars, it is the similarities and differences of these forms that will be the focus of study. Most rim sherds in the assemblages are small and fragmentary, representing less than 10 percent of the vessel from which they originated. As a result, only limited data regarding decoration and appendages are available.

Lawrence Vessels

Rim sherds were recovered from 27 of 65 total features and represent 67 discrete vessels. The sample consists of several vessel forms, including jars, bowls, pinch pots, a bottle, and a palette. Most of the assemblage consists of shell-tempered pottery with smoothed-over cordmarked exterior surfaces. These sherds are representative of the Fisher series. Intermixed with shell-tempered ceramics are seven grit-tempered Langford series vessels, consisting of 6 jars and 1 bowl. The rim fragments were recovered from Features 16, 24, 27, 41, 45, and 49, with the ratio of grit to shell for each feature being 2:163, 1:12, 18:148, 4:127, 3:25, and 4:36, respectively. The ratios indicate that the Langford vessels were probably traded to the Lawrence inhabitants through a peaceful, reciprocal exchange system.

Jars predominate within the Lawrence assemblage, making up 51 (76%) of the total vessels. Only 2 hemispherical bowls (3%) and 1 bottle (2%) could be identified. Rim sherds of 13 small pinch pots (19%) were recovered from six pits. They are irregularly shaped, crudely fashioned forms with plain surfaces. Most vessels are tempered with crushed mussel shell, comprising 48 (72%) of the specimens. Twelve rims (18%) exhibit no tempering, while 7 (10%) are grit tempered. Two basic categories of surface treatments are represented. Ceramics with smoothed-over cordmarked exterior surfaces are predominant, comprising 45 (67%) of the vessels. The specimens are cordmarked to the lip. The remainder exhibit plain exterior surfaces. Interior surfaces are typically plain, being smoothed with a dull finish. The vessels were classified into four rim form categories: vertical (N=38, 57%), everted (N=11, 16%), flared (N=10, 15%), and outcurved (N=8, 12%). The large number of vertical, everted, and flared rims reflects the high proportion of jars in the assemblage. Outcurved rims reflect the presence of bowls. The four lip forms observed were flattened, flat-thickened, rounded, and outward beveled. Most lips are flattened (N=39, 58%). Flat-thickened (N=17, 25%) and rounded (N=10, 15%) are also common; only one outward beveled form was observed. Thirty-six specimens (54%) exhibit lip decoration. Decorative techniques associated with the lip design field include smoothed-over cordmarking, dowel notching, and punctation. Smoothed-over cordmarked specimens are most common (N=34), and punctated and plain-dowel impressed are represented by single examples.

Keeshin Farm Vessels

Twenty-six vessels recovered from 16 of 31 total features compose the Keeshin Farm assemblage. The sample consists almost entirely of jar forms, with the exception of one pinch pot bowl. The tempering materials present in the Keeshin Farm assemblage consist largely of angular particles of dark, crystalline grit. In terms of surface treatment, sherds with plain exteriors predominate (N=24, 92%). The surfaces are smooth, and the finish is primarily dull. One specimen exhibits brown slipped surfaces, and another had a smoothed-over cordmarked exterior surface and plain interior surface. Temper particles frequently appear on the surface. The vessels were classified into six rim form or shape categories: vertical (N=15, 58%), everted (N=4, 15%), incurved (N=2, 8%), flared (N=2, 8%), inslanted (N=2, 8%), and outcurved (N=1, 3%). All are associated with jars except for the outcurved type, a shape characteristic of a pinch pot. The three lip forms observed were flattened, rounded, and outward beveled. Flattened forms predominate in the assemblage, comprising 81 percent (N=21), which is typical of other Langford assemblages (Fenner 1963:61). Other lip forms are rounded (11%) and outward beveled (8%). The only lip decoration visible in this assemblage consists of notching oriented obliquely to the exterior lip surface of a single jar. The notching was executed with a plain dowel or stick.

INTERSITE COMPARISONS OF FISHER AND LANGFORD SERIES JARS

Jars typically predominate to the near exclusion of other vessel types within Oneota assemblages, as exemplified in the Lawrence and Keeshin Farm samples. They are wide-mouthed, globular containers with subangular or rounded shoulders, constricted necks, thin walls, and rounded bases (Fenner 1963:55; Griffin 1946:15). Jars were the basic utilitarian vessels of the Mississippi period, serving as all-purpose cooking and processing containers given their context in domestic refuse deposits including a wide range of foodstuffs. Others may have been used for storing liquids, solids, or other items. The similarities and differences in jar rim forms and associated surface finishes, decoration, and appendages have been shown to be significant as spatiotemporal markers for Mississippian vessels in the American Bottom (Jackson 1992a; Milner 1984; Vogel 1975) as well as distinguishing the Prairie Peninsula as a culture area during late prehistoric times.

The most important information in the ceramic assemblages can be obtained by comparing jar attributes from Lawrence with those from the Keeshin Farm site. The Lawrence assemblage is dominated by sherds attributed to the Fisher ceramic series, represented by Fisher Trailed and those segregated based on tempering and surface finish but not assigned a type name. Ceramics of the Langford series, specifically Langford Trailed and Langford Collared, predominate within the Keeshin Farm component. Table 13 indicates that the relative percentages of certain attributes by ceramic series are nearly identical, especially in terms of rim form and lip form. Differences arise in other tabulations, which may be attributable to sample size and spatiotemporal differences between the two occupations. A general overview of each ceramic series will be followed by type-by-type comparative discussions based on rim forms.

Table 13.

Jar attributes by site and series.

| Attributes | LAWRENCE | | KEESHIN FARM |
	Fisher Series N (%)	Langford Series N (%)	Langford Series N (%)
Rim Form			
Vertical	31 (69)	5 (83)	15 (60)
Everted	11 (24)	-	4 (16)
Flared	3 (7)	1(17)	2 (8)
Inslanted	-	-	2 (8)
Incurved	-	-	2 (8)
Lip Form			
Flattened	28 (62)	6 (100)	21 (84)
Flat-thickened	15 (33)	-	-
Rounded	1 (2)	-	2 (8)
Out-beveled	1 (2)	-	2 (8)
Ext. Surface Finish			
Smoothed-over cordmarked	38 (84)	6 (100)	-
Plain	7 (16)	-	24 (96)
Brown-slipped	-	-	1 (4)
Appendages*			
Lug/Semicircular	9 (60)	-	-
Lug/Tab	1 (7)	-	-
Lug/Indeterminate	1 (7)	-	-
Loop Handle	2 (13)	-	-
Strap Handle	2 (13)	-	-
Decoration			
Decorated	39 (87)	6 (100)	11 (44)
Indeterminate	6 (13)	-	14 (56)

* Some specimens exhibit more than one appendage; therefore, totals do not represent actual number of specimens.

Lawrence Fisher Series Jars

Jars assigned to the Fisher series ceramic group dominate the Lawrence assemblage, comprising 67 percent (45 vessels) of all vessels (Table 13). The vessels are shell tempered, with not much leaching noted. Their exterior surfaces are predominately smoothed-over cord-marked, and the remaining jars exhibit plain, smoothed surfaces. Interior surfaces are plain and not well finished. Three rim types were identified: vertical, everted, and flared. Lip forms are predominately flattened to flat-thickened, although single examples of rounded and outward beveled forms also occur. A total of 39 vessels are decorated, representing 87 percent of the specimens. Decorative techniques consist of incision, punctation, plain-dowel notching, and smoothed-over cordmarking. The three design fields identified were lips, shoulders, and appendages.

Lip decoration is associated with 30 vessels. The majority of the jar rims exhibit smoothed-over cordmarking (N=28, 93%) on either exterior (13 vessels) or superior/exterior (15 vessels) surfaces. One specimen is decorated by small, dotlike punctations and straight incised lines on the superior lip surface, and vertical notching occurs on the exterior surface. Another displays vertical notching on the interior surface produced by a small plain dowel.

Decoration on the shoulder area is present on 25 vessels. All are trailed, and one also has punctations. Thus, the sherds conform to the Fisher Trailed type. Motifs associated with the shoulder design field often consist of simple parallel curvilinear trailing on a smoothed-over cord-marked surface (11 vessels). The curvilinear motifs are sometimes bordered by punctates and a horizontal line at the base of the neck. This design probably would have been repeated in a series encircling the vessel. Fourteen incised specimens were too small for the design motif to be identified, although the design elements could be identified.

Eight specimens have decorated appendages, comprising seven semicircular lugs and one tab lug and strap handle. Decorative techniques consist of trailing, smoothed-over cordmarking, and notching. The tab lug and strap handle from a single rim specimen exhibits a smoothed-over cordmarked surface.

Keeshin Farm Langford Series Jars

Twenty-five jars are present in the assemblage. These sherds are representative of the Langford series, consisting of grit-tempered specimens with primarily plain surface finishes. Eight are assigned to the Langford Collared category, and two belong to Langford Trailed. Rim form was used as the basis for category divisions because other attributes of vessel form were often unknown. Several rim forms are present, including vertical, everted, flared, incurved, and inslanted. Three jar subtypes were identified on the basis of lip form: flattened, rounded, and outward beveled.

Decoration was observable on 11 jar specimens, representing 44 percent of the vessels. Lip decoration was observed on only 1 vessel. It was characterized by oblique dowel impressions on the exterior lip surface. Decoration on the upper rim design field of 8 jar fragments consists of folds applied to the vessel exterior at the lip. These sherds conform to the Langford Collared type as defined by Fenner (1963:63). The boundary between the lip fold and the vessel body is barely discernible in the profile of these vessels because they are flattened in cross section. Rim fold thickness ranges from 0.2 to 2.7 mm, with a mean of 0.9 mm. Rim fold height ranges from 2.9 to 15.5 mm, with a mean of 8.3 mm. No additional decoration is associated with the rim folds.

Decoration was also observable on the shoulder area of two specimens. The decoration consists of slightly wide, incised or trailed curvilinear lines. Thus, the sherds conform to the Langford Trailed type. Most rims were too small to exhibit decoration in this area, since they extended only a few centimeters below the lip.

Vertical-Rimmed Jars

This jar type is predominant at both sites. At Lawrence, it accounts for 69 percent (31 vessels) of all Fisher series jars. There are 14 specimens assigned to the Fisher Trailed type and 17 that were segregated based simply on shell tempering into a generalized Fisher series category. Also, 83 percent (5 vessels) of all Langford series jars at Lawrence can be placed within this type. Similarly, this category represents 60 percent (15 vessels) of all jars at the Keeshin Farm site.

Lawrence Fisher Series   Three jar-lip subtypes were identified within the Fisher series: flattened, flat-thickened, and outward beveled. Jars with flattened lips constitute about 55 percent (17 vessels) of all vertical-rimmed jars and about 38 percent of all Fisher jars. Most exhibit smoothed-over cordmarked exterior surfaces (12 vessels), although 3 exhibit plain surfaces and 2 have poorly eroded exterior surfaces. Decorative techniques consist of incision and smoothed-over cordmarking. Twelve lips exhibit smoothed-over cordmarking, which occurs on the exterior surface of 7 specimens and superior/exterior surface of 5 others. Decoration on the shoulder field was present on 5 specimens. All exhibit trailing, with a simple curvilinear line motif found associated with this field on 2 vessels. Appendages occur on 3 rims assigned to this type. One semicircular lug is present on vessel 38-3-49 and is decorated by vertical plain-dowel impressions on the exterior surface. Two rims exhibit discrete semicircular lug fragments as well as complete loop handles that are undecorated and molded to the vessels at the inferior surface of the lug. The lug of vessel 53-1-59 is decorated by vertical incisions, and another on vessel 63-1-64 is decorated by vertical plain-dowel impressions on the exterior surface.

Jars with flat-thickened lip forms represent about 42 percent (13 vessels) of all vertical-rimmed jars and about 29 percent of all Fisher jars. Most jars of this type exhibit a smoothed-over cordmarked exterior surface (12 vessels), although 2 exhibit plain surfaces. Decorative techniques consist of trailing, smoothed-over cordmarking, and plain-dowel notching. Lip decoration consists of cordmarking, which occurs on the superior/exterior (3 vessels) and exterior (2 vessels) surfaces, or vertical notching on the interior surface (1 vessel). Decoration on the shoulder field was present on 9 vessels. All exhibit trailing, with a simple curvilinear line motif common to this field (6 vessels). Appendages occur on 2 rims assigned to this type. A semicircular lug fragment associated with vessel 20-1-20 is decorated by vertical incisions on the exterior surface. Another rim specimen, vessel 28-2-37, exhibits 2 undecorated appendages: a semicircular lug with a strap-handle fragment molded to its inferior surface.

Only one outward beveled lip form (vessel 8-2-3) is present. This fragmentary specimen is characterized by plain, undecorated surfaces.

Lawrence Langford Series Five jars exhibit vertical rims with flattened lip forms and smoothed-over cordmarked exterior surfaces. They are representative of the Langford Cordmarked type. All lips are decorated with smoothed-over cordmarking, with three exhibiting vertical cordmarking on the exterior surface only. The others display cordmarking on both exterior and superior surfaces.

Keeshin Farm Langford Series Three jar-lip subtypes were identified within the Langford series: flattened, rounded, and outward beveled. Jars exhibiting flattened lip forms constitute about 46 percent (12 vessels) of all Langford vessels. Most have plain surface finishes except for 1 specimen exhibiting brown-slipped surfaces (vessel 27-1-10). Three Langford Collared and 1 Langford Trailed vessels are associated with this subtype. The Langford Collared specimens are decorated by rim folds on the upper rim design field.

The Langford Trailed specimen (vessel 22-1-8) is decorated on the shoulder design field with a wide (a mean width of 5.6 mm) trailed curvilinear motif (Figure 8). The meandering trailed lines are very shallow, suggestive of painting for decorative effects, as exemplified by painting thought to be visible on four sherds from the Plum Island site (Fenner 1963:59). This specimen was not large enough for a specific design motif to be identified.

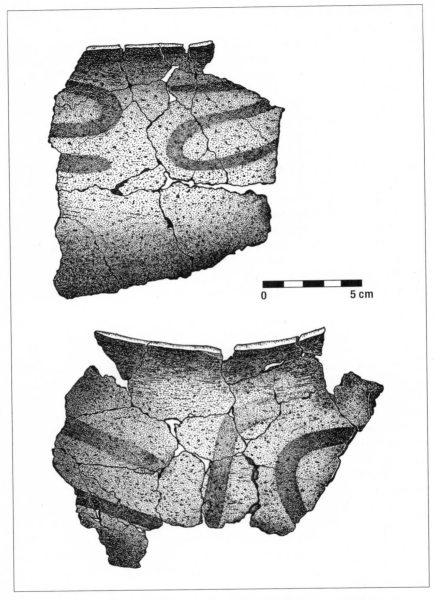

Figure 8 Langford Trailed jars: vessel 22-1-8 (above) and vessel 3-1-2 (below).

Two other subtypes were identified. One vertical-rimmed jar with a rounded lip form possesses plain surface finishes and lacks lip modification. Two other jars exhibit outward beveled lip forms, comprising only about 8 percent of all Langford vessels. Both grit-tempered jars exhibit plain surface finishes and also lack lip modification.

Everted-Rimmed Jars

Everted-rimmed jars rank second in frequency at both sites. They are characterized by a distinct break on the interior surface contour near the rim body and neck juncture that gives each rim a characteristic angled appearance. This form includes the angled and everted rims of Vogel (1975). Moffat and Koldehoff (1990a:129) distinguish between broadly and more sharply everted forms, with the latter possibly associated with later Oneota sites. This type represents about 24 percent (11 vessels) of all Fisher jars in the assemblage. Nine specimens were assigned to the Fisher Trailed type. Two could not be given a type name because of their fragmentary nature. The everted type accounts for 16 percent (4 vessels) of all Langford jars, which are all broadly everted forms.

Lawrence Fisher Series   The three lip form subtypes identified in the sample are flattened, flat-thickened, and rounded. Flattened lips comprise about 73 percent (8 vessels) of everted-rimmed jars and about 18 percent of all Fisher jars. Most exhibit smoothed-over cordmarked exterior surfaces, although one plain specimen is present.

Decorative techniques consist of incision, smoothed-over cordmarking, and punctation. Six lips exhibit smoothed-over cordmarking, which occurs on the superior/exterior surface of 5 specimens and the exterior surface of 1 specimen. One specimen exhibits punctation and incision marks on the superior surface and vertical notching on the exterior edge, which is described below. Decoration on the shoulder field was present on 6 specimens. All exhibit trailing, with a simple curvilinear line motif common to the field of decoration (3 vessels). No appendages were observed for this subtype.

One shell-tempered, everted-rimmed jar (vessel 5-1-1) is typical of the Fisher Trailed type, with a shoulder motif consisting of curvilinear trailing over a smoothed-over cordmarked exterior surface (Figure 9). The trailing consists of five wide (a mean width of 5.5 mm) parallel curvilinear lines running horizontally along the shoulder. They, in turn, are paralleled above by shallow, widely spaced punctates (about 15 mm in width). The combination of these elements may represent the tail of the thunderbird and thereby association with upperworld power through metonymy as discussed in chapter 7. Decoration in the lip design field is complex, involving the exterior and superior (often referred to as interior by researchers) lip edges. The exterior edge is decorated by notches or

U-shaped indentations that cut perpendicular to the lip. This boldly executed modification resembles that found on Fisher and Langford vessels from other sites as well as the type Moccasin Bluff Impressed Exterior Lip from southwestern Michigan (Bettarel and Smith 1973:114, Plate 25), the Fifield series from northwestern Indiana (Faulkner 1972:188–192), and the type Carcajou Curvilinear from extreme southern Wisconsin (Hall 1962:60–61, Plate 22A).

The superior surface of the lip is decorated by a row of small dotlike punctations associated with three narrow straight incised lines in the form of chevrons, which have a rounded apex pointing inward to the vessel orifice. The elements may represent a segment of the cross-in-circle motif (James A. Brown, personal communication, 1996). The motif is simultaneously a sun symbol, represented by the central circle and indentations or dot punctations that may represent the rays of the sun, and a symbol of the four cardinal directions (see Brown et al. 1967:33; Penney 1985:192). Notably, the dot and chevron motif interior rim design has been reported in other Oneota ceramic assemblages (Benn 1989:243). For example, Moffat and Koldehoff (1990a:153, 163, Figure 46A; 1990b:282, Figure 28C) have noted its occurrence in Moingona

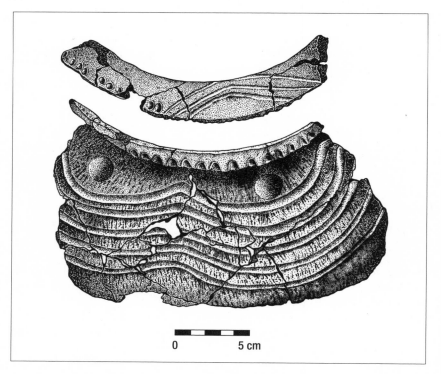

0   5 cm

Figure 9 Fisher Trailed jar, vessel 5-1-1, with possible thunderbird and cross-and-circle motifs.

phase Oneota Wildcat Creek and Dawson site ceramic assemblages of the Central Des Moines River valley. The cross-in-circle motif also occurs on Middle Mississippian jar shoulder design fields of Ramey Incised vessels (Pauketat and Emerson 1991:Figure 10F) as well as those from the Spoon River region (Fulton County) of Illinois (O'Brien 1993:Figure 2). The co-occurrence of cross-in-circle and chevron (hawk/thunderbird) motifs on the lip design field may convey a unified theme regarding a sky arch or dome synonymous with the upperworld (Pauketat and Emerson 1991:928–929).

Two other lip subtypes were noted. Flat-thickened lip forms comprise 15 percent (2 vessels) of everted-rimmed jars and about 4 percent of all Fisher jars. Both specimens exhibit smoothed-over cordmarked exterior surfaces and lips decorated with vertical smoothed-over cordmarking on the exterior surface. Trailing occurs on the shoulder field, with a simple curvilinear motif observed on one specimen. No appendages were observed for this subtype. An everted-rimmed jar with a rounded lip exhibits plain surface finishes and decoration appearing on the shoulder field in the form of trailing. One appendage fragment consists of a semicircular lug.

Keeshin Farm Langford Series   Two lip subtypes were identified in the sample. Everted-rimmed jars with flattened lips comprise about 11 percent (3 vessels) of all Langford vessels. All exhibit plain surfaces. One Langford Collared specimen (vessel 7-1-3) is decorated by a rim fold on the outer lip surface. Another everted-rimmed jar exhibits a rounded lip form. It possesses plain surface finishes and no lip modification.

Flared-Rimmed Jars

This category ranks third in frequency in both assemblages, representing 7 percent (3 vessels) of all Fisher jars in the Lawrence assemblage. It is distinguished by an open or gradual, smooth outcurving of its upper portion. Also, flared rims have an inflection point where the curvature changes from concave to convex. All are assigned to the Fisher Trailed type. One flared type of the Langford series was also found in the Lawrence assemblage. Flared rims account for 8 percent (2 vessels) of all Langford series jars at Keeshin Farm.

Lawrence Fisher Series   Three flared-rimmed jars exhibit flattened lips and possess smoothed-over cordmarked exterior surfaces. The lip forms exhibit smoothed-over cordmarking on the superior/exterior surface of two vessels and the exterior surface of another specimen. Shoulder decoration consists of simple curvilinear line motifs. Two attached appendages occur on vessel 16-2-15 assigned to this type. One is a strap handle decorated with smoothed-over cordmarking, which is attached to a tab lug projecting horizontally outward from the lip.

Lawrence Langford Series   A flared-rimmed jar (vessel 27-1-27) with a flattened lip is decorated on the shoulder field with a set of five medium (a mean width of 3.1 mm) curvilinear lines over a smoothed-over cordmarked exterior surface. The trailing is bordered by an inferior single row of large, widely spaced chevrons. Another distinctive chevron motif appears on a shoulder of a Langford jar from the Keeshin Farm site (Figure 10).

Keeshin Farm Langford Series   The low frequency of flared rims (2 vessels) at the Keeshin Farm site is in marked contrast to their prevalence in the Gentleman Farm site (Brown et al. 1967:23) and Plum Island site (Fenner 1963:59) assemblages. Both rims exhibit flattened lips. One (vessel 3-1-2) can be assigned to the Langford Trailed type. It is deco-

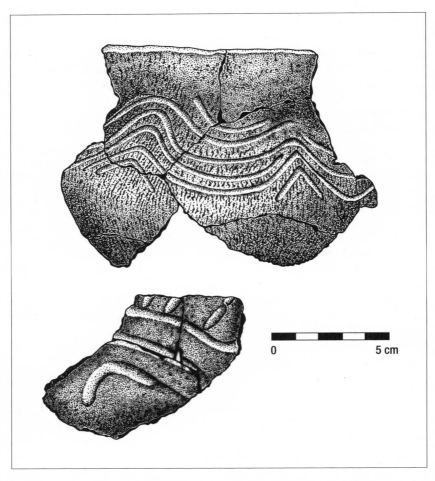

Figure 10   Lawrence Langford Trailed jar, vessel 27-1-27 (above), and chevron motif on a Keeshin Farm Langford Trailed jar shoulder (below).

rated on the shoulder design field by trailed curvilinear meanders. The wide (a mean width of 7.6 mm), shallow trailed-line motif could not be determined. The other specimen exhibits plain surfaces and lip modification restricted to a flattened fold, thus corresponding to the Langford Collared type.

Incurved-Rimmed Jars

Only two rims were placed in the incurved category, both present in the Keeshin Farm assemblage. The Langford series vessels exhibit flattened lips. One specimen has a smoothed-over cordmarked exterior surface and plain interior surface (vessel 19-1-7). The exterior lip surface is decorated by oblique dowel impressions. The other rim fragment exhibits plain surfaces and was decorated on the upper portion with a flattened fold (vessel 13-1-4), thus the vessel was assigned the type Langford Collared.

Inslanted-Rimmed Jars

Inslanted-rimmed jars are present in the Keeshin Farm assemblage only. The two Langford series vessels associated with this type have flattened lips and exhibit plain surfaces. The only recognizable decoration consists of lip modification visible on one rim segment as a flattened fold (vessel 32-2-16), therefore it was considered to be Langford Collared.

CERAMIC TRADITIONS AND EXTERNAL RELATIONSHIPS

The interaction and creative processes within and between ceramic traditions (Oneota, Middle Mississippian, and traditions extending back to Woodland times) is evident in the vessels at Lawrence and Keeshin Farm. The archaeological literature has suggested that the two contemporaneous ceramic traditions of Fisher and Langford are very similar in many attributes (e.g., shape, surface treatment, and decoration) with the exception of tempering agents (Griffin 1943; Griffin 1946). This study identified the similarities and differences between the two traditions by comparing Lawrence and Keeshin Farm utilitarian vessels. Variation exists, but there are some striking similarities or patterns in stylistic attributes. Importantly, it is the execution of similar Oneota jar compositions that define the Prairie Peninsula and its environs as a *distinct culture area*. The vessel shapes and associated decorative patterns as plastic art compositions communicate the potters' power of creativity as well as conformity to communal tradition or regulation across space and time (e.g., horizons). In common with visual art forms throughout history, potters created order or unity out of chaos by controlling, organizing, and integrating lines and shapes through the binding principles of balance (horizontal, vertical, and radial), harmony (rhythm, repetition, and dominance), variety, movement, proportion, and space (see Ocvirk et al. 1968:19). The organization of the parts fits into the order of a whole pot and, in essence, the order of the cosmos.

The dominance of globular or *spherical* shapes for Oneota jars suggests conformity to rules and regulations by communities found within the Prairie Peninsula and its environs extending from Late Woodland through Mississippian times. The spherical pots and associated designs appear to express an "ideology of the people" or self-image of a community, a means of social solidarity ("us" versus "them") (see Braun 1991:366–367). They may also, at times, have provided a model of the cosmos as a balanced, ordered entity similar to that found later in other material culture objects such as Cheyenne shields of the Plains (Nagy 1994) and twined fiber bags of the Eastern Woodlands (Wilson 1982). A common, ordered worldview would serve the interests of the people, giving them some sense of reality by which they could live in communication with others (Bell 1992:192).

Oneota jar decoration was placed on the lip, upper rim, shoulder, and often appendage design fields. Preferences for these fields were probably based on visibility from a normal viewing position, the relation of vessel contour to the design field, and the sooting of vessels below the shoulder. The vessels often depict a unified decorative theme based on curvilinear (circles, concentric arcs, scrolls) or rectilinear (chevron, nested chevrons, inverted chevrons, zigzags) line motifs along with other decorative techniques repeated serially around the vessel.

A comparison of jar shapes in other Mississippian and Late Woodland cultures of the same time period as the Oneota Emergent and Developmental horizons shows significant differences (Figure 11). Since vessels were often used as cooking pots for processing cultivated seeds into gruel (as indicated by their context in domestic refuse pits), there is no relationship between shape and function. Instead, they reflect the aesthetic preferences of potters working within the bounds of tradition. Their choices in vessel shape were influenced, in part, by the plan or position of decoration on particular design fields.

The Middle Mississippian Cahokia pottery types of Ramey Incised (A.D. 1050–1250) and Powell Plain are characterized by subglobular or *ellipsoid,* shallow jars with rolled lips, inslanted rims, and pronounced shoulders. The design field is restricted to the exterior surface of the inslanted rim, with decorations meant to be viewed from above. Ramey Incised symbols include both curvilinear (circles, nested arcs, scrolls) and rectilinear (chevrons, parallel diagonal and horizontal lines) incised or trailed shapes. They are often accentuated by the use of polished slips and the absence of appendages (Jackson 1992a:172; Pauketat and Emerson 1991:929; Vogel 1975:95).

The Oneota jar style contrasts with the Fort Ancient Croghan (A.D.

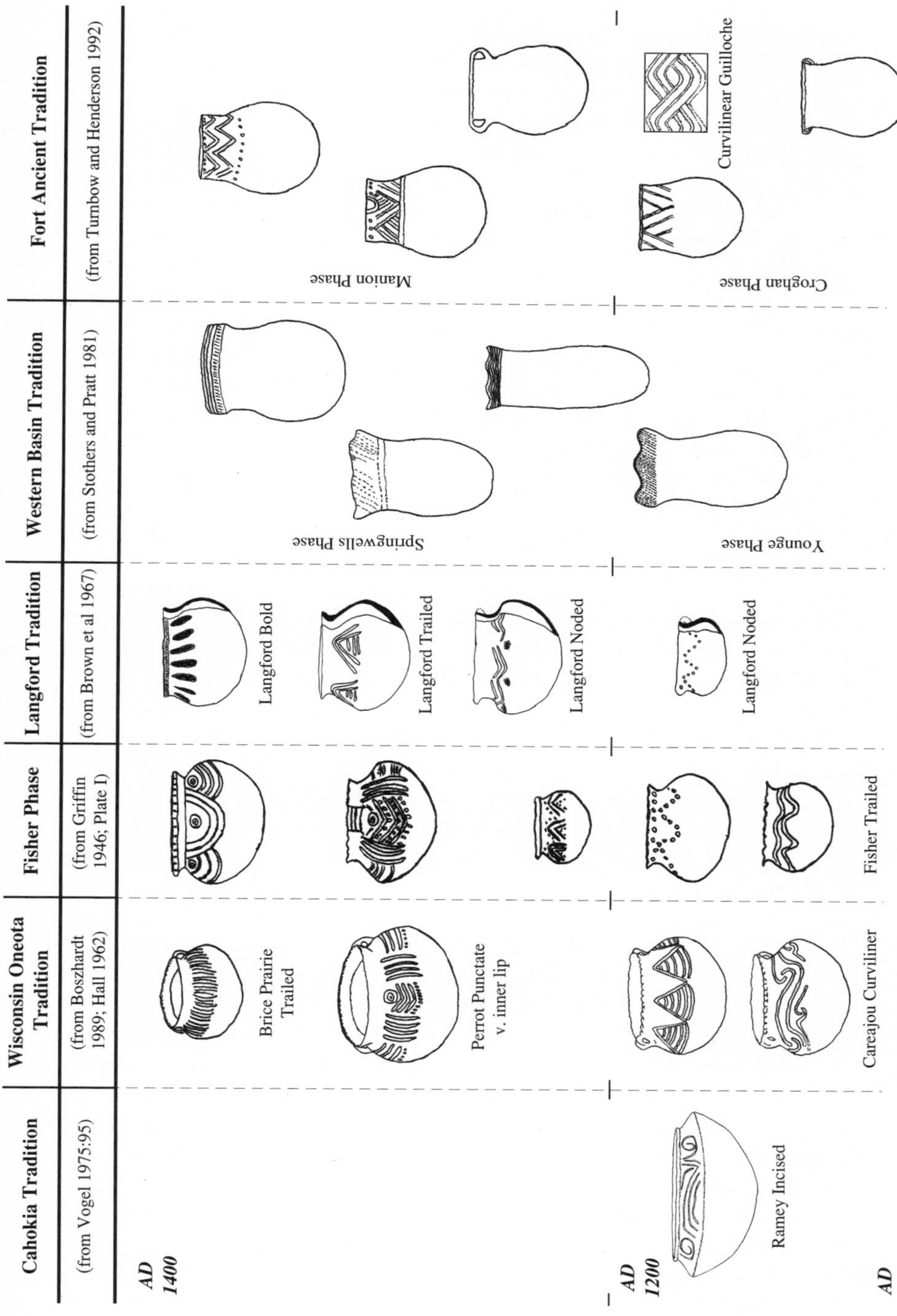

Figure 11 Comparison of jar shapes in Mississippian and Late Woodland assemblages.

1000–1200) and Manion (A.D. 1200–1400) phase forms of the Central Ohio Valley. They are characterized by slightly elongated or *ovaloid* jars usually with flat or rounded lips, vertical rims, and weakly developed shoulders. The design fields include lip, rim, and neck surfaces, with the viewer's attention guided to the side of the vessel. Rectilinear geometric shapes are often used on jar necks including line-filled triangles and chevrons; curvilinear guilloche motifs occur less frequently. Appendages may include vertical lugs, although loop and strap handles also are present (Henderson et al. 1992:258, 264).

In even greater contrast to Oneota spherical jars are those of the Western Basin tradition of the western Lake Erie basin. Jars of the Younge (ca. A.D. 1000–1200) and Springwells (ca. A.D. 1200–1400) phases are characterized by elongated or *ovaloid* forms (some being extremely elongate and bag shaped), with flattened lips, uncollared to well-developed collared vertical to flared rims, and weakly developed shoulders. The design fields include the lip and collared area, although neck decorations can occur. Rectilinear decorative shapes include multiple bands of oblique stamped impressions or one or more bands of horizontal motifs. Marked differences from Mississippian assemblages also occur in the complete lack of appendages (e.g., lug or strap handles) and common use of large castellations. The differences may be attributable to terminal Western Basin tradition peoples being cultural "kinfolk" of the western branch of the Ontario Iroquois tradition (Stothers and Graves 1983; Stothers and Pratt 1981).

Variation in the Keeshin Farm and Lawrence assemblages is mainly attributable to slight differences in their position in time and space and, thus, their relationship to different horizon styles. The Langford ware at Keeshin Farm is characterized by trailed curvilinear motifs on plain exterior surfaces of shoulder design fields. The visually distinctive motifs share elements with Emergent horizon Oneota ceramics in eastern Wisconsin, specifically the Carcajou Curvilinear sherds from the Carcajou site (Hall 1962:Plate 22A, 22B; Gibbon 1986:Figure 6-2). In contrast, Fisher ware is often characterized by decoration on smoothed-over cordmarked surfaces. Aside from these general differences, there are similarities within the Lawrence assemblage, with smoothed-over cordmarking clearly dominating both Fisher and Langford series vessels (N=6, 100%). The observed pattern reflects shared information between Fisher and Langford potters within the Middle Rock River region during the Developmental horizon. Temporal trends identified for exterior surface treatment indicate that plain exteriors increase in popularity, clearly dominating in Huber assemblages (Bluhm and Fenner 1961:145; Emerson and Brown 1992; Faulkner 1972; Herold et al. 1990:88).

Differences also occur in the decoration of the upper rim design field of Langford series jars from the Keeshin Farm site. These vessels display intentionally and carefully worked rim folds, representing excess clay folded over from the lip and pressed almost even with the exterior surface. Folded or weakly collared rims have been reported at other Langford sites, including Robinson Reserve (Fowler 1952:52), Oakwood Mound (Skinner 1953:10), Plum Island (Fenner 1963:63), Cooke (Markman 1991:194), and Reeves (Craig and Galloy 1995) but are absent in the Lawrence and other Fisher phase assemblages. They are also associated with other areas of the Midcontinent, such as the Younge and Springwells phases of the western Lake Erie region (Stothers and Pratt 1981:95) and wares from the Central Ohio Valley. It appears that this decorative form is a development from both earlier and contemporaneous Late Woodland collared wares, like Starved Rock Collared, and is restricted to the Oneota Emergent and Developmental horizons.

Jar similarities are most apparent in rim form. Both sites have a preponderance of vertical rim profiles, with everted rims also frequently occurring. This dominance—93 percent of Fisher series and 76 percent of Langford series rims from the Lawrence and Keeshin Farm sites, respectively—reflects Oneota rather than Fort Ancient or Western Basin tradition interaction. Vertical and everted forms are typical of Emergent horizon Oneota assemblages from eastern Wisconsin (Overstreet 1995:36). Importantly, everted or angled rims are also typical of other Oneota and Middle Mississippian assemblages (Milner et al. 1984; Moffat and Koldehoff 1990:129). Such forms, however, are notably absent in Fort Ancient assemblages of the Middle Ohio Valley (Griffin 1943; Turnbow and Henderson 1992:298) and the Western Basin tradition assemblages of the western Lake Erie region (Stothers and Pratt 1981). The prevalence of vertical and everted rims in Fisher and Langford assemblages (Brown et al. 1967; Emerson and Brown 1992:85, 86; Fenner 1963; Skinner 1953) is consistent with Huber phase ceramics (Emerson and Brown 1992:88; Faulkner 1972:66; Herold et al. 1990; Michalek and Brown 1990), thus showing temporal continuity between ceramic industries.

Four lip forms were identified during this study: flattened, flat-thickened, rounded, and outward beveled. In general, these data show that flattened lips occur most frequently, and rounded and outward beveled lips occurr least frequently. Also, flat-thickened lips are only present in the Fisher series vessels from Lawrence. Flattened lip forms are predominant in other Fisher assemblages (Fenner 1963:55) and are also common in Langford assemblages like the Gentleman Farm (Brown et al. 1967) and Reeves (Craig and Galloy 1995) sites. Temporal trends identified for lip forms appear to indicate that rounded lips increased in popularity through time, although they still occurred in either less frequency than or nearly equal proportion to flattened forms in Huber assemblages (Faulkner 1972:65; Michalik and Brown 1990:208).

Upperworld cosmological themes sometimes appear to be expressed graphically through symbols on the upper portion of Oneota jars, with their variability noted cross-culturally and through time in the North

American Midcontinent. This is exemplified by the presence of curvilinear and rectilinear (e.g., chevron) decorative motifs repeated serially around vessel shoulder design fields of Langford and Fisher jars. They are common during the Mississippi period (Brown et al. 1967:22) and show continuity with earlier Woodland vessel motifs (Benn 1995; Overstreet 1995:60).

Scrolls, spirals, and meandering or undulating curvilinear lines occur on Carcajou Curvilinear jars (Koshkonong phase pottery) from Carcajou Point, Wisconsin (as noted above), and are common on Ramey Incised subglobular jars. The motifs are also found farther afield in the guilloche decorative motifs of the Fort Ancient cultures (Henderson et al. 1992:258), in the Oliver phase of Central Indiana (McCullough 1991:28), and on vessels as distant as the Fort Walton culture, Florida (Berlo and Phillips 1998:84). Curvilinear lines may indicate winds (Anonymous 1897:119–120; Willoughby 1897:10–11), the seasons, or the revolving motion of the sky (Berlo and Phillips 1998) associated with the upperworld.

The chevron motif may be interpreted as an abstract symbol (metonym) of a raptorial bird or thunderbird of the upperworld in Oneota iconography (Benn 1989, 1995). Hall (1991:29) and Gibbon (1995:191) have suggested that the chevron is a stylistic rendering of predatory bird's tail, apparently a thunderbird of falcon form—an abstract rather than representational form perhaps attributable to the reduced size of the ceramic body design field as elongated Woodland vessels become globular in Mississippian times (Benn 1995). However, Lame Deer and Erdoes (1972:111) state that, among the Sioux nation, "abstract designs are always women's work. Men draw figures of humans and animals realistically, the way they see them." The chevron motif is noted in Langford ceramic assemblages at the Fisher (Griffin 1946:18), Zimmerman (Brown 1961:Figure 8A), Plum Island (Fenner 1963:61), Gentleman Farm (Brown et al. 1967), and Reeves (Craig and Galloy 1995) sites. It has also been observed in the Fisher assemblage at the Fisher site (Griffin 1946:15). The motif and its possible association with the thunderbird will be discussed more fully in the next chapter.

What gives the curvilinear and rectilinear motifs their distinctive meanings and emotional responses is how they are combined (attention to symmetry, complexity, color, and space) on the jar shape, the Oneota *spherical* shape. They appear to express fundamental cosmological beliefs dealing with an ordered world with four cardinal directions (sometimes represented by handles) surrounding a central circular form of the sun (the vessel orifice). But this assumption needs testing by examining large numbers of vessels.

•   In the production of utilitarian jars as a visual, plastic art form, Oneota potters were affected by historical factors of tradition and interrelationships along with religious, cosmological, and aesthetic value considerations. Each potter sought to create *unity* or oneness out of chaos through technical skills and inspiration or creativity from dreams. The result was beauty found in the *spherical* jar shapes exhibiting smoothed-over cordmarked or plain, smoothed surface finishes and decoration on the upper body and rim segments by incision, trailing, punctation, dowel notching, smoothed-over cordmarking, and/or appliqué. The most elaborate decoration occurs on the shoulder and superior surfaces of everted rims, capturing the viewer's attention from above. Here, curvilinear (spirals, festoons) and/or rectilinear (chevrons) motifs were repeated often enough in a rhythmical way to make them the dominating feature of the artist's expression. The proportionally related composition provided a means of visual communication, often with the meaning apparently focused on cosmological themes relating to the upperworld (wind, sun, thunderbird) and an ordered cosmos (see Holmes 1883:268; Willoughby 1897; Wissler 1907), themes that appear to have a long tradition cross-culturally in Native American societies and should be viewed in a religious ideological sense. The power of creativity could have been granted as a gift to the potter by a supernatural being(s) and shared by the community in culturally appropriate ways. For archaeologists, the vessels produced by Oneota peoples can be easily recognized from those of other areas of the North American Midcontinent, making the Prairie Peninsula and environs a true culture area.

CHAPTER SEVEN

Thunderbird Symbolism and Material Culture

As Native American men and women actively exchange collective meanings of culture, symbols of power are seen in imagery and creativity cross-culturally and across temporal dimensions (see Whitten and Whitten 1993). Symbols are used to regulate and organize relations between people and to communicate about human relations with the supernatural world. According to Ian Hodder (1992:208), "The symbolic meanings are built upon, by association and metaphor, the material world," or, in other words, a practical knowledge of the social and natural world. Therefore, each symbol is to be taken as a power unto itself. Such power can be observed in material symbols associated with creative events and objects (pottery, textiles, metalwork) embellished with symbols communicating inner personal and community strengths used to interact with cosmic powers, such as the mythical thunderbird of the upperworld.

The interpretation of thunderbird power and symbolism presented in this discussion rests on the assumption that everything in the universe of the small-scale, Native American society is connected with everything else. That is, there is a theme of continuity, of integration, of interaction between humans and animate nonhuman forms that exist in the "natural" and "supernatural" worlds (Dugan 1985). This view contrasts with that of traditional Western thought regarding the relationship between culture and nature, especially the Judeo-Christian belief that man has ultimate "power over" nature. As the anthropologist Roy Willis (1990:6) states, "This religious legitimation of human domination and exploitation of the world of nature is now frequently contrasted with a nonhierarchic relation of interdependence between human beings and nature that is held to characterize the world-views of many small-scale, 'tribal' societies." The culturally constructed cosmologies of Eastern Woodland and Plains societies are shown here to have been interrelated in what Willis (1990:8–9) terms "complementary dualism," which holds that everything in the tangible, material world—people, animals, things—has a counterpart in the other, spiritual world. These two worlds are equally "real" and intimately interrelated across time and space. Thus, thunderbirds readily become people, and vice versa. Complementary dualism appears to be a common conceptual framework, although the content of the dual demiworlds, the nature of the unifying principle, and the location of the cosmological divide varies among groups.

THE MYTHICAL AND HISTORICAL REALITY OF THE THUNDERBIRD

Access to supernatural power was through certain zoomorphic forms perceived as being capable of moving between the vertical strata of the cosmos as "dynamic" mediators. Among Native American societies of the Plains and Eastern Woodlands, the dominant and most enduring symbol of the upperworld has been the celestial bird (King 1982:11; Lame Deer and Erdoes 1972:136–137; Overstreet 1995:53; Penney 1985; Wilson 1982). The celestial bird may be perceived as a prime mediator between the opposed and complementary domains of the visible and the invisible, natural and supernatural, human and nonhuman, or "life" and "death," similar to the role of the python in Kom cosmology of Cameroon, West Africa (Willis 1990:14–15) or the shaman in South American rituals (Langdon 1992:12). Among the Ojibway, the spiritual "masters" among avian creatures, the thunderbirds, are inherently powerful and capable of metamorphosis or transformation to human form, and they are the sources from which humans (particularly shamans) may seek to enhance their personal power for good or evil (Hallowell 1967:226–227, 1992:66). This concept was also held by the Winnebago. Paul Radin (1923:439) states that, among the Winnebago, thunderbirds (*wakandja*) "are always represented as appearing to men as bald-headed individuals wearing a wreath made of the branches of the arbor vitae. They are in control of almost all the powers that man can imagine, but they generally bless him with success on the warpath and with a long and honorable life. They are represented as having a spirit village in the west and as intermarrying with the Night Spirits who have a village in the east. Powerful shamans and warriors not infrequently claim that they are merely reincarnated Thunderbirds."

Myth and legends of Plains and Eastern Woodlands societies are often derived from nature. For example, the avian attributes given thunderbirds by various societies are explicit in that the linguistic stem for "bird" is often identical to "thunderbird" (e.g., Illiniwek, *pineusen;* Mississagua, *pinesi;* Ojibway, *binesi;* and Ottawa, *pinasi*) (Chamberlain

1890:51; Hallowell 1967:220). To the Ojibway, the avian characteristics attributed to thunderbirds are based on behavioral observations, especially regarding migrations that are phased on an annual cycle, or a circannual rhythm. Thunderbirds are classified with temperate-zone birds that migrate south before the onset of winter. Their migratory behavior corresponds with temperate-zone hibernators, like snakes, that also follow similar circannual rhythms as a key to survival. Also of importance, Hallowell (1967:220, 1992:62) found a very high correlation between the occurrence of thunderstorms in the meteorological records from April to October and periods when migratory birds return to summer in the mid- to northern latitudes (i.e., northwestern Ontario and Manitoba). This phenomenon would explain why thunderbirds were only heard from spring through fall by the Ojibway. A somewhat different version is given by the Menominee, with informants telling Skinner (1913:77) that there was a high correlation between the occurrence of thunderstorms and the flight of young thunderbirds: "Their eggs hatch in July and the thunderstorms so prone to occur at that season are due to the activity of the young birds in learning to fly."

The cross-cultural Native American view explaining the phenomenon of thunderstorms appears to be very similar, with the thunderbird being closely linked to thunderstorms and associated rain, lightning, hail, and tornadoes in Plains and Eastern Woodlands mythology. Thus, the thunderbird possesses generative and destructive power. Swanton (1910:746–747) states that, among such societies, "the phenomenon of thunderstorms . . . were supposed to be caused by birds of enormous size, which produced thunder by flapping their wings and the lightning by opening and closing their eyes. The great downpour which generally accompanies thunder was often accounted for by supposing that the bird carries a lake of fresh water on its back." According to W. H. Holmes (cited in Eells 1889:335), the Dakota believe that "the storm bird dwells in the upper air beyond human sight, and carries on its back a lake of fresh water. When it winks its eyes there is lightning, when it flaps its wings there is thunder, and when it shakes its plumage there is rain." Dorsey (1894:508) notes a similar belief in such a creature among the Mandan. A slightly different version exists respecting the Cree, as exemplified by F. V. Hayden's (cited in Chamberlain 1890:54) statement:

> Indeed, these Indians do not seem to fear any natural phenomena except thunder, which is supposed to be the screaming and flapping of the wings of a large bird, which they represent on their lodges as a great eagle. Wind is supposed to be produced by its flying, and flashes of lightning are caused by the light of the sun reflected from its white and golden plumage, and when strokes of lightning are felt they are thunderstones cast down by this bird. All storms, tornadoes, etc., are caused by its wrath, and fair winds, calm and fine weather are regarded as tokens of its good humor.

In a study of Teton Dakota myth, Dorsey (1894:441) suggests an association between thunderbirds and fertility when he states, "They [thunderbirds] created the wild rice and a variety of prairie grass, the seed of which bears some resemblance to that of the rice." Landes (1970:59–60) reports on this concept for the Prairie Potawatomi: "Thunderbird enjoyed a contrasting exaltation, symbolizing everything noble and virile. . . . Master of the Skies, Thunderbird was solicited during drought (Kansas suffered drastically from the 1930s dust storms) on occasions that even Mayetta whites described to me as effective . . . and he was solicited during flood." Among the Ojibway, Hoffman (1891:219) notes that the thunderbird is "the one who causes the rains, and consequently life to vegetation, by which the Indian may sustain life." Menominee informants told Hoffman (1896):

> Ina'maqki'u^v (the Big Thunder) lived at Winnebago Lake, near Fond du Lac. The Good Mystery made the Thunderers laborers, and to be of benefit to the whole world. When they return from the southwest in the spring, they bring the rains which make the earth green and cause the plants and trees to grow. If it were not for the Thunderers, the earth would become parched and the grass would wither and die.

Thunderstorms are not related to the thunderbird alone but tend to be interpreted as a life-and-death struggle between the thunderbird(s) and the plumed or horned serpents (Arikara, Assiniboin, Bungi, Dakota, Fox, Menominee, Ojibway, Sac), underneath, underground, or underworld panther (Fox, Kickapoo, Ioway, Ojibway, Menominee, Prairie Potawatomi), water monsters (Dakota, Wichita, [Kathlamet?]), and water spirit (Winnebago) (Michelson 1930:54–55). For example, on the Plains a thunderstorm was thought to be caused by a contest between the thunderbird and a gigantic rattlesnake-like creature, or an underground or underwater horned monster called "Unktehi" by the Dakota and "Waktceqi" by the Winnebago (Dorsey 1894:425, 438, 442). Ojibway informants told Hallowell (1967:221), "When there is lightning and thunder this is the prey [includes all snakes, but particularly Great Snakes] the Thunder Birds are after." Midwest Native American tribes believed, according to Skinner (1914:72), "It is the duty of these birds to guard man, to rake the earth with hail and water it with rain, and above all, to prevent the evil horned snakes from destroying mankind." Menominee informants told Skinner (1913:77), "As the elder brothers of the Indians, the thunderers are always active in their behalf, slaying the evil snakes from the underworld whenever they dare to appear on the surface."

According to John R. Swanton (1910:747), the accounts of this struggle between these mythic beings have led some ethnohistorians to mistakenly assume "a mystic significance from this, such as the war between light and darkness or good and evil." They failed to see the ambiguity and heterogeneity in power associated with such mythical creatures. Their power is derived, in part, from ambiguity, because they do not fit into the mutually exclusive categories that organize the world. They are neither inherently good nor evil because they work for the benefit as well as the detriment of others.

As shown above, the thunderbird theme was geographically wide-spread among historic Native American groups, being present among Arctic, North Pacific Coast, Southwest, Plains, and Eastern Woodlands societies. In most of these cases, the thunderbird has been envisioned as a gigantic raptor whose wings created thunder and whose flashing (wink-ing, twinkling) eyes emitted lightning (e.g., Arapaho, Cheyenne, Co-manche, Cree, Dakota, Hare, Kiowa, Mandan, Mississagua, Ojibway, Ot-tawa, Tlingit, Winnebago) (Chamberlain 1890; Dorsey 1894:508; Eells 1889:330, 335; Hall 1977:501; Hallowell 1992:61; Michelson 1930; Mooney 1896:968; Penney 1985:180; Radin 1923:287; Swanton 1910:746; Wintemberg 1928:27). The kind of bird it resembled, how-ever, varies cross-culturally from a gigantic eagle, or "supereagle," (Hare, Menominee, Ojibway, Omaha, Ottawa, Potawatomi, Sac and Fox, Win-nebago), falcon (Ojibway), hummingbird (Lillooet), jackpine partridge (Beaver), crane (Pawnee), to a raven (most Alaskan Native Americans) (Chamberlain 1890; Eells 1889; Fletcher and La Flesche 1911:42; Hoff-man 1891:230; Michelson 1930:54; Skinner 1914:72).

THUNDERBIRD TAILS AS SYMBOLS
OF POWER IN HISTORIC ARTWORK

In religious and symbolic Oneota artwork, abstract designs of the thunderbird may have been derived from a stylization of the bird's tail, giving free expression to this great spiritual power. The abstract or geo-metric designs may include arch, festoon, chevron, and triangular motifs. Archaeologists Robert Hall (1991:29) and Adolph Link (1995:20) sug-gest that the distinctive chevron motif in Oneota art is derived from a stylization of a thunderbird tail that could have represented the entire bird, which is an example of metonymy, "the substitution of an attribute, effect or association for a thing" (Hodder 1992:203). In other words, a part is used to symbolize the whole. This is exemplified by a "crown" or "throne" being used to stand as a symbol for the monarch or for monar-chy, which is a cultural symbol known and understood by all the mem-bers of the society (see Leach 1976:14; Rosman and Rubel 1995:58).

There are many historic Native American examples of this symbolic representation. Headgear displaying eagle tail feathers were used by the Oglala Dakota leaders for social and ceremonial events as a sign of power, which are shown in their pictographic records by Garrick Mallery (1893:587, 750–751). The Oglala drawings or paintings usually depict the center tail feather(s), which may denote gens, personal designation, or social status. Colin Taylor (1991:95) illustrates a "real" Lakota head-dress containing some seventy tail feathers from an immature golden eagle. It was worn by Sinte Maza, or Iron Tail, an Oglala Sioux who was born in northwest Nebraska about 1860. Highwater (1983:145) notes, "A head band of stiff tail and wing feathers was used by many tribes from Virginia to the St. Lawrence River." Some Ottawa warriors of the Great Lakes region also wore headdresses made of the tails of eagles or other birds (Kinietz 1940:252). Fanlike arrangements of golden eagle tail feathers were used as ceremonial ornamentation on red pipestone pipes and paired calumets (supposedly representing the oppositions of male and female, sky and earth, day and night) for the Pawnee Hako and Omaha Wa'wan ceremonies (Fletcher and La Flesche 1911:376–377; Hall 1997:50–52). The Ioway eagle dance, called Ha-Kon-E-Crase, required that each male dancer carry a fan made of the eagle's tail in his left hand as he imitates the movements of a soaring eagle (Skinner 1915:716). Frances Densmore (1929:83–85) states that an elderly Ojibway man, Niskigwun, attributed his success in war and acquisition of a new home to a dream of a bald eagle (*wabicuckwe*) and the tail feathers that he constantly kept with him. Turkey tail feather fans were used by the Creek and Yuchi as a sign of leadership (Swanton 1979:456), and the Sac leader Black Hawk (Makataimeshekiakiak) frequently used a hawk-tail fan as his portrait was being painted by George Catlin, perhaps signifying either his power (Hall 1991:29–30) or an attempt to obtain spiritual guidance and protection.

The perception of the chevron or triangle as a symbol of power, because of their association with a thunderbird's tail, may be supported by historic Plains and Eastern Woodlands art, especially pictographs. According to Henry W. Henshaw (1910:242–243), "Pictography may be defined as that form of thought-writing which seeks to convey ideas by means of picture-signs or marks more or less suggestive or imitative of the object or idea in mind. Significance, therefore, is an essential element of pictographs, which are alike in that they all express thought, register a fact, or convey a message." Thus, the primary purpose of pictography was the conveyance of ideas concerning a system of beliefs through imagery. To those Native Americans with esoteric knowledge concerning their culture's worldview, the figures in picture writing were invaluable memory aids that were passed down through successive generations. Thunderbirds can be seen in some pictographic records of Algonquian and Siouan societies, and their spiritual nature is often indicated by certain symbols (e.g., zigzag lines representing lightning bolts and slightly angular, wavy, or straight individual lines denoting communication, or "spirit power").

The most notable pictographs have been reported for the Ojibway (Densmore 1929; Hoffman 1891; Mallery 1893), with thunderbirds depicted in the mnemonic drawings etched on ceremonial song scrolls of the Ojibway Midewiwin, or Grand Medicine Society. The images are a result of the shamans' visions in the quest for medicine, gaining a knowledge of which was a primary objective of Midewiwin members (Densmore 1929:175; Hoffman 1891:156–164; Rajnovich 1989). The Ojibway pictographer was a man or woman shaman who expressed visions and journeys to the "otherworld" using the symbolic metaphor. Important to this study are the similarities between the Ojibway birch bark pictographs of thunderbirds as seen in Figure 12A–H, with chevron and triangular-shaped tails depicted along with triangular or diamond-shaped bodies. Figure 12A is the sign for the song "I brought the medicine to bring life" and means, as Hoffman was told (1891:203), that the thunderer, Mide' Man'ido, after bringing some of the plants—by causing rainfall—returns to the sky. The short line represents a segment of the circular line often used to denote the imaginary vault of the sky. Figure 12B would be read "I brought life to the people" and refers to the fact that thunderbirds are responsible for rainfall and, therefore, give life to vegetation so that Native Americans can survive. Figure 12C is sung "I am sitting like a sparrow-hawk." It is interpreted as "The singer is sitting upright, and is watchful, like a hawk watching for its prey. He is ready to observe, and to acquire, everything that may transpire in the Mide' structure" (Hoffman 1891:230). Figure 12D reads "The bird, the crow bird's skin is the reason why I am a spirit." The thunderbird (eagle) is depicted in this etching even though the crow is mentioned (Hoffman 1891:264). Figure 12E is the sign for the song segment "The thunder is heavy," which refers to the thunderbird who causes rain (Hoffman 1891:209). Figure 12F would be read as "The spirit is flying," which can be interpreted as "The Thunder Bird, who causes the rain, is away at some remote place (Hoffman 1891:210)." Figure 12G is sung "The bird as I promise the falcon the reason he is a spirit" and apparently would be interpreted as "Ki'tshi Man'ido [Great Spirit] promised to create the Thunder-bird, one of the man'idos [spirits]. The falcon is here taken as a representative of that deity" (Hoffman 1891:230). Figure 12H shows the thunderbird occupying the highest point over the shamans' medicine lodge, indicative of its primacy in power among the spirits in the Shaking Tent ceremony (Hoffman 1891:252). Communion or communication within the spiritual realm are depicted by "power lines" linking the hearts of animal spirits with the Jessakkid or shaman, who is a seer and prophet (i.e., "revealer of hidden truths," or interpreter of dreams).

Pictographic records of the thunderbird were by no means unique to the Ojibway but were also represented in the work of other peoples of Central Algonquian stock. For example, the Menominee created birch bark records, accompanied by songs, as mnemonic reminders of interaction with thunderbirds. Among them were three birch bark strips in-

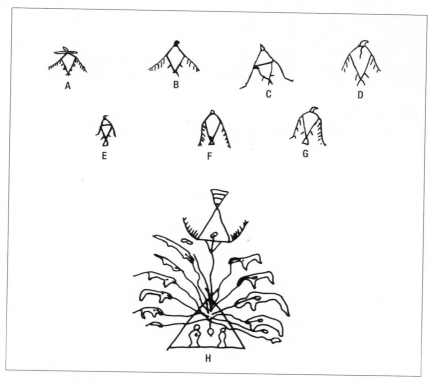

Figure 12   Ojibway birch bark records relating to the thunderbird in songs (Hoffman 1891): A, "I brought the medicine to bring life"; B, "I brought life to the people"; C, "I am sitting like a sparrow-hawk"; D, "The bird, the crow bird's skin is the reason why I am a spirit"; E, "The thunder is heavy"; F, "The spirit is flying"; G, "The bird as I promise the falcon the reason he is a spirit"; H depicts the Shaking Tent ceremony, in which the thunderbird is drawn directly above the shamans' lodge, showing its primacy in spiritual power.

structing people in the lore of the thunderers. They were obtained from an elderly male informant who provided the songs that accompany each pictograph series. These barks could be traced back as far as his great-grandfather. Alanson Skinner (1913:74–75) was told that Figure 13A depicts Wickano, the leader of the thunderers, as a man on earth who receives the power to create rain and lightning in a vision. In a repetition of forms demanding attention or emphasis, Wickano is shown holding rain, lightning, and wind in his hands. The dividing vertical lines symbolize torrential rainfall. A lodge (k) is shown near the end of the series, which contains the destructive forces needed by the thunderers. The song accompanying this pictograph group is "Takame'sao [a personal name among the thunderers] he is a god."

Figure 13 Menominee mnemonic drawings of the thunderbird on birch bark.

Figure 13B relates the thunderbird's destructive power to create lightning, floods, hail, wind, and tornadoes (c–h, j) as well as its constructive power to make such forces cease, resulting in a rainbow appearing above him (i). The next pictograph is a great tree where thunderers rest and watch for the evil serpent monsters (k). In the remainder of the sequence, the thunderers are shown traveling together (l–p) with their leader guiding the way (q). The series of ideograms is sung "Vapour I do walk with animal like (with thunder power)."

Figure 13C shows the thunderbird's village in the sky (a) and its power to control wind (c), clouds (d), rain (g), and a tornado or whirlwind (i). The thunderbird is portrayed in several ideograms: Wickano standing alone (b), at his resting place on a large rock (e), in human-like form (h), and in the process of capturing one of the evil serpents, which the thunderers eat (k) (although the form looks more like another underwater supernatural known as the Great Fish). The song for this bark strip is "Oh cloud! you that are god animal like."

Thunderbirds were also represented in Plains Native American pictographs, which often show thunderbirds with a chevron or triangular tail. Figures 14A–C represent Dakota drawings of thunderbirds. Figures 14A and 14B were discovered in 1883 among the Dakota near Fort Snelling and were drawn and interpreted by people of that nation. Both exhibit wings and waving lines issuing from the mouth downward, perhaps signifying communication. The one in Figure 14C is more abstract, lacking the head and wings (Mallery 1893:483). Figure 14D shows a thunderbird that was painted on the side of a Cree tipi in Saskatchewan. It has a triangular body and chevron tail. Zigzag lines at the left of the bird signify lightning or thunder, a sign for the presence of mysterious supernatural power (Wintemberg 1928; Wissler 1907:46–47).

Thunderbirds are commonly depicted in their geometric bird-form on carrying bags or pouches of North American groups. The elaborately patterned containers were often manufactured on a simple square frame from the bast or inner bark of basswood trees, although other fibers were used, such as cedar bark, slippery elm bark, Indian hemp (apocynum) made of rotted nettle fiber, dark brown bison hair, and commercial wools and yarns obtained from traders or blanket ravelings (Densmore 1929:157–159; Feest 1984:14–15; Highwater 1983:129; King 1982:25; Skinner 1913, 1921:232; Whiteford 1977; Wilson 1982). Woven bags were formerly used for carrying and storing food or personal belongings as well as for holding medicines and ritual paraphernalia, called sacred packs or medicine bundles.

Medicine bundles were the focus of power relationships as indicated by studies of the Prairie Potawatomi by Skinner (1924:55-56, 1927:356) and Landes (1970), of the Menominee by Skinner (1913, 1921), and of the Winnebago by Radin (1923:442, 550). Ruth Landes (1970:42) states that, to the Prairie Potawatomi:

> A medicine bundle, in the 1930's, was a pack of charms, herbs, and symbolic objects. A few individuals privately owned or were trustees of these, and a number of men and women were associated with each "owner" or trustee in the bundle's secret rites. The bundles were regarded as the oldest surviving cult-altars. A person cared for one or more at a time (more than one, however, was seen as a vast responsibility, so laxness was expected, though condemned fiercely). A man with several bundles tried to amalgamate them, to consolidate their "power" and increase efficiency. When they were merged, the same membership continued. People followed intently the activities of the medicine bundles and of the personalities linked to them.

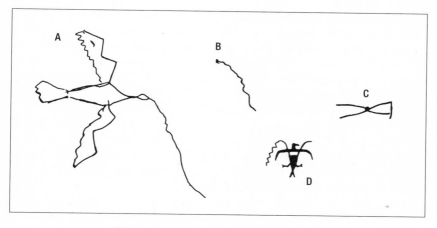

Figure 14   Dakota drawings of thunderbirds.

Among the Menominee, sacred or medicine bundles were of four basic types—war bundle, hunting bundle, witchcraft bundle, and good luck bundle—that contained small personal charms or fetishes. Each bundle was accompanied by songs and rituals. The bundles and their contents belonged to individuals who dreamed the right to possess them and were thought to be gifts from the thunderbird or morning star (Skinner 1913:91–96; 1921:310). Skinner (1913:93–94) states:

> With the Menomini, as among the Blackfoot, all medicines originate in dreams, and "the material part of each is after all but an objective part of a ritual." Thus, theoretically, there would be no objection to parting with any medicine or charm, provided the songs accompanying it, and through which alone it can be made effective, were retained, except for the fact that through its use with its ritual and by its contact with the animating power of the supernatural donors which it represents, the object itself acquires a degree of sanctity in proportion with its antiquity and the services which it has performed. . . . In other words, any medicine bundle or charm has three distinct qualities—first, the object itself, powerful, as we have explained above, through use and contact with the beings who gave it; second, an additional power given by the dream; and third and greatest, the animating force of songs. To possess the songs is enough to permit the owner to use the power of the bundle.

WEAVING, WOMEN, AND BALANCE OF SUPERNATURAL POWER

Mythological themes relating to the thunderbird have been remarkably preserved on similar twined fiber bags that were made by the Great Lakes Native American groups like the Menominee, Miami, Ojibway, Ottawa, Sac and Fox, and Winnebago as well as the Plains groups of the Omaha, Osage, Oto, and Ioway. The artists are assumed to be almost exclusively women (see Benn 1995:94; Densmore 1929:152, 159; Drooker 1992:12; La Flesche 1889:9; Mason 1904:191, 314–316; Skinner 1921:256) using ancient symbols and their creativity in presentation. Benn (1995:94) points out that gender was often ignored in ethnohistoric sources despite evidence that women were doing the weaving. The association of women with weaving is supported by one of Densmore's (1929:159) Ojibway informants: "This woman, Magidins by name, was more than 70 years old at the time and said that she learned this work [weaving] from her grandmother when a child." Perhaps the most compelling argument comes from a statement made by W. Vernon Kinietz (1940:177) regarding the manufacture of bundles by the Miami: "The war mats or bundles carried by the young men and in which they placed their tutelary birds were made by the women. They took round reeds which grew in the swamps, dyed them black, yellow, and red and made mats three feet long and two feet wide; they folded over one end for about a foot in the form of a comb case."

The designs depicted on the woven bags usually consist of geometrical figures arranged in bands, with different images placed on opposing sides. The geometrical shape of the figures are primarily due to the technique and materials used in twined weaving. Shapes are effected by the bark or yarn warp strands, which are often of zigzag or vertical types (Feest 1984:15; Mason 1904:385). Thus, geometric decorations were produced, such as zigzag lines, chevrons, triangles, squares, rectangles, and rhomboidal figures. The repetition of rhythmical, dominating thunderbirds and underworld panthers demands attention or emphasis, and it allows pause for examination. The visual elements are usually organized in pure symmetrical balance so that unity (the whole or total effect of an artwork) and harmony are easily attained. Therefore, the artist is able to communicate effectively, perhaps giving the viewer some order and coherence in the stream of sensations, emotions, and ideas entering their consciousness. Several examples of this kind of Native American artwork are given below.

Among Central Algonquian groups, the upperworld thunderbirds often occur in association with underworld panthers, reflecting the opposition and ambiguity of these two powerful mythical beings. These figures are often represented on opposite sides of the fiber bag and in visually opposing manners. The thunderbird is usually depicted with a frontal body and profile head; the underworld panther in most instances has a profile body and frontally viewed head. It is possible that these opposing "otherworld" powers were intended to neutralize one another, indicating that good and evil were equalized and balanced supernatural forces in the middleworld, or "this world" (Wilson 1982:440).

A Menominee basswood bark twine bag is decorated on one side with a woman and eagle designs and on the other with underworld or underground panthers (Figure 15). This specimen, dated post-1850(?), is the enveloping bag of a medicine bundle for hunting called Kitagase Muskiki, or "Spotted Fawn Medicine." It contained various ritual items, including wolf-tail medicine, fawnskin medicine in wrappers of fawn hair, a small medicine pouch, two dolls representing the powers of the ancestors (grandparents), and a wooden male figurine (Skinner 1913:141–143).

At the top of the obverse side of the bag are motifs consisting of a woman flanked by two thunderbirds or eagles. The figures are clasping hands, which may signify that this sacred container was made by a woman or women (Skinner 1913:142). Skinner (1913:78) notes, "Because of their friendliness, figures of the thunderbirds themselves, or rather their relatives, the eagles, are placed on the woven bags owned by the women as a sign of respect and as a prayer for their protection." It is also possible that the "clasped hands" that are placed on gift bags may symbolize "friendship" (Skinner 1921:261). Thunderbirds are represented below the woman and the two eagles. A single zigzag line

Figure 15 Menominee sacred bundle with designs of a woman and thunderbirds on obverse side (top) and underground panthers on reverse side (bottom). Neg. Nos. 34085 and 34086 (photographs by J. Kirschner), courtesy the Library, American Museum of Natural History.

above the head of each of the four elaborate geometric forms is a symbol for lightning (Skinner 1921:261; Wintemberg 1928:30). On the reverse side of the bag are four pairs of mythical giant underground panthers with horns and skeletal markings. According to Howard (1960:217), the underwater panther was "generally described as being of an enormous size, with short yellow fur (or brassy scales), a long panther-like tail, and horns like a bull's." The bison-like horns may indicate power or spirituality above the ephemeral plane of existence as viewed among the Ojibway (Hoffman 1891:196; Mallery 1893:757–758). Skinner (1921:263–265) reports that the Menominee believe that panthers with horns represent supernatural creatures while those without horns depict ordinary animals. The figures also display long, curling tails drawn under their feet, which are similar to those depicted by the Fox. According to Skinner (1921:263) and Wilson (1982) this tail was often referred to as "the panther's road through life" and sometimes said to be made of copper. The animal used as a model for the giant underground panther was probably the mountain lion (*Felis concolor*) whose exceptionally long tail, 30 to 36 inches long (76–91 cm), was viewed as its most distinguishing feature (Wilson 1982).

A Sac and Fox woven fiber sacred pack is shown with four geometric thunderbird figures (Figure 16), which dates to about 1860. All exhibit hooked beaks, indicative of a raptorial bird, with their wings or arms linked. This sacred bundle contains a copper effigy (perhaps of an underworld panther or underworld bear); copper may have been viewed as a powerful spiritual substance derived from the underworld (Penney 1985:149).

Similar woven bags depicting the association of thunderbirds with underworld supernatural beings were created by the Ottawa and Winnebago (Figures 17–18). There is slight variation in the pattern (i.e., combinations of elements), balance, proportion, and movement of motifs on each bag. Still, the principles of organization providing unity and harmony are very similar. According to Ocvirk et al. (1968), "Unity in art results from practicing, knowing, and selecting the 'right' visual devices and using the best principles to relate them." Such Native American creations were strongly influenced by traditions.

Certainly, the cross-cultural regularities in cosmology and understandings of the symbolic meanings associated with the thunderbird suggest extensive interaction among Siouan and Algonquian groups. These regularities also suggest great antiquity, as originally proposed by Skinner (1921:262), which indeed may be relevant if one assumes that ideologies, religious beliefs, and ritual institutions are particularly conservative and slow to change among small-scale Native American societies.

Figure 16 Sac and Fox twined sacred bundle, ca.1860. Photograph
© The Detroit Institute of Arts, a Founders Society Purchase.

THE MATERIAL REALITY OF THE THUNDERBIRD
IN PREHISTORIC ARTWORK

A comparison of ethnohistoric artwork to the archaeological evidence reveals that the domain of celestial bird symbolism shows significant continuity through time in the Midcontinent (Benn 1989, 1995; Hall 1977; Penney 1985:183; Sampson 1988:182–183). The power of the mythical thunderbird apparently was expressed as part of a long-standing symbolic system through the processes of creativity and imagery in a wide range of media, including monumental earthworks, sheet copper, marine shell, petroglyphs, pictographs, and conventionalized or geometric representations (cordmarking or trailing) on ceramics (Benn 1995; Brose 1985; Brown 1985; Link 1995; Sampson 1988; Sampson and Esarey 1993). Some archaeologists have pointed out that avian symbolism extends as far back as the Late Archaic period (3000–1000 B.C.), as exemplified by ground and polished stones, called birdstones, that functioned as atlatl appendages (Penney 1985). Representations of raptorial birds or mythical thunderbirds increase dramatically during the Middle Woodland period. The images of eagles and falcons executed in a remarkably naturalistic style appear in Hopewell contexts as carved effigy bowls of platform pipes, sculpted boatstones, copper cutouts, and repoussé plaques and on the exterior surfaces of ceramic vessels (Brose 1985). Most occur as grave goods and express a religious aspect of the Hopewellian interaction sphere. Whether such objects actually reflect thunderbird representations is debatable. However, the data do show how conservative and slow to change those aspects of culture relating to the realm of the sacred were, at least among small-scale societies.

The antiquity of thunderbird symbolic representation was originally interpreted by Radin (1911, 1923:287) and Skinner (1921:264) as extending back through time to at least the Late Woodland Effigy Mound tradition (ca. B.C. 650–1300). Earthen mound effigies in the form of birds are noted as occurring throughout portions of the Upper Mississippi River and Lake Michigan basins (Hurley 1970; Mallam 1976;

Figure 17 Ottawa woven bag with a stylized thunderbird, ca.1860. Photograph
© The Detroit Institute of Arts, a Founders Society Purchase.

Radin 1923; Rowe 1956). The bird type is often represented with out-stretched or drooping wings and rectangular bodies. Examples can be seen in Radin's (1923) plan maps of effigy mounds at Pishtaka, Wingra, and other sites in Wisconsin. They appear to have been symbols of power, a focus of festival activities, and embodiments of worldview. As Hall (1995:51) notes, "Effigy mounds were monumental expressions of the cosmology of their builders." The bird effigies were probably associated with the guardian spirit (cosmic mediator) concept advocated by Rowe (1956) and were the foci of multilineage social cohesion and individual reciprocal relations with the supernatural.

The thunderbird form also stands out as a cosmic agent in the art of Oneota and Middle Mississippian cultures (Hollinger and Henning 1998; Cheryl Munson, personal communication, 1998). Of importance in this study are the metaphoric abstractions occurring on pots, which may have involved the use of chevron or concentric arc and punctate motifs as symbolic substitutions for the power of the thunderbird. Among Oneota symbolic and religious artwork, the chevron grouping is dominant throughout the Prairie Peninsula (see Benn 1989, Table 1; Brown 1965). It is represented by many forms, including nested lines and/or dots, pendant triangles, chevrons crammed at oblique angles, and sometimes fields of vertical or oblique lines substituted for the chevron (Benn 1989). An arch or U-shaped form is sometimes referred to as an inverted curved chevron (Link 1995:6) or chevron (Hall 1991:29). A horizontal sequence or band of arches may be referred to as festoons. The motifs are often repeated around the shoulder and/or rim of a vessel to create or reinforce meaning.

Using the artistic media to communicate their cosmology, Fisher and Langford potters may have conveyed their access to power (knowledge or cultural meaning) by their use of imagery and symbolic metaphor. The symbolic motifs taken from nature (i.e., Prairie Peninsula) probably were used to express the cosmic powers in their world. The Fisher phase ceramics often have shoulder decorations consisting of horizontal bands of concentric arcs or festoons with the use of punctates (circular motifs) as superior border elements, a combination of motifs that probably signifies the power of the thunderbird. The design has been identified and described at the Lawrence site (vessel 5-1-1) and also occurs on vessels at the Fisher site as described and illustrated by Griffin (1946:15, Plate I) and Brown (1965:123, Table 65). An example from the Fisher site is illustrated in Figure 19. This shell-tempered Fisher Trailed jar (Item #1078) exhibits a vertical rim, a flattened lip with exterior vertical notching, and a shoulder decorated by medium width (4 mm) trailing over a smoothed-over cord-marked surface. The concentric circle motifs ("targets") have been described for Moingona phase (Gradwohl 1974; Moffat and Koldehoff 1990a:159) and Brice Prairie phase (Boszhardt 1994:194, 197) components and may denote the sun, as Mallery (1893:695) and Willoughby

Figure 18 Winnebago twined storage bag with four sacred thunderbirds, ca.1850. Nettle fiber, bison hair yarn, commercial yarn. Courtesy of Cranbrook Institute of Science, Cat. No. 2311.

(1897:9–10) report for the Ojibway and Omaha, respectively. The concentric arcs may symbolize "the arch of the sky," where supernaturals live, as recorded for the Ojibway (Hoffman 1891:196–197; Mallery 1893:239, 694), or the thunderbird, which Radin (1923:443, Plate 48) shows appearing on a Winnebago buckskin offering as a "rainbow motif." Another rainbow motif decorated the tent of an Omaha shaman named Nikucibca[n], who claimed to have had a vision of the "Thunder-being" before creating the symbol on the tent (Dorsey 1894:400, Figure 167). Its exact significance has never been explained, although it could represent the sky vault or the thunderbird. Because the thunderbird had a strong mythical association with the sun among historic Native Americans, the tail motif may symbolize through metonymy ultimate power and knowledge that emanates from the upperworld.

The chevron motif commonly occurs as a decorative pattern on the rim, neck, and shoulder areas of Langford jars. Only two specimens were identified and illustrated in the Langford assemblage from Keeshin Farm, which is probably attributable to extremely small sample sizes. However, they were a common motif found in the Gentleman Farm (Brown et al. 1967) and Fisher (Griffin 1946) site assemblages. A complete grit-tempered Langford Noded vessel (Item #3EM20) from the Fisher site exhibits dot-filled

0   5 cm

Figure 19 The thunderbird tail motif as expressed on a Fisher site vessel.

chevrons or zigzags similar to the motifs associated with the Oneota Orr phase in northeastern Iowa (Wedel 1959; see Benn 1989: Figure 3b). This vessel exhibits a flared rim and a rounded lip with exterior-superior oblique notching. The decoration is meant to be viewed from the side, since no shoulder decoration is seen from above the vessel (Figure 20).

WOMEN AND ONEOTA POTTERY PRODUCTION

The foregoing discussion clearly shows that most avian imagery has a strong abstract or geometric character, suggesting that many simple motifs (e.g., chevron, triangle) were probably taken from textiles and basketry and applied to pottery. The symbols retained their shapes as modified by the technical requirements of the medium of weaving (Highwater 1983:84; Mason 1904:314–316). Importantly, they may also have retained their distinctive meanings and emotional responses. Such artistic expressions may be identified primarily with women. Lame Deer and Erdoes (1972:108–118) point out that abstract art is used exclusively by Siouan women to convey information about life experiences, as in the words of literature or the numbers of mathematics. Kathryn Browning-Hoffman (1979:31) has reported on the geometric designs produced in

Figure 20 Langford Noded vessel decorated with chevrons from the Fisher site.

historic Chitimacha basket making: "Daughters are taught to make the [geometric] designs from the pattern baskets of their mothers." Women's creativity in abstract art across media (especially pottery, textiles, basketry, beadwork, and porcupine quillwork) has also been noted for other Plains and Eastern Woodlands societies (Chandler 1973; Conklin and Patraka 1977:34–37; Densmore 1929:120, 155–156; Dickason 1974:71–72; Drooker 1992:12; Mason 1904:188, 191; Skinner 1921:241–242, 256).

Thus, women probably were the principal producers of pottery in Woodland and late prehistoric politico-economic systems (Benn 1995:93; Sassaman 1992:74; Wright 1991:200, 214). This concept of women as primary potters is also based on cross-cultural ethnographic studies of tribal societies (Murdock and Provost 1973) as well as ethnohistorical sources (Blair 1912:324; Deetz 1965, 1968; Driver 1961:172; Holmes 1903; Mason 1904:372; Neill 1884:251; Swanton 1979:549–555). For example, James Deetz (1965, 1968) has presented evidence that the spread of a series of pottery designs among the protohistoric Pawnee reflected a pattern of manufacture and design procedures transmitted along female lines. Elisabeth Tooker (1964:59) describes how early-seventeenth-century Huron women made earthenware cooking pots or kettles (called *anoo*). Iroquois women also made pottery jars for cooking that had globular bodies, round bottoms, constricted necks, and straight rims usually topped by projecting collars (Underhill 1971:89). Edward Neill (1884:251) quotes from an unpublished journal of a North West Company English trader, Alexander Henry, that early-nineteenth-century Mandan women "make use of large earthen pots of their own manufacture, made of black clay, of which they have plenty near their villages."

Among tribal- and chiefdom-level societies of the southeastern United States, John R. Swanton (1979) notes that women were primarily responsible for making pottery vessels, in such societies as the Natchez, Pascagoula, Creek, and Cherokee. Also, Swanton (1996:157–159) has provided seventeenth-century Spanish explorer accounts of pottery production by women of the Caddo culture (from the Red River region of Arkansas, Louisiana, Texas, and Oklahoma):

> Espinosa mentions "earthen vessels, some large and some small, in which to serve the old and the young," and notes that bear's fat was kept in some of them (Espinosa, 1927, pp. 155, 157). Among the furnishings of the temple were "earthen-ware vessels" which are evidently incense burners in which they burn fat and tobacco (Espinosa, 1927, p. 160). The importance of this industry to women is demonstrated by the same missionary when he says: "From clay, they make by hand all the utensils they need for their household use" (Espinosa, 1927, p. 177) . . . that Caddo women at least had real artistic ability of a high order is witnessed by some of the exquisite ceramic remains that are constantly being dug up in the former territory of these people.

Women's knowledge and vision among the Oneota may have been derived from ancient tradition and female-to-female exchange relationships outside their domestic economy and might also have drawn upon the imagination, perception, and myriad other sources of differences between individuals. The transmission takes place primarily on the household level in such small-scale (i.e., no centralized production, complex technologies, large workshops, or markets), kin-based societies (see Neff 1992:150–151). As such, ceramic customs could have been transmitted from the senior potter in the family, being a mother, aunt, or grandmother, to a young female member (Deetz 1965, 1968; Neff 1992). The pottery production process would have required extensive knowledge concerning (1) the location of clay sources, (2) the selection of proper materials to be used, (3) the extraction and transport of materials to the site of manufacture, (4) the preparation of materials for use as vessels by forming, drying, and open firing, and (5) choosing from myriad vessel attributes, including vessel form and the decoration type, to use for functional, aesthetic, and symbolic purposes (Arnold 1985; Rye 1981).

Women master potters of Langford and Fisher societies may have gained power and prestige personally as well as for their household and community. However, it is unlikely they attained the relatively high status attributed to Iroquois women (e.g., female ownership of land, control over horticultural production, and authority in making formal political decisions) (Brown 1970; Wallace 1969). Instead, community leadership may have entailed such roles as organizing feasts and subsistence activities, controlling domestic household activities, and influencing political decisions through informal channels (see Maltz and Archambault 1995). Such power could have been legitimized through carefully arranged marriage alliances (affinity) and through birth lines (consanguinity) (Benn 1989:236; Staeck 1993), as exemplified ethnohistorically by the Ioway (Skinner 1926:251) and Oto (Whitman 1937:85) and ethnographically by the Canelos Quichua of Amazonian Ecuador (Whitten 1985:118–122). It is important to note, however, that power could never be attained in small-scale Native American societies without visions or dreams (Lame Deer and Erdoes 1972:13; Rosman and Rubel 1995) or maintained without the consensus of the group, which makes power ambiguous.

• The most striking feature of the various historic Native American cultures is the sharing of an anthropomorphic cosmology and common religious beliefs, which is consistently expressed in the artwork of central Algonquian and Siouan groups. All shared the concept of a multilayered cosmos consisting of "otherworld" realms inhabited by powerful supernatural beings and this world of human beings. The great thunderbird of the upperworld was antithetical to underworld creatures like the underwater panther or great serpent. Their struggle for power in "this world" was fraught with ambiguity and uncertainty between good (generative) and evil (destructive) forces—a struggle that created a very tenuous balance of nature or cosmic unity and threatened the physical, social, and spiritual well-being of humans. One may assume that Oneota peoples maintained similar beliefs, because of the conservative nature of religious tradition and the patterning of symbolic reproduction in various media.

The thunderbird is shown to have remarkable continuity in religious symbolism through time and cross-culturally. Raptorial birds, such as the eagle and falcon, often served as a symbol for the thunderbird. On fiber bags, the figures of this avian mythological creature were geometric, highly stylized, and angular, because curves are almost impossible in the weaving technique. Still, the thunderbird was often clearly and boldly depicted through rhythm, repetition, dominance, and pure symmetrical balance. Its identifying attributes are easily recognized by using a series of triangles or chevrons for the wings, body, and tail (Whiteford 1977). The thunderbird tail motif is viewed as signifying the supernatural power of the upperworld through metonymy. It occurs on Oneota vessels in a variety of geometric forms (i.e., chevrons, lines, and concentric arcs) reflecting variability in the multitude of Oneota societies existing throughout the Prairie Peninsula and its environs.

Women were agents creating Oneota culture. Women appear to have been the artists producing the historic woven bags, and so it is assumed that they were probably the primary producers of Oneota ceramic vessels. This is based on the fact that the geometric symbols used in weaving and attempts to achieve unity and harmony through pure symmetrical balance of motifs are essentially the same as those depicted on the rims, necks, and shoulders of pottery vessels. Also, there are ethnohistoric and ethnographic accounts that women were the primary producers of pottery in small-scale Native American societies. Thus, their "power to" transform formless natural clay matter (nature) into objects with order or oneness (culture) is interpreted as showing remarkable continuity within the environmental contexts of the Prairie Peninsula. Apparently, the essence was to *unite* earth and sky realms in this plastic medium and to communicate that constructive power to "others." It was a ritual dramatization of life by "the people" living at the center of the universe, with sacred, culturally safe places being the ordered, egalitarian world of the household and the community. Such creativity was inspired by visions and songs, providing access to mythic time and space, emotions (meaning and feeling) about the beauty and power of natural phenomena (e.g., thunderstorms), and knowledge transferred through successive generations.

Migration and the Power of Mortuary Ritual

The similarities in cultural material observed in the Langford and Fisher archaeological assemblages reveal powerful integrative relations and ideologies. These similarities persist as elements of traditions, which occur when numerous people make and use similar objects for many successive generations. This process of socialization within traditions has been shown to be continually created and re-created in power-laden situations (Paynter and McGuire 1991:6–7). Oneota peoples probably attempted to exercise power over one another and, concomitantly, in resistance to domination in all facets of daily life. Their social relationships may be largely understood through inferences obtained using ethnohistoric and ethnographic sources concerning small-scale Native American societies, particularly information relating to societal migration and funeral rites. Power relations may revolve around the ambiguity, insecurity, and uncertainty associated with access to valuable social and natural resources as well as vision knowledge of realities associated with the supernatural.

SOCIAL POWER AND ITS RELATION TO MIGRATION

Societal fissioning, migration, and interaction are integral parts of nonhierarchical societies, as demonstrated in ethnolinguistic (Coe et al. 1986:42–45), ethnohistoric (Blaine 1979:276; Blair 1911:293–300; Deliette 1934:307, 312; Kinietz 1940:60, 245; Trigger 1969:108), and ethnographic (Chagnon 1968; Jackson 1983:100) studies. Certainly, evidence of these processes are mounting in the archaeological record (see Esarey and Santure 1990; Finney and Stoltman 1991; Jackson 1992b:515; Snow 1995;

White 1985:39). Recent discussions involving migration as a demographic process, however, have suffered by attributing demographic movements strictly to ecological or economic factors such as environmental degradation, conquest, population pressure, trade, or subsistence risk buffering mechanisms. But movements of people, particularly non-hierarchical groups, may often be linked to social power relationships involving either intracommunity conflict or festivals (centered around feasts) focused on intersocietal activity. Both causes are based on concepts of power. This is applicable to the times of the Oneota Emergent and Developmental horizons (ca. A.D. 1000–1300/1400) within the area occupied by Langford and Fisher folk (as determined by the absence of palisaded villages and limited evidence of trauma-induced death among their burial populations).

A definition of *migration* is necessary at this time to avoid confusion over its usage. For many scholars, the word *migrate* may simply imply permanent human population movements in a single direction, as exemplified by the peopling of the New World. But the word has a broader, more dynamic meaning of changing location periodically, passing from one region to another (see New Lexicon Webster's Dictionary of the English Language 1989; American Heritage Dictionary of the English Language 1992; Random House Dictionary of the English Language 1966). Thus, a migration of peoples can involve movement in two directions, with the initial migration followed by a return to the migrants' place of origin (Anthony 1990:897–898). Migrations are dynamic by providing people the "power to" habitually gather at an agreed time and place from which the participants would normally return to their respective communities.

An understanding of migration can come from studies of the location of Fisher and Langford sites. This may be exemplified by the Lawrence site, which is the only Fisher phase village known in the entire Rock River valley. The site represents a western outlier of Fisher phase components located along the Upper Illinois River drainage and so probably resulted in a population movement from that area (Figure 2). The Lawrence ceramic assemblage clearly indicates interaction with local Langford peoples. This active interaction is also demonstrated at the site by a mixture of Langford grit-tempered and Fisher shell-tempered ceramics in 24 pit features. The Langford occupation of the Noble-Wieting site in north-central Illinois (the only Langford occupation located within the Sangamon River drainage) is another clear-cut example of migration, and it resulted in interaction with regional Mississippian populations (Schilt 1977). This site is a southern outlier of Langford tradition components. The causes for such migrations are difficult to discern but may involve either intracommunity conflict or festivals.

In kin-based societies, leaders may promote their power and authority through manipulation of their lineage's or kindred's productive power (e.g., cooperative labor ventures, exchange of foods and raw materials) and by establishing, through marriage, intergroup alliances. However, the communal mode of production in such societies limits the extent of debts or inequalities that can be accumulated within a community, thereby limiting the scale of power and authority exerted by an individual. The internal social tensions associated with debts and attempts at domination by a leader, or anyone, may take the form of resistance to power, which would be a positive process of societies "holding to" ways of being and relating in traditions (Bender 1990; Cobb 1993:48). Rather than hostility in face-to-face situations (e.g., verbal threats, gestures, or physical assault), resistance to would-be dominators could involve mild forms of social control: malicious gossip leading to accusations of malevolent sorcery, innocuous forms of violence, repudiation, malingering, rough humor and derogation that is used to counteract achievement (as among the Ojibway) or a system of decision-making checks and balances (as among the Iroquois) (Barnouw 1963:149–150; Marquardt 1992:106; Trigger 1990:143; Upham 1990:10). Elisabeth Tooker (1979:69) finds that "the most explicit statements of Indian moral standards are to be found in the admonitions of the people to one another." Resistance to domination may take more extreme measures, such as the fissioning of a community; thus, migration is induced (McGuire 1989:47).

Perhaps least recognized in the archaeological record is the importance of festivals and ceremonies in leading to migration. Festivals provided a great opportunity for historic intertribal visiting that extended from a few days to weeks (Blaine 1979). Thus, their importance among Oneota groups may have been to forge intervillage solidarity and mutual interdependence (see Cobb 1993:81; Sassaman 1995:185–186). A model may exist in the interethnic relations of prairie-adapted Assiniboin, Cree, and Ojibway peoples in northern Montana and North Dakota for the eighteenth and early nineteenth centuries (see Albers 1996). These northeastern Plains peoples did not conform to typical tribal models in which territories were divided, claimed, and defended by discrete ethnic groups; instead, the peoples collaborated in trade, combat, subsistence, and *ceremony*. Religious ceremonies, feasts, and dances associated with sacred bundles (with their protective powers) also provided opportunities for migration and social interaction among the Sac and Fox (Harrington 1914:132). Equally important among historic groups were mortuary ritual performances in which each individual experienced a transcendent fusion of drama and the art of life.

MORTUARY RITUAL PERFORMANCES

The concepts of power and transformation are present in the cultural performances given by all Native Americans of all time periods. The festival, in particular, is a major creative diversionary event that provides a means of both renewing time and reaffirming life. It is a medium for producing and remembering social meaning. The sequence of events that occur in the festival requires a careful interplay of religious (sacred) and secular (profane) powers in an orchestrated way, offering the awareness of order on many levels, including acoustic, kinesic, linguistic, semantic, and so on. The festival provides people a special, periodically recurrent sociopolitical and ceremonial occasion that transforms "daily or mundane time" to "time out of time"—a time to reveal and celebrate their passage from one state of being to another within the dangerous world of nature and supernature. Symbolism permeates all the senses through power-enhancing performances like dance, music, art, feasting, debates, exchanges, and games, where the participants become literally one with the universe. The mythic and ritual correspondences provide participants with the opportunity to reflect on life, to commune, and to communicate information to one another. The spaces and times of everyday life are viewed as a paradox wherein the "end" becomes the "beginning"—from chaos and death spring order and life. There is no end to life, but only changing forms or transformation (Allen 1986; Falassi 1967; Guss 1989:47–48, 96; Hall 1987b; Jackson 1983:202–204; Sullivan 1986; 1988:164–170). As anthropologist Lowell John Bean (1992:23) states, "Without individual or community action by man through such rituals as world renewal ceremonies, the balance of power in the universe would be upset, and one side of the system might be disproportionately favored over another." Festivals, then, promote social solidarity and communal identity and serve as psychic anchors for the self through shared play, ritual, and celebration.

The images of power in the festival are evident in the rites of passage (e.g., public ceremonies held to mark the changes in the status of an individual progressing through the life cycle, such as birth, death, adoption, initiation into age groups, and naming) and rites of intensification (e.g., ceremonies performed to mark planting, in hope for a good crop, or the "first harvest," in thanks for what has been given) performed by historic Eastern Woodlands and Plains groups (Blaine 1979:172; Blair 1912:168–169, 234; Hall 1987b; Herman 1967:586–589; Jones 1989:70–71; Kinietz 1940:100–101, 276–277; Radin 1923:141–142; Swanton 1979:775; Trigger 1969:93–96; Yarrow 1881:190–198).

Archaeologists have often focused attention on death, since it is prominent in the archaeological record. There is an understanding that mortuary ritual is *not* simply related to the status of the deceased as an elite or nonelite member of society (Cobb 1993:81; Trigger 1969:112) but involves important ceremonial aspects reflecting relations of power (see Charles 1948; Stothers 1999:202). Death is usually inseparable from religious rites and beliefs (Dial 1978). Among tribal societies, festivals associated with death involve *communally* sponsored ceremonies, because no full-time priesthood or extensive religious hierarchy exists (Wallace 1966:86–87, 97–99).

Festivals relating to the "cult of the dead," or ancestor worship, were common among North American tribal societies and involved acts of worship concerned with spirits of deceased persons who were thought to have power to help or harm the living. All dead were deemed common ancestors, so any attempt to distinguish ancestor worship (involving specific kin) from the cult of the dead (whether they are kin or not) is purely academic (Hultkrantz 1981).

Mortuary ritual and ceremonies were considered by Native Americans as showing respect for the death and subsequent rebirth of the human spirit, the most dramatic moment in life. The rituals were directed to the problem of the human transformations of that dramatic moment (Wallace 1966:106). They involved scenes of mourning (usually immediately after death, renewed at the burial site, and again when the mourning feast occurs) (Fletcher 1907) as well as scenes of celebration and happiness, strengthening and encouraging the spirit of the deceased (La Flesche 1889:10). Among the Iroquois, Anthony F. C. Wallace (1966:105) states, "The ritual was intended to ensure the passage from a state of mourning to a state of normal social activity of the bereaved." Songs, speeches, dances, feasts, and games were conducted during the course of mortuary ceremonies, according to ethnohistoric accounts (Densmore 1929:73–78; Radin 1923:140–155; Skinner 1913:63–72; Trigger 1969:109; Yarrow 1881:190–198). The climax of the ceremonies was the giving of gifts from which the mourners could accrue new power (Charles 1948:170). Thus, funeral rites were essential in the interaction of people as well as of the souls of the living with those of the dead.

Religious festivals as life-cycle rites of passage, transition, or deliverance exhibit the following features, as described by Levinson (1996:3–6, 69–75) and Thomas (1987:458):

1. Liturgical drama with its actors and their scripts, an audience, and place and scene of performance, which was filled with rich symbolism expressing core values of the community.
2. Ability to reorganize the society disturbed by death and to console the survivors by bringing people together physically and spiritually, thus reinforcing a sense of community solidarity.
3. Opportunity for people to exchange gifts through reciprocity and provide a public arena for establishing power relations between local groups and allies.
4. An educational tool for children to teach them about religious tradition.

Certainly, the most poignant examples of Fisher and Langford festivals are their mortuary ritual practices that show Woodland influence (Fowler 1952). In such rites of passage, most Langford burials were within and/or below low, broad mounds located near the village, although some individuals were also placed in pits scattered throughout a habitation area. In comparing the Oakwood Mound with the Fisher Mounds, Robinson Reserve mound (Ck°2), and Gentleman Farm mound, Robert Skinner (1953:7) notes that "in principal the discernible stages in burial and mound-building are the same." A similar pattern has been suggested for the Oneota Developmental horizon in eastern Wisconsin based on excavations at the Walker-Hooper (Brown 1993; Brown et al. 1967:37) and Pipe sites (Overstreet 1995). An accretional burial mound has also been documented for the Bold Counselor phase Oneota cemetery at Norris Farms 36. The mounds and their monumentality were foci of communal ritual ceremonies. Here, the use of graveside fires and inclusion of foodstuffs with the deceased were common religious practices having a long tradition.

An aspect common to Bold Counselor and Langford mortuary ritual is the presence of burned areas or hearths near some graves. These features indicate that mortuary fires may have aided the spirit of the deceased on its perilous journey to the otherworld. Graveside fires were a consistent part of the funeral rites of many historic tribal groups (Hartland 1912:432; Thomas 1907:947), including the Menominee (Skinner 1913:66), Missouri, Oto (Yarrow 1881:97), Ojibway (Densmore 1929:75), Omaha (La Flesche 1889:10), Sioux (Yarrow 1881:198), and Winnebago (Radin 1923:141, 148). Fire was an important element in many Native American rituals and stories because of its resemblance to living things, its relationship to the sun, and its creation of light (Gill and Sullivan 1992:89). The use of fire at the grave served as a means to release their spiritual essence (Hultkrantz 1981:95), to warm the spirit, to light and comfort the spirit, to enable the spirit to prepare its food, and/or to drive evil-disposed beings from the grave (Hartland 1912:432). Frances Densmore (1929:75) states that the Ojibway graveside fires were to be used for warmth and cooking by the deceased spirit. Among the Omaha, funeral fires were to light the spirit to the land of happiness, with the fire fueled by the mother or a close female relative without weeping so that the spirit would not be distressed (La Flesche 1889:10). A fire was built on top of an Iroquois grave so that the spirit could prepare its food (Bushnell 1920:89).

Small mortuary fires of historic tribal groups were usually kept burning near or on the grave for four days and nights (La Flesche 1889:10; Yarrow 1881). H. C. Yarrow (1881:198) quotes a writer concerning the custom of these fires among Native Americans:

> The Algonkins believed that the fire lighted nightly on the grave was to light the spirit on its journey. By a coincidence to be explained by the sacredness of the number, both Algonkins and Mexicans maintained it for *four* nights consecutively. The former related the tradition that one of their ancestors returned from the spirit land and informed their nation that the journey thither consumed just four days, and that collecting fuel every

night added much to the toil and fatigue the soul encountered, all of which could be spared it.

A Dakota wife was also obligated to keep a fire burning for four nights on her husband's grave and to ensure that it did not burn out before dawn (Fletcher 1907:952).

Reference to the sacred number *four* may relate to the fact that a vision quest usually requires four days and nights without food or water, at which time communication occurs with the spirits (e.g., *Wakan Tanka*, a Supreme Being or Great Spirit, who is the source of all power among the Sioux) (Black Elk and Lyon 1991:123; Hultkrantz 1983:42; Lame Deer and Erdoes 1972:11). It may also relate to the four sacred quarters, marked by the cardinal points, or the four winds, which are basic concepts organizing the Native American universe in time and space (Holmes 1911:365–367; Powers 1987:68–70; Skinner 1921; Sullivan 1988; Willoughby 1897). Among the Seneca, Mohawk, Oneida, Onondaga, and Cayuga, the word *four* meant "complete, right, perfect," which extended to the sacred tree of the confederacy, with its four roots extending north, south, east, and west (Hewitt 1889). In any event, the four days and nights in mortuary ritual are great symbolic vehicles marking a particularly sacred, liminal period in which the individual is in a kind of limbo—literally, "in between"—no longer among the living and not yet reborn (Rosman and Rubel 1995:199).

Evidence for feasts are often present at Oneota mortuary sites. Grave goods from Oneota burials generally represent common artifacts, such as the association of shell spoons with complete ceramic vessels (Brown et al. 1967:16–17; Kreisa 1993:42–43; Santure and Esarey 1990:106). It is assumed that foodstuffs were placed within these containers. For example, the Norris Farms 36 mound, relating to the Bold Counselor phase Oneota occupation, contained 45 individuals (17% of the population, including men, women, and children) that were buried with pottery vessels. Eight vessels were associated with shell spoons that were found either beside, inside, or on top of the vessel. Santure and Esarey (1990:106) suggest that other vessels lacking shell spoons could have had spoons of perishable wood and, conversely, graves containing shell spoons could have had wooden or gourd containers.

The Gentleman Farm mound (Figure 21), relating to the Langford occupation, contained 13 individuals (8% of the population) directly associated with pottery vessels. Ten burials contained complete vessels with shell spoons, with seven spoons inside and three beside the vessels. Brown et al. (1967:16–17) suggest that there were two cases where the spoon was found in the mouth of the container, indicating that the vessel was filled with food or other substances at the time of burial. Complete vessels and shell spoons were also associated with burials at the two Robinson Reserve mounds (Fowler 1952) and the Material Service

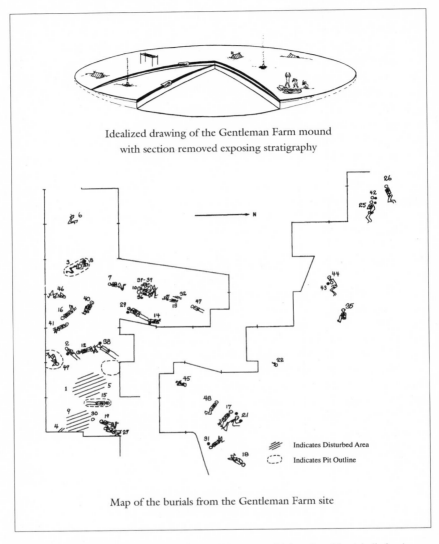

Idealized drawing of the Gentleman Farm mound
with section removed exposing stratigraphy

Map of the burials from the Gentleman Farm site

Figure 21   Drawings of the Gentleman Farm mound (above) and burials (below).
Courtesy of Illinois State Museum.

Quarry site (Bareis 1965), both relating to Langford occupations. The
Huber phase Oneota occupations of the Hoxie Farm (Herold et al.
1990) and Anker (Bluhm and Liss 1961) sites also contained complete
pottery vessels with human burials. Certainly, this pattern suggests feasts
and, in specific reference to Norris Farms 36 and Hoxie Farm, little
marked social stratification in Oneota societies. But what other interpretations can be deduced from this pattern?

The inclusion of food with burials was a common practice among North American tribal groups (Hartland 1912:428; Thomas 1907:947). This association was shared by the Dakota (Dorsey 1894:489), Huron (Trigger 1969:109–111), Menominee (Skinner 1921:80), Sac and Fox (Yarrow 1881:95), Omaha (La Flesche 1889:11), and the Algonquian tribes of the "Illinois country" (Bushnell 1920:39). According to Winnebago myths, the inclusion of food with burials was necessary for the spirit of the deceased on its long, complicated journey to the otherworld (Kreisa 1993:42; Radin 1923:141, 144). Among the Siouan Omaha, Francis La Flesche (1889:11) found:

> Food and water are placed at the head of the grave for several days after the burial. The spirit is supposed to partake of this food. No Indian would touch any article of food thus exposed; if he did, the ghost would snatch away the food and paralyze the mouth of the thief, and twist his face out of shape for the rest of his life; or else he would be pursued by the ghost, and food would lose its taste, and hunger ever after haunt the offender.

Among the Dakota, J. Owen Dorsey (1894) notes:

> A woman who attends in collecting the food . . . is careful to put the best part of the food on the bowl or dish under the scaffold near the head of the corpse. Should anyone eat before the food has been put aside for the ghost, all the ghosts become angry with him, and they are sure to punish him; they will make him drop his food just before it reaches his mouth, or they will spill the water when he tries to drink, and sometimes they cause a man to gash himself with a knife.

Interestingly, the anthropologist Lawrence Sullivan (1988:665) notes that, in South American religions, "While the living sustain the dead in memory with food offerings, the dead give life to the living through dream images during the deathlike state of sleep. . . . Having joined the ranks of unmanifest supernatural beings, the dead become the source of symbolic life." This reciprocal relationship between the "souls" of the living and the dead is also present in North American societies, as exemplified by the Dakota and the Ojibway (Yarrow 1881) and the Winnebago (Radin 1923:314). Among the Dakota, appeasement of the dead was deemed necessary for an affirmative quality of family life, especially to aid them in hunting and other work activities (Hultkrantz 1981:105; Yarrow 1881:108). James Dorsey (1894:489) quotes J. W. Lynd:

> The belief in the powers of some Dakotas to call up and converse with the spirits of the dead is strong in some, though not general. They frequently make feasts to those spirits and elicit information from them of distant friends and relatives. Assembling at night in a lodge, they smoke, put out the fire, and then, drawing their blankets over their heads, remain singing

in unison in a low key until the spirit gives them a picture. This they pretend the spirit does; and many a hair-erecting tale is told of the spirit's power to reveal, and the after confirmation.

Among the Ojibway, the soul (called *Ochechag,* the core of the self) of the dead was thought to visit the living through apparitions to either invite them to the "otherworld" or forewarn them of approaching loss of power or death (Yarrow 1881:200). Radin's (1923:313–314) study of Winnebago concepts of death and the afterlife notes: "Although the Winnebago know that after death they will never see people again, they do not feel that all kinds of intercourse have ceased. The deceased may appear to a living individual in dreams or visions; he may talk to him or make his presence felt in a multitude of ways; and since . . . the test of existence is the consciousness of some kind of contact, such intercourse may be of a very intense type."

Important large communal rituals of the Feast of the Dead were practiced by seventeenth-century tribal groups of the Upper Great Lakes area (i.e., Huron, Nipissing, Ottawa, Saulteur) to honor the deceased as intermediary beings (Hultkrantz 1981; Tooker 1964:135). Their performances were clearly different from those of the Prairie Peninsula and Plains areas but still served an important function of promoting sociopolitical and economic integration and reciprocity (Stothers 1999:202). The Huron Feast of the Dead was held at intervals of about 8 to 12 years, whenever the villagers decided to move. Bones of the dead from the last such ceremony were removed from the village cemetery, cleaned, and wrapped in hides or fine new beaver skins. The elaborately decorated bone bundles were then transported on the backs of female relatives to the site of the feast where they were interred in a common grave pit, which the Huron generally referred to as "the kettle" (Tooker 1964:134–135; Trigger 1969:106–112). Hind (cited in Yarrow 1881:191) relates an account of a Huron mass burial witnessed by the Jesuit priest Jean de Brebeuf in 1636:

> The ceremony took place in the presence of 2,000 Indians, who offered 1,200 presents at the common tomb, in testimony of their grief. The people belonging to five large villages deposited the bones of their dead in a gigantic shroud, composed of forty-eight robes, each robe being made of ten beaver skins. . . . Before covering the bones with earth a few grains of Indian corn were thrown by the women upon the sacred relics. According to the superstitious belief of the Hurons the souls of the dead remain near the bodies until the "feast of the dead"; after which ceremony they become free, and can at once depart for the land of the spirits, which they believe to be situated in the region of the setting sun.

The precursors of such ceremonies are associated with ossuary burials found within the territory occupied by the western branch of the Iroquois tradition (Tooker 1964:134), the Pickering populations of Ontario. However, ossuary burial practices also have been identified in the western Lake Erie region (northwest Ohio, northcentral Ohio, and southeast Michigan) suggesting a long tradition extending back at least to the Wolf phase of the Sandusky tradition (ca. A.D. 1200–1400), if not earlier. It is suggested that such practices may have resulted from a reorientation of social organization and an awareness of villages as corporate entities, which were necessary to cope with competitive pressures as hostilities increased between peoples (Stothers and Graves 1983:115, 118).

• The concept of power in nonhierarchical Native American cultures, such as Oneota, should be viewed in terms of its heterogeneity or ambiguousness. There were many types of power that were often obtained through visions, inspiration, and social relationships. It was *not* based on the control or domination of resources (minimizing costs while maximizing gain) or on symbols that represent the power of elites. It was a "power to" carry out specific tasks rather than simply "power over" people and resources, and this power was constrained by cultural tradition. The unequal social relations involving coercive power (i.e., the use of threats to compel people to cooperate and provide resources) and ideological power (i.e., dependent on the concealment of elite interests through ideology) that largely define complex societies, such as states, did not exist. Power was in the form of resistance that could result in peoples' fissioning from the main group to avoid conflict. The power of the festival, and particularly religious ceremonies associated with the cult of the dead, was of central importance in Native American cultures. Festivals were collective undertakings often leading to the migration of distant villagers invited to participate by the host village. Peaceful intertribal gatherings render possible the borrowing of esoteric knowledge concerning ceremonial routine, songs, dances, and art symbols (Lowie 1915), which is seen in the similarities of early Oneota mortuary ritual (e.g., mound burials).

Funerary ritual was based on reciprocity to maintain the world of human beings in balance and harmony. The dead were to be honored at mortuary ceremonies, for they were viewed as intermediaries between humans and the supernatural powers (Brown 1997:468; Wallace 1966:65), which was especially true for the Central Algonquian area (including the Siouan Winnebago) (Hultkrantz 1981). Historic and Oneota tribal male and female burials were treated equally. There is no reason to assume a ranked society based on the distribution of grave goods, since the accoutrements often consist of ceramic vessels and shell spoons, suggesting offerings of foodstuffs for the afterlife, associated with men, women, and children. The widespread burial of grave goods with the deceased (comprising necessities for the afterlife) was often intended to appease the soul in the hope of bringing good luck

(Wallace 1966:64–65). Another notable ritual pattern occurring in the archaeological record is that Langford tradition and Bold Counselor Oneota phase cemeteries sometimes had graveside fires, used to help the deceased to the otherworld. Oneota mortuary ritual would have provided people a means of renewing time and reaffirming life and a time to create and celebrate through song, dance, music, art, debates, feasting, and games. The power of men and women in society would have been defined in relation to symbolic systems like festivals (Hodder 1992), and, as we have seen, it was also expressed with sophistication and style in archaeological and historical art objects relating to a mythological avian creature, the thunderbird.

The Story of Community, Tradition, and Dreams

Following the example set by Kitchi-Manitou, every person is to seek a dream or vision within the expanse of his or her soul-spirit being and, having attained it, bring it into fulfillment and reality. Otherwise the dream or vision will be nullified.

—*Basil Johnston* 1995:3, *Ojibway orator*

CROSS-CULTURAL RELATIONSHIPS AND TRADITIONS

A study of power relations in past Native American societies of northern Illinois requires an intensive cross-cultural survey of ethnographic and ethnohistorical data about Plains and Eastern Woodlands tribal societies, which is then examined and utilized in conjunction with archaeological data. In some cases, this information is combined with ethnographic documentary sources like the Human Relations Area File, which is cross-indexed for hundreds of cultural features among more than 300 societies worldwide (Barnouw 1963:343; Costin 1996; Nanda 1994:43). The point of a holistic social science (with its complementary scientific and humanistic goals) is to reveal both cross-cultural regularities and particularistic, historical differences (Kepecs 1997:195; Knapp 1992; Trigger 1986a). One should try to capture the subjective world of human experience (O'Meara 1989), something that the processualists, with their "hard science" approach, refuse to acknowledge. It means defining culture as "the patterned and learned ways of life and thought shared by a human society" (Bodley

1994:7). Culture has several properties that researchers must take into account: it is shared, learned (not biologically inherited), filled with symbolic meanings, adaptive, transmitted to future generations through traditions, and integrated (Bodley 1994:8–9).

Critics of using ethnographic analogy have pointed out its problems for studying cultures of the New World, problems that are important and deserve attention. Ethnographic reports prepared by earlier anthropologists as well as historical documents by government officials, explorers, missionaries, and traders represent secondhand data with cultural biases that may include ethnocentrism: the tendency to evaluate a culture in reference to one's own presumably superior culture (i.e., Western middle- to upper-class rational thinking and self-interest) (Bodley 1994:10–11; Trigger 1986a:254–255). Also, because the information often comes from just one segment of the community—men—androcentrism or gender bias may result in interpretations of a culture dominated by men and thus made more homogenous than it really is (Klein and Ackerman 1995; Nanda 1994:24–25; Wright 1996). Another problem is presented by acculturation, the process of culture change resulting from contact between two cultures with different lifeways. Acculturation varies considerably, with changes ranging from the incorporation of a few traits into a culture to cases where there is rapid, sweeping transformation of an individual culture in contact with a more powerful one (superordinate-subordinate relations). Of course numerous examples exist in the history of Native American–white relations in the United States (Ember and Ember 1990:476–477; Hallowell 1952). Finally, another problem applicable to this study is the limited data on Illiniwek and Miami groups that once lived in the area, making a more historic contextual approach difficult.

Despite the criticisms that have been made here and elsewhere, many anthropological archaeologists have shown that the use of early ethnographic and ethnohistoric sources with archaeological data can be very productive (see Knapp 1992; Rogers and Wilson 1993; Spores 1980; Trigger 1986a, 1989). Some misunderstanding in the use of such sources by processualists (focused on ecological and economic concerns) may reflect a lack of attention to Native American religious institutions and structures (e.g., myths). Religious arguments for the existence of supernatural beings and the importance of faith violates the laws of scientific logic. Ake Hultkrantz (1983:109), a major Swedish scholar on Native American religion, and Sam Gill (1987), an American religious scholar, argued that an appropriate academic study of Native American religion and ritual had barely begun in the 1980s. Little progress has occurred in archaeology since then (Brown 1997), with the exception of Robert L. Hall's (1997) work *An Archaeology of the Soul*. The importance of communicative powers and the immediate effects of the performance of religious acts has been neglected, particularly in feasting and

mortuary ritual. For example, archaeologists have continued to view burial mounds as simply territorial markers, even though more complex relationships and religious practices are evident in the archaeological record
that can be explained through ethnohistoric analogs, or models.

Religion is a social institution that enhances the "fitness" of its followers by reducing fear and anxiety while increasing a sense of esteem, security, and empowerment of belonging to a powerful group that can unify
action in the face of adversity, whether sociopolitical, physical, or psychological. It is a product of tradition that is extremely conservative and so
embodies the traces of past religious developments, with some traits linking America with Siberia (Hultkrantz 1983:104). The French anthropologist Claude Levi-Strauss's (1963:206–231) cross-cultural analyses of
New World mythology (sacred narratives) revealed widely shared patterns of underlying themes that are of major cultural and historical significance (see Boas 1914). Recent cross-cultural studies have examined religious symbolism in the art of small-scale societies, such as feline
symbolism (Saunders 1998) and basic tribal art motifs (Schuster and
Carpenter 1996), with uniformity in certain themes and schematic designs suggesting a common origin in the ancient past rather than numerous independent inventions. Importantly, the studies also provide arguments for differences that can only be understood by reference to the
way a society's system of symbols is constructed and utilized. I have
shown in this study that the thunderbird concept was widespread among
small-scale societies of the Eastern Woodlands and Plains regions and so
probably of ancient origin. Although one cannot offer conclusive proof
that the chevron motifs on Oneota vessels symbolize the thunderbird,
their context on ceramic vessels (along with other thunderbird imagery)
presents strong *inferences* that cannot be dismissed because of the inability to demonstrate direct continuity between Fisher and Langford and
historic tribal groups.

Studies to delineate and explain cross-cultural regularities and differences among Native American societies is not new to anthropology. It
was stressed in the holistic works of the early-twentieth-century cultural
anthropologist Franz Boas and his prominent students Ruth Benedict,
Edward Sapir, Robert H. Lowie, Alfred L. Kroeber, Paul Radin, John R.
Swanton, and A. Irving Hallowell. Hallowell's dissertation (1926) "Bear
Ceremonialism in the Northern Hemisphere" is clearly a Boasian product, presenting detailed cross-cultural comparisons and historical implications. Each culture was found to exhibit its own particular combination of features (variation) regarding bear rituals, but there were also
some important patterns that only could be explained through a view of
nature that was not just economic but psychological. The ritual patterns
were structured by cultural tradition and conveyed by messages through
successive generations in art, ceremonies, and myth. The reverence afforded the bear was emphasized and reiterated by community elders as

the necessary and proper thing for continued success in hunting or healing the sick, a religious tradition that remained intact even in the face of acculturation (Barnouw 1963:150; Casagrande 1952; Wallace 1949:38). Its antiquity is demonstrated in the archaeological record (Berres et al. 1999).

Using cross-cultural ethnohistoric and ethnographic research and archaeological data, power relations among the small-scale, kin-based Fisher and Langford societies have been examined here within the contexts of historicity or cultural continuity through time and space (cultural traditions). The concept of power was shown to be heterogeneous and ambiguous; it would have been shared by many and would have taken many forms in the growth and development of the people. Their religious institutions apparently stressed the balanced or reciprocal relationship between human beings and a natural world infused with supernatural power, which would have occurred in many facets of Oneota lifeways (e.g., animal taboos). In the early Oneota sociopolitical realm, there was probably a distinct absence of permanent positions of status and leadership (as found in other tribal societies and verified in the Oneota mortuary record), with power relations cutting across various dimensions of society, including lineage or clan groupings and gender and age categories. As such, tribal leadership would have been based on consensual power, the assent of the people (see Lewellen 1983:95). In terms of gender roles, Daniel Maltz and JoAllyn Archambault (1995:245) argue that in "Native North America, 'domination' and 'inequality' are not the most useful concepts for examining the nature of gender, or the relationship between gender and power" and that "'autonomy,' 'complementarity,' and even 'egalitarianism' are more useful." All individuals possessed the "power to" resist domination either through simple difference or migration and to create and re-create culture through festivals, ritual, works of art (songs, dance, oration, and ceramic styles), subsistence activities, exchange of knowledge (spiritual, esoteric, and practical), among other things, and thus make history. The concepts of freedom and equality and the value of dreams appear to have been perpetuated in small-scale historic Native American societies as part of a tradition or continuity that extended back to at least Mississippi times, if not to the first crossing of Beringia.

Archaeologists can interpret late prehistoric lifeways with the goal of finding "historical reality." Such interpretations require a thorough examination of the cultural patterning evident in archaeological data sets, often hidden by variability (the noise) or biases either in the sample or by the researcher, along with the use of cross-cultural ethnohistoric and ethnographic accounts as analogs. Spores (1980:579–580) points out the importance of being more explicit in describing inferential processes involved in interpreting the patterns, thus providing clarity. Their meaning can then be explored in terms of human relationships, particularly relations of power, and how they changed through time from the perspective of Emergent, Developmental, and Classic horizons within the major Oneota cultural tradition.

ETHNICITY OR MOIETY

As shown in this study, Fisher and Langford societies were roughly contemporaneous, spatially interspersed along the northeastern portion of the Prairie Peninsula (particularly along the Upper Illinois Valley), and shared many aspects of material culture, settlement-subsistence patterns, sociopolitical structure, mortuary ritual beliefs and practices, and reciprocal exchange systems with other contemporary Emergent and Developmental horizon Oneota societies. Archaeologists differentiate the two based on tempering agents because there apparently is no other criteria. From an emic perspective it is unlikely they could separate themselves into distinct ethnic groups on this basis alone. Ethnicity is defined as "a group identity based on culture, language, religion, or a common attachment to a place or kin ties" (Nanda 1994:467). Ethnicity involves an emotionally charged sense of self and group identity that is transmitted through successive generations. Outsiders clearly recognize ethnic group membership and their boundaries (Doob 1988:231; Nanda 1994:303). Importantly, ethnicity primarily emerges as a significant aspect of social hierarchy and the struggles for economic resources and power in nation-states throughout the world (Nanda 1994:310; Rosman and Rubel 1995:302–303), so it is a concept for our times. The relevancy of its usage for prehistoric small-scale Native American societies is highly problematic.

If not ethnicity then perhaps a moiety system may explain Fisher and Langford relationships, specifically their involvement in the exchange of ceramic vessels. A *moiety* is a type of social structure characterized by an entire society (tribe, clan, or community) being divided into two halves. It represents the largest type of unilineal kin grouping, in which membership may be assigned through the mother (matrimoiety) or father (patrimoiety) or by generation level (Bodley 1994:38; Driver 1961:299; Rosman and Rubel 1995:95; Turner 1972:86). The division into moieties may be simple or complex and may coincide with clan organization. According to Levi-Strauss (1963:10), "Almost as many kinds of dual organization are known as peoples possessing it." It is not a spurious category, because it can result from the fusion between two neighboring groups (for economic, ceremonial, demographic, or other reasons) or the need for organizing ritual activities and specifying roles in initiation ceremonies, funerals, and marriages (Bodley 1994; Levi-Strauss 1963).

An amazing variety of moiety systems or dual organizations occurred among Eastern Woodlands and Plains societies (Callender 1978b:615–616; Driver 1961:299–302; Swanton 1979:663–665;

Underhill 1971:150–151). True moieties characterized the Winnebago, Menominee, Miami, and probably the Illiniwek, with clans grouped into two moieties associated with the Earth and Sky (Callender 1978b). The Winnebago exogamous moieties were formerly segregated spatially within the village, the northeast half being occupied by the Lower or Earth clans (Bear, Snake, Water-spirit, Wolf, Deer, Elk, Buffalo, and Fish) and the southwest half by those of the Upper or Sky moiety (Thunderbird, Eagle, War, and Passenger Pigeon). Both were linked by reciprocal obligations, like requirements to hold funerals for deceased members of the opposite moiety (Radin 1923). Most Sioux camps were likewise organized with the segregation of Earth and Sky moieties (Callender 1978b; Levi-Strauss 1963). The Creek Nation possessed two moieties termed Peace and War, the colors white and red associated with each respectively. Towns were divided along lines determined by the two moieties. At one point in their history, there were 31 Peace towns and 18 War towns for which moiety affiliation was known. Both acted reciprocally to perform ball games (a derivation of lacrosse) and other ritual acts (Swanton 1979:664, 674). With the widespread historic evidence of dual organization, the challenge is to find its presence in the archaeological record. Until more Fisher and Langford sites are excavated, materials analyzed, and the data reported, the question of whether they represent two moieties cannot be answered.

FISHER AND LANGFORD CERAMICS AS ONEOTA

Oneota is widely known as much as a "pottery culture" as a true culture, but there is increasing evidence that there was indeed an Oneota society. The Fisher and Langford ceramics and other archaeological data observed at Lawrence and Keeshin farm in particular strongly support this position. The ceramic jar attributes in both the Lawrence and Keeshin Farm assemblages, and Fisher and Langford domestic ceramic production in general, show a much closer relationship to Oneota than other Mississippian (Cahokia and Fort Ancient) or Late Woodland (Western Basin and Oliver phase) ceramic traditions. James B. Griffin (1943:283–284) was the first to acknowledge that Fisher should be considered Oneota based primarily on similarities in vessel form, rim form, surface treatment, and decoration. By extension, the same similarities between Fisher and Langford ceramic attributes would also place the latter within Oneota cultural contexts. The utilitarian vessels described here provide evidence that the Prairie Peninsula was a *distinct culture area*, a concept that had been originally proposed by James A. Brown. The vessels are art forms with decorative styles appearing to convey similar messages relating to the power of the upperworld across a number of societies.

The composition of both ceramic traditions show continuity with some aspects of Late Woodland production. First, there was a continuation of smoothed-over cordmarked exterior surface treatment, which perhaps allowed ease of holding and moving pots. The greater amount of smoothing contrasts with pottery from the American Bottom, a distinction noted between the Middle Mississippian assemblages of the Central Illinois Valley and the American Bottom (Harn 1980:21). Second, there was a complete developmental change away from generally thicker-walled, elongated earthenware jars of Woodland times to thin-walled, globular-bodied vessels. The ubiquity of these jars in Oneota assemblages apparently corresponds with a satisfactory level of performance sought and achieved for effectively cooking starchy seeds, like maize. Accumulated knowledge and skills pertaining to mechanical strength and resistance to thermal stress in cooking pots was probably transmitted on the household level from senior to junior generations (as part of ceramic traditions) in such small-scale societies (Braun 1991; Neff 1992:150–151; Rands 1994).

The Langford tradition assemblages show further continuity with the Late Woodland period in the use of small rim folds or collars along with grit tempering (Fowler 1952; Markman 1991b; Skinner 1953). The high rim folds appear to be a development from Late Woodland collared wares such as Starved Rock Collared, Aztalan Collared, and Maples Mills Collared. However, the folded collars are flattened almost even with the vessel wall by folding the upper portion of the rim outward from the vessel and then back upon itself rather than a thickening fashioned by modeling or "pinching." Therefore, Langford vessels share similarities with contemporaneous ceramics of the Oliver phase Bowen site of central Indiana (Dorwin 1971:Figure 10f), the late prehistoric ceramics from the Aztalan site of southeast Wisconsin (Richards 1992:Figure 5.6), and the Fort Ancient tradition (Turnbow and Henderson 1992:Figure A-7). Folded or thickened collared rims occur on numerous pottery types across the northern United States and southern Canada, from the Prairie Peninsula eastward (Brose 1978; Stothers 1995). They are, however, notably absent in Middle Mississippian Cahokia tradition assemblages (Milner et al. 1984).

There are only a few vessel forms in Oneota assemblages, limited to jars, bowls, pinch pots, and water bottles. Jars predominate within the samples as they do at Lawrence (76%) and Keeshin Farm (96%). Their ubiquity has been documented for the Langford tradition sites of Cooke (Markman 1991b), Reeves (Craig and Galloy 1995), Robinson Reserve (Fowler 1952), Oakwood Mound (Skinner 1953), and Gentleman Farm (Brown et al. 1967:23) and may be viewed as successfully fulfilling a number of needs as all-purpose cooking and storage containers. Bowls, pinch pots, or water bottles occur either infrequently or are absent in Oneota collections. Their presence suggests interaction with Middle Mississippian groups, because they are common forms in the Illinois River valley (Harn 1980; Morgan 1985) as well as Cahokia (Milner 1984;

Vogel 1975). Pinch pots and water bottles are notably absent in Fort Ancient ceramic assemblages (Turnbow and Henderson 1992:297–298). Particularly noteworthy, however, are the absence of beakers, hooded water bottles, juice presses, seed jars, and stumpware in Oneota and Fort Ancient collections, all of which are present in the Lohmann and Stirling phase assemblages of the American Bottom (Milner et al. 1984:161, 168). Their distinctive sizes and shapes appear to have fulfilled a number of specific needs for Middle Mississippian peoples.

A significant aspect of the Fisher and Langford cultures are the similarities in rim form and shoulder decoration they bear to other early Oneota cultures. Shared characteristics include the dominance of everted and vertical rims at the Lawrence and Keeshin Farm sites. The prevalence of these forms in Fisher and Langford assemblages has been reported for Oakwood Mound (Skinner 1953:Figure 7), Cooke (Markman 1991b:194), Reeves (Craig and Galloy 1995:6–8), and Plum Island (Fenner 1963:55, 61). They have also been noted in Huber phase assemblages at Griesmer (Faulkner 1972:64, 66), Hoxie Farm (Herold et al. 1990:Figures 2.1 and 2.2), and Oak Forest (Michalik and Brown 1990:Figure 10.3), which shows continuity between ceramic industries. The low, broadly everted forms present at Keeshin Farm closely resemble those of the early Koshkonong phase of southern Wisconsin (Hall 1962) as well as the Apple River Bennett and Mills phase profiles of northwestern Illinois (Emerson 1991a). It is important to note that everted or angled rims are absent in Fort Ancient assemblages (Griffin 1943; Turnbow and Henderson 1992:298) while dominant at the Oliver phase Bowen site (Dorwin 1971:250, Table 9), located along the southeastern margins of the Prairie Peninsula and a transitory zone between Oneota and Fort Ancient.

Fisher phase jars often have shoulder decorations consisting of wide to medium curvilinear trailing in conjunction with the use of punctates as fringe or border elements and the chevron design as a common motif. This is not a unique style of Oneota decoration but one that is shared with the Moingona phase in the Central Des Moines Valley of south-central Iowa (Benn 1991; De Vore 1990; Gradwohl 1974; Moffat and Koldehoff 1990c), the Correctionville–Blue Earth phase of northwestern Iowa and southern Minnesota (Fishel 1995; Henning 1970), the Burlington phase in southeastern Iowa (Tiffany 1979), and the assemblage represented at the Guthrey site in Missouri (Henning 1970). In contrast, the early Langford vessels at Keeshin Farm show a close relationship with the Emergent horizon Oneota ceramics in eastern Wisconsin by sharing wide curvilinear trailing elements (similar to the type Carcajou Curvilinear). A distinctive feature of Fort Ancient is the prevalence of two- to four-line curvilinear guilloche decorative motifs incised on jar necks (Henderson et al. 1992), which do not occur on Oneota ceramics.

Also, trailed decoration on the inner lip design field (e.g., Lawrence

Fisher Trailed jar, vessel 5-1-1) seems to be distinctive of the Upper Mississippi River basin in Iowa, Minnesota, and Wisconsin (Henning 1970; Michalik and Brown 1990:213; Moffat and Koldehoff 1990c). Moffat and Koldehoff (1990c:432) state that one of the more striking differences between Cahokia (Moorehead and Sand Prairie phases) and Oneota is that the Middle Mississippians rarely decorated their cooking vessels and other utilitarian wares, which is a fundamental difference needing further study.

The absence of shell-tempered ceramics in Langford assemblages, like Keeshin Farm, has often been used by archaeologists classifying the societies as non-Oneota. However, Oneota societies are known to manufacture ceramics with a variety of tempering agents rather than exclusively shell as dictated by the McKern system. Grit-tempered ceramics are known in Minnesota Oneota assemblages (Anfinson 1979), and grog tempering is a consistent trait in Oneota pottery from Mississippi Alluvial Plain sites of southeast Iowa (Henning 1995). Grog-tempered sherds were also found in the Oneota Huber phase Huber and Hoxie Farm assemblages (Herold et al. 1990:30), and grit-tempered Huber ware occurred at the Griesmer site (Faulkner 1972:66).

MUNDANE LIFE: SOCIAL CHOICES AND GENDER INTERDEPENDENCE

The Fisher and Langford settlement patterns appear comparable with other Oneota societies, consisting of relatively large permanent or semi-permanent villages (or multiseasonal base camps), seasonal or specialized extraction locations, and bivouacs (Benn 1989). Village sites, like Lawrence and Keeshin Farm, are usually associated with elevated terraces along major streams that afforded easy access to nearby prairie-forest ecotones, aquatic/wetland resources, and arable, rich forest soils (Alfisols) with high agricultural productivity. They also served as important points of communication along major waterways. Although Oneota village site size varied, there is no indication that a larger polity exerted hegemony over a smaller one through ranking. In other words, no data support the existence of a series of smaller groups or communities integrated and dominated by an elite group at a large, centrally located settlement or nodal center (the locus of political leadership for the cluster as a whole). The villages were relatively self-sufficient because of the people's ability to efficiently exploit seasonally available resources located primarily within the river valley. It was up to the leader(s) of each Oneota village to initiate and maintain a balance of power across the landscape through active interaction with "others," which could be realized by organizing village feasts (as reciprocal exchanges) with lavish displays of food and inviting other peoples to participate.

The faunal samples from the Lawrence and Keeshin Farm sites show that a variety of fauna were exploited and utilized, with some patterns typical of other Oneota sites in the Prairie Peninsula. The inhabitants focused on floodplain resources, particularly those associated with aquatic/wetland habitats near the sites, and prairie species were rarely utilized. Perhaps this should not be surprising since a great abundance and diversity of fauna, highly concentrated on a spatiotemporal scale, are available in this habitat. Aquatic/wetland resources dominate at most Oneota sites, including the Chicago area Huber phase sites of Huber (67%), Anker (60%), Hoxie Farm (45%), and Oak Forest (60%) (Michalik 1982; Neusius 1990:277) as well as the Bold Counselor phase components at the Morton site (59%) in the Central Illinois Valley (Styles and King 1990:59) and the Sponemann site (68%) in the American Bottom region (Kelly 1992:498). Most assemblages reflect an emphasis on large fish, such as channel catfish and suckers (Catostomidae), which could be most easily captured during their spring-spawning concentrations.

Large herbivore prairie resources, elk and bison, are often poorly represented in early Oneota assemblages. Possibly, that is because the village occupations represent only the part of the economic cycle during which subsistence activities were focused on aquatic/wetland and woodland species. However, it is more likely that changes in grassland productivity associated with the Pacific climatic episode affected bison and elk herd opportunistic migration and availability. An increase in droughty conditions may have enhanced the growth of dominant "warm season" C_4 grasses (e.g., big bluestem, little bluestem, Indian grass, buffalo grass, side-oats grama), which bison are known to preferentially graze.

The significance of forest and forest-edge animals in the assemblages is attributed largely to white-tailed deer, a large mammal that was transported whole to the habitation areas for butchering, distribution, consumption, and disposal of remains. Deer proved vital to prehistoric societies as a source of meat, fat, bone marrow, grease, and large hides. The many furbearing species that were valued historically (e.g., beaver, muskrat, and river otter) appear to have been relatively unimportant, although the scarcity or complete absence of their remains in the archaeological record may actually represent cultural practices that can confound any simple generalization. For example, historic and ethnographic records show that the remains of semiaquatic mammals (after they were skinned and the meat consumed) were often thrown back into the water at their place of capture so as not to offend the animal's spirit. Another problem limiting our understanding of mammal procurement and utilization stems from the fact that studies are restricted to villages inhabited from spring through the fall, ignoring the winter segment of the seasonal rounds (Wright 1987).

The low ranking of birds in the Lawrence and Keeshin Farm assemblages is perplexing, as it is for Oneota assemblages throughout the Prairie Peninsula and environs, especially given the fact that most sites appear to represent warm-season occupations located in proximity to productive habitats for waterfowl and wading birds. Therefore, availability would not present a problem. Also, certain bird skeletal parts have been shown to have a high survivability rate under fire and so would be preserved in the assemblages rather than completely consumed, as traditionally assumed (Michalik 1982:34). Perhaps it reflects a cultural bias against eating birds, as Kelly (1990:399) suggests. Still, ethnohistoric sources indicate that many bird species were probably procured for decoration, ritual, and clothing use (Highwater 1983; Parmalee 1977; Swanton 1979). It is conceivable that the paucity of avian remains may reflect ritual disposal away from habitation refuse pits due to the sanctity of birds as creatures of the upperworld. For example, the Hopi captured eaglets for feathers and, after ritual sacrifice, buried them with appropriate rites in special cemeteries (Hough 1911:409). The infrequent pattern of natural bone modification (animal gnawing, root etching, and weathering) suggests that animal refuse was rapidly buried by the occupants to keep the habitation areas clean, and so this planned behavior may provide support for this interpretation.

Based on ethnohistorical and ethnographic accounts, one can argue that male hunters' decisions to target certain mammals were influenced by women, who managed household activities. Power was contained in the interdependence of both genders working for the survival and continuation of the family and community. The large prey species, including bison (weighing from 800 to 2,000 pounds) and elk (weighing from 500 to 1,000 pounds), would have been butchered at the kill site, with selected cuts taken back to the village (Wing and Brown 1979:132). It is assumed that the amount of meat, fat, marrow, and grease associated with each skeletal part and how certain bone elements were to be used as tools, ornaments, or other paraphernalia would influence choices on how the large carcasses were to be butchered, stored, and transported (Lyman 1994b:225). White-tailed deer and smaller whole animals, as shown in this study, were transported whole to the village, where the labor of women would be indispensable in the preparation of meals and hideworking for clothing and other paraphernalia.

DIVERSIONARY LIFE: THE POWER OF FESTIVALS AND DREAMS

Because the Emergent and Developmental Oneota peoples lacked defended territories, they do not exactly fit our Western concept of a "tribe." The data show that freedom of migration or mobility (not bound to catchment areas) was extremely important in the lifeways of Langford and Fisher peoples as well as Oneota in general. This mobility can be seen in outlier sites like Lawrence, which is the only Fisher village site located in the midst of Langford sites in the Middle Rock River region. Migration is viewed as a structural behavior typically performed by defined subgroups (often kin-recruited) with specific goals and targeted on known destinations (Anthony 1990). Migrations may move in two directions and need not involve an invasion of another's territory, which may be exemplified by the Fisher phase occupation of Lawrence. Thus, there were many other factors involved in site placement besides subsistence strategies and displacement of another cultural group through warfare (a focus of archaeological research for the Classic Oneota horizon and early historic period). Perhaps most important were friendly intertribal festivals, which rendered possible the borrowing of ceremonial routine, dances, songs, and other acts (Lowie 1915).

Festivals provided an opportunity for peoples to reflect on life, thereby expanding individual consciousness, to integrate and communicate through various activities, and to celebrate life through ceremonies of world renewal. Time is renewed by multiplying the times of existence (e.g., through historicity), and the spaces and times of the mundane world are viewed as a paradox wherein the "end" becomes the "beginning"—from chaos and death come order and life. Members of a society are linked through past, present, and future. Communal ritual and ceremonial performances are necessarily universal among cultures because it gives people purpose in life and communicates the group's most traditional values across time. They transcend the ordinary course of events. The diversions require a careful interplay of religious and secular power relations to restore the isolated, private self into conscious harmony with the universe (Allen 1986; Falassi 1967; Sullivan 1986). Communal ritual has proven difficult to identify in the archaeological record when dealing with habitation sites such as Lawrence and Keeshin Farm, perhaps owing to biases in recovery techniques and/or problems of organic material preservation caused by natural or cultural processes (Wright 1987:4). In contrast, there is a rich archaeological data set concerning mortuary ritual, with the cultural meanings of the *patterns* well documented in historical records.

Information regarding mortuary ritual in Fisher and Langford societies indicates general patterns or similarities with other Emergent and Developmental Oneota societies. Their common interests of maintaining the world in balance were grounded in the knowledge and practice of similar religious institutions. Individuals were often buried within or below low, broad mounds near villages, and the burials were associated with graveside fires and common utilitarian goods. The mound environs or nearby villages were probably the scene of festivals, which would have included dances, songs, speeches, feasts, and games based on ethnohistoric accounts (Densmore 1929; Lowie 1915; Radin 1923; Skinner 1913; Trigger 1969). It provided an opportunity for intertribal cohesiveness as people commune, communicate, celebrate, mourn, and thereby transform "daily or mundane time" to "time out of time." People came to participate, through intimate personal contact, in the knowledge and beauty of the ceremony. Because it is a rite of passage, death would not be perceived as an end of things but as a transition or rebirth to a new state of being. Thus, family members would continue to be a part of the group even after death, with the survival of the living based on mutual dependence (Holsbeke 1997:12).

The Langford tradition sites of Gentleman Farm (Brown et al. 1967), Material Service Quarry (Bareis 1965), Oakwood Mound (Skinner 1953), and Robinson Reserve (Fowler 1952) did not show evidence that the mound burials represented an elite group either by exotic grave goods or by age and sex. At Gentleman Farm, complete ceramic vessels and/or mussel shell spoons occur in association with female and male adults as well as children, showing equality by age and gender (Brown et al. 1967:16–17, Table 6). A similar pattern of mortuary behavior occurred at the Oneota Bold Counselor phase Norris Farms 36 cemetery, in which pottery vessels and/or shell spoons were associated with 45 individuals, including adults and children of both sexes (Santure and Esarey 1990:106). The occurrence of these common grave offerings can be explained as attempts by the living to provide foodstuffs to the soul of the dead, who then could give life to the living through the power of dream imagery (Boas 1910b:617–618). Having gone ahead of the living, the dead serve as ideal mediators between the "higher" powers of the otherworld and humans (Holsbeke 1997; Hultkrantz 1981).

The reciprocal relationship of people to the souls of the dead and to one another was also applied to the relationship of people to other non-human supernatural beings that was essential for maintaining the world in balance or harmony (Black Elk and Lyon 1991; Trigger 1986:255–256; Whelan 1993:256–259). In the Native American worldview, human beings were not superior to nature but regarded all phenomena as having life and thus power. This is especially true in regard to mythological thunderbirds (in the form of raptorial birds), infused with sacred powers of the upperworld that humans sought to acquire through dreams or visions. Dreams and visions (as liminal states of being) gave each individual access to mythic time and space and to the powerful non-human beings that live there (Berlo and Phillips 1998:25; Hultkrantz 1986). The *art of dreaming* has been shown *not* to be an irrational act, but rather it was necessary to overcome the anxieties and uncertainties of existence (see Hartmann 1998). Such experiences were just as real as those of waking life and provided an important subject of discussion as to their meaning among the community (Feest 1986:12). Problems must be resolved and the unity of the world maintained.

NOT ART FOR ART'S SAKE

Among small-scale Native American societies, the beauty of art permeates all aspects of life and is devised to convey particular messages about the world (Berlo and Phillips 1998:7–9; Rosman and Rubel 1995:229). Artistic production has a collective and thus anonymous quality. The power of imagery is inherent in every person and finds expression in the creation of aesthetics of art (Boas 1910:617). It includes all pottery vessels manufactured by Langford and Fisher peoples regardless of whether they exhibit decoration, for other qualities may be more important (see Berlo and Phillips 1998:9). Imagery is used as a means of linking members of society through past, present, and future (perpetuating cultural traditions) and provides a religious dimension that bridges the worlds of the natural and the supernatural (Holsbeke 1997; Nanda 1994:396).

It is argued in this study that the strong abstract or geometric character of symbols (triangles, chevrons) depicted on Oneota globular jars represent the thunderbird through metonymy; these symbols were probably taken from textiles and basketry and produced primarily by women. It should be recognized that analogy is a dangerous tool, because meanings attached to such geometric symbols may vary over space and time. Still, the regularity of globular jar forms and geometric decorative patterns often associated with them are clearly evident in the archaeological record throughout the Prairie Peninsula and its environs. An image was created that resonates even in the memory of archaeologists today. The artists' skill in handling materials and manipulating stylistic conventions created order out of chaos and may have been derived from ancient shared traditions and from individual creativity. As seen in imagery, dreams give birth to creation.

The motifs associated with the thunderbird are viewed as ancient and enduring across the Plains and Eastern Woodlands. Ethnographic and ethnohistoric sources indicate that the thunderbird was associated with the upperworld and the benevolent, fertile forces of rainfall as well as the life-threatening powers of tornadoes, lightning, hail, and floods. The power of the thunderbird was opposed yet complementary to the great underworld spirits, such as the underwater panther associated with the historic Woodland tribes and replaced by the underwater horned monster among the Plains tribes. Their perpetual struggle for existence and the ambiguity of their power provided a very tenuous balance of nature on earth. It was important for Native American peoples to both placate and use some of this mysterious power.

Other forms of symbolic communication of religious ideology include the circle-and-cross motif found throughout the New World in pre-Columbian times (Harrod 1987:53; Holmes 1911; Mallery 1893; Ridington and Ridington 1970; Willoughby 1897). The circle-and-cross motif symbolizes the Native American cosmic structure, composed of the sacred cardinal directions of north-south and east-west (the four winds associated with the directions and responsible for sustaining and perpetuating the life cycle) and a central vertical axis that connected the upper and lower supernatural realms with this world of human beings.

Such symbolic forms helped to organize Native American individual and collective experiences at the center of the world, from which creation began. It was a world *within* which Fisher and Langford peoples could dwell and where power relations could take many positive forms. Individuals could produce beautiful things, bring about pleasure, promote traditional values and knowledge, and share personal experiences of the harmony and unity of life. The use of a more anthropological archaeology in the twenty-first century focusing on power and gender will provide a better understanding of Oneota culture and Native American heritage in its entirety.

References Cited

Abrahams, Roger
  1984   Equal Opportunity Eating: A Structural Excursus on Things of the Mouth. In *Ethnic and Regional Foodways in the United States: The Performance of Group Identity*, edited by Linda Keller Brown and Kay Mussell, pp. 19–36. University of Tennessee Press, Knoxville.

Adams, William Y., Dennis P. VanGerven, and Richard S. Levy
  1978   The Retreat from Migrationism. *Annual Review of Anthropology* 7:483–532.

Albers, Patricia A.
  1996   Changing Patterns of Ethnicity in the Northeastern Plains, 1780–1870. In *History, Power, and Identity: Ethnogenesis in the Americas, 1492–1992*, edited by Jonathan D. Hill, pp. 90–118. University of Iowa Press, Iowa City.

Alex, Lynn Marie
  1980   *Exploring Iowa's Past: A Guide to Prehistoric Archaeology*. University of Iowa Press, Iowa City.

Allee, Mary N.
  1949   *The Gentleman Farm Site and the Fisher-Heally Series in Northern Illinois*. Unpublished Master's thesis, Department of Anthropology, University of Chicago, Chicago.

Allen, Joel Asaph
  1876   *The American Bisons, Living and Extinct*. Memoirs of the Geological Survey of Kentucky, vol. 1, Pt. 2. University Press, Cambridge, Massachusetts.

Allen, Paula Gunn
  1986   *The Sacred Hoop: Recovering the Feminine in American Indian Traditions*. Beacon Press, Boston.

American Ornithologist's Union
  1982   Thirty-fourth Supplement to the American Ornithologists' Union Check-list of North American Birds. *Auk* 99(3):supplement.

Anderson, David G., David W. Stahle, and Malcolm K. Cleaveland
  1995   Paleoclimate and the Potential Food Reserves of Mississippian Societies: A Case Study from the Savannah River Valley. *American Antiquity* 60(2):258–286.

Anderson, Richard C., and John M. Masters
  1985   Terraces of the Rock River Valley in Southern Wisconsin and Northern Illinois. In *Illinoian and Wisconsinan Stratigraphy and Environments in Northern Illinois: The Altonian Revised*, pp. 21–34. Illinois State Geological Survey Division Guidebook 19. Illinois Department of Energy and Natural Resources, Champaign.

Anfinson, S. F. (editor)
  1979   *A Handbook of Minnesota Prehistoric Ceramics.* Occasional Publications in Minnesota Anthropology No.5. Minnesota Archaeological Society, St. Paul.
Anonymous
  1897   The Swastika in America. *American Antiquarian* 19(2):116–120.
Anthony, David W.
  1990   Migration in Archeology: The Baby and the Bathwater. *American Anthropologist* 92:895–914.
Arens, William, and Ivan Karp
  1989   Introduction. In *Creativity of Power: Cosmology and Action in African Societies,* edited by William Arens and Ivan Karp, pp. xi–xxix. Smithsonian Institution Press, Washington, D.C.
Armelagos, George J.
  1994   You Are What You Eat. In *Paleonutrition: The Diet and Health of Prehistoric Americans,* edited by Kristin D. Sobdik, pp. 235–244. Occasional Paper No. 22. Center for Archaeological Investigations, Southern Illinois University, Carbondale.
Arnold, Dean E.
  1988   *Ceramic Theory and Cultural Process.* Cambridge University Press, Cambridge.
Ashbrook, Frank G.
  1955[1892] *Butchering, Processing, and Preservation of Meat.* D. Van Nostrand, New York.
Bailey, Kenneth D.
  1987   *Methods of Social Research.* 3d ed. Free Press, New York.
Balkin, J. M.
  1998   *Cultural Software: A Theory of Ideology.* Yale University Press, New Haven.
Balter, Michael
  1998   Digging into the Life of the Mind. *Science* 282:1444.
Bamforth, Douglas B.
  1987   Historical Documents and Bison Ecology on the Great Plains. *Plains Anthropologist* 32:1–16.
  1988   *Ecology and Human Organization on the Great Plains.* Plenum Press, New York.
Barbeau, Charles M.
  1914   Supernatural Beings of the Huron and Wyandot. *American Anthropologist* 16:288–313.
Bareis, Charles J.
  1965   Excavation of Two Burials at the Material Service Quarry Site, La Salle County, Illinois. *Wisconsin Archeologist* 46(2):140–143.
Barker, Philip
  1993   *Michel Foucault: Subversions of the Subject.* Harvester Wheatsheaf, New York.
Barnes, Barry
  1988   *The Nature of Power.* University of Illinois Press, Urbana and Chicago.
Barnouw, Victor
  1963   *Culture and Personality.* Dorsey Press, Homewood, Illinois.

Barr, Kenneth A.
1979   *An Analysis of the Faunal Assemblage from the Elam Site: An Upper Mississippian Seasonal Encampment on the Kalamazoo River in Allegan County, Michigan.* Unpublished Master's thesis, Department of Anthropology, Western Michigan University, Kalamazoo.

Bean, Lowell John
1992   Power and Its Application in Native California. In *California Indian Shamanism,* edited by Lowell John Bean, pp. 23–32. Anthropological Papers No. 39. Ballena Press, Menlo Park, California.

Beauchamp, William M.
1893   Notes on Onondaga Dances. *Journal of American Folklore* 6(20):181–184.
1895   Mohawk Notes. *Journal of American Folklore* 8(28):217–221.

Bebb, M. S.
1860   The Flora of Ogle and Winnebago Counties, Illinois. *Prairie Farmer* 22:182–183.

Becker, C. D., and D. A. Neitzel
1992   *Water Quality in North American River Systems.* Battelle Press, Columbus, Ohio.

Bell, Catherine
1992   *Ritual Theory, Ritual Practice.* Oxford University Press, New York.

Bellrose, Frank C.
1976   *Ducks, Geese, and Swans of North America.* Stackpole Books, Harrisburg, Pennsylvania.

Benchley, Elizabeth D., and Robert A. Birmingham
1978   *Preliminary Predictive Model of Archaeological Site Locations in the Rock River Drainage, Illinois.* Report of Investigations No. 20. Archaeological Research Laboratory, University of Wisconsin, Madison.

Benchley, Elizabeth D., Lynne Goldstein, Robert A. Birmingham, Mark J. Dudzik, and William Billeck
1981   Rock River, Upper Mississippi River, Little Wabash River, Lower Wabash River Units (I, III-North and VIII). In *Predictive Models in Illinois Archaeology: Report Summaries,* edited by Margaret K. Brown, pp. 1–20. Illinois Department of Conservation, Springfield.

Bender, Barbara
1990   The Dynamics of Nonhierarchical Societies. In *The Evolution of Political Systems,* edited by Steadman Upham, pp. 247–263. Cambridge University Press, Cambridge.

Benedict, Ruth Fulton
1922   The Vision in Plains Culture. *American Anthropologist* 24(1):1–23.

Benn, David W.
1989   Hawks, Serpents, and Bird-Men: Emergence of the Oneota Mode of Production. *Plains Anthropologist* 34:233–260.
1991   The Christenson Oneota Site, 13PK407. *Journal of the Iowa Archaeological Society* 38:16–55.
1995   Woodland People and the Roots of the Oneota. In *Oneota Archaeology: Past, Present, and Future,* edited by William Green, pp. 91–140. Report No. 20. Office of the State Archaeologist, University of Iowa, Iowa City.

Benson, Gunnar, A.
  1972   *Sinnissippi Mounds, Sterling, Illinois.* Ms. on file, Northern Illinois University, DeKalb.
Bent, Charles
  1877   *History of Whiteside County, Illinois, from Its First Settlement to the Present Time.* L. P. Allen, Morrison, Illinois.
Berlo, Janet C., and Ruth B. Phillips
  1998   *Native North American Art.* Oxford University Press, Oxford.
Bernabo, J. Christopher
  1981   Quantitative Estimates of Temperature Changes over the Last 2700 Years in Michigan Based on Pollen Data. *Quaternary Research* 15:143–159.
Berres, Thomas E.
  n.d.   *Faunal Remains from the Old Edwardsville Road Site (11MS1291).* Report submitted to the Illinois Transportation Archaeological Research Program, University of Illinois. Ms. on file, University of Illinois, Urbana.
  1984   *A Formal Analysis of Ceramic Vessels from the Schlemmer Site (11-S-382): A Late Woodland/Mississippian Occupation in St. Clair County, Illinois.* Unpublished Master's thesis, Department of Anthropology, Western Michigan University, Kalamazoo.
  1995   *The Lawrence Site: A Fisher Upper Mississippian Habitation in the Rock River Valley of Northern Illinois.* Paper presented at the Annual Meeting Midwest Archaeological Conference, Beloit, Wisconsin.
  1996   Faunal Remains. In *The Vaughn Branch Site: Late Woodland and Mississippian Occupations in the American Bottom (11-Ms-1437),* edited by D. K. Jackson, pp. 115–119. Research Reports No. 42. Illinois Transportation Archaeological Research Program, University of Illinois, Urbana.
Berres, Thomas E., David M. Stothers, and Brad W. Bodoh
  1999   *Bear Imagery and Ritual in the Midcontinent: Reflections on A. Irving Hallowell's Work.* Paper Presented at the 45th Annual Midwest Archaeological Conference, Michigan State University, East Lansing.
Bettarel, Robert L., and Hale G. Smith
  1973   *The Moccasin Bluff Site and the Woodland Cultures of Southwestern Michigan.* Anthropological Papers No. 49. Museum of Anthropology, University of Michigan, Ann Arbor.
Bianco, William T., and Robert H. Bates
  1990   Cooperation by Design: Leadership, Structure, and Collective Dilemmas. *American Political Science Review* 84(1):133–147.
Binford, Lewis R.
  1965   Archaeological Systematics and the Study of Cultural Process. *American Antiquity* 31:203–210.
Binford, Sally R., and Lewis R. Binford (editors)
  1968   *New Perspectives in Archaeology.* Aldine, Chicago.
Bird, M. Catherine
  1997   *Broken Pieces: Langford Settlement System and the Role of Material Culture in the Maintenance of Social Boundaries.* Unpublished Ph.D. dissertation, Department of Anthropology, University of Wisconsin—Milwaukee.

Birmingham, Robert A.
1975   *The Langford Tradition and Its Environmental Context in the Rock River Valley, Illinois.* Unpublished Master's thesis, Department of Anthropology, University of Wisconsin-Milwaukee.

Black Elk, Wallace H., and William S. Lyon
1991   *Black Elk: The Sacred Ways of a Lakota.* HarperCollins, San Francisco.

Black-Rogers, Mary
1988   Ojibwa Power Interactions: Creating Contexts for Respectful Talk. In *Native American Interaction Patterns,* edited by Regna Darnell and Michael K. Foster, pp. 44–68. Canadian Museum of Civilization, National Museums of Canada, Hull, Quebec.

Blaine, Martha Royce
1979   *The Ioway Indians.* University of Oklahoma Press, Norman.

Blair, Emma Helen (editor)
1911–12 *The Indian Tribes of the Upper Mississippi Valley and the Region of the Great Lakes.* 2 vols. Arthur H. Clark, Cleveland.

Blessing, Fred K.
1956   Some Uses of Bone, Horn, Claws, and Teeth by Minnesota Ojibwa Indians. *Minnesota Archaeologist* 20(3):1–11.

Bluhm, Elaine A., and Gloria J. Fenner
1961   The Oak Forest Site. In *Chicago Area Archaeology,* edited by Elaine A. Bluhm, pp. 138–161. Bulletin No. 3. Illinois Archaeological Survey, University of Illinois, Urbana.

Bluhm, Elaine A., and Allen Liss
1961   The Anker Site. In *Chicago Area Archaeology,* edited by Elaine A. Bluhm, pp. 89–138. Bulletin No. 3. Illinois Archaeological Survey, University of Illinois, Urbana.

Bluhm, Elaine A., Michael P. Hoffman, and Margaret J. Hoffman
1961   Preliminary Report on the Archaeological Survey of the Rock River Valley. Ms. on file, Department of Anthropology, University of Illinois, Urbana.

Boas, Franz
1910a   Religion. In *Handbook of American Indians North of Mexico, Part II,* edited by Frederick Webb Hodge, pp. 365–371. Bulletin No. 30. Bureau of American Ethnology, Smithsonian Institution, Washington, D.C.
1910b   Soul. In *Handbook of American Indians North of Mexico, Part II,* edited by Frederick Webb Hodge, pp. 617–618. Bulletin No. 30. Bureau of American Ethnology, Smithsonian Institution, Washington, D.C.
1914   Mythology and Folk-Tales of the North American Indians. *Journal of American Folklore* 27(56):374–410.

Bock, Philip K.
1974   *Modern Cultural Anthropology: An Introduction.* 2nd ed. Alfred A. Knopf, New York.

Bodley, John H.
1994   *Cultural Anthropology: Tribes, States, and the Global System.* Mayfield, Mountain View, California.

Bohlen, H. David
1989   *The Birds of Illinois.* Indiana University Press, Bloomington.

Bonhage-Freund, Mary Theresa, and Jeffrey A. Kurland
1994   Tit-for-Tat among the Iroquois: A Game Theoretic Perspective on Inter-Tribal Political Organization. *Journal of Anthropological Archaeology* 13:278–305.

Borchert, John R.
1950   Climate of the Central North American Grassland. *Annals of the Association of American Geographers* 40:1–39.

Boszhardt, Robert F.
1989   Ceramic Analysis and Site Chronology of the Pammel Creek Site. *Wisconsin Archeologist* 70(1–2):41–94.

1994   Oneota Group Continuity at La Crosse: The Brice Prairie, Pammel Creek, and Valley View Phases. *Wisconsin Archeologist* 75:173–236.

Boszhardt, Robert F., Wendy Holtz, and Jeremy Nienow
1994   A Compilation of Oneota Radiocarbon Dates. Paper presented at the Workshop in Oneota Archaeology, Iowa City, Iowa.

Bozell, John R.
1993   Vertebrate Fauna. In *Temples for Cahokia Lords: Preston Holder's 1955–1956 Excavations of Kunnemann Mound*, edited by Timothy R. Pauketat, pp. 107–123. Memoir No. 26. Museum of Anthropology, University of Michigan, Ann Arbor.

1995   Culture, Environment, and Bison Populations on the Late Prehistoric and Early Historic Central Plains. *Plains Anthropologist* 40(152):145–163.

Braun, David P.
1983   Pots as Tools. In *Archaeological Hammers and Theories,* edited by James A. Moore and Arthur S. Keene, pp. 107–134. Academic Press, New York.

1991   Why Decorate a Pot? Midwestern Household Pottery, 200 B.C.–A.D. 600. *Journal of Anthropological Archaeology* 10:360–397.

Breitburg, Emanuel
1992   Vertebrate Faunal Remains. In *Fort Ancient Cultural Dynamics in the Middle Ohio Valley,* edited by A. Gwynn Henderson, pp. 209–242. Monographs in World Archaeology No. 8. Prehistory Press, Madison, Wisconsin.

Brew, John O.
1971   The Use and Abuse of Taxonomy. In *Man's Imprint from the Past: Readings in the Methods of Archaeology,* edited by James Deetz, pp. 73–107. Little, Brown and Company, Boston.

Brewer, Douglas J.
1986   *Cultural and Environmental Change in the Fayum, Egypt: An Investigation Based on Faunal Remains.* Unpublished Ph.D. dissertation, Department of Anthropology, University of Tennessee, Knoxville.

1992   Zooarchaeology: Method, Theory, and Goals. In *Archaeological Method and Theory,* vol. 4, edited by Michael B. Schiffer, pp. 195–244. University of Arizona Press, Tucson.

Britton, W. A., and A. S. Messenger
1969   Computed Soil Moisture Patterns in and around the Prairie Peninsula during the Great Drought of 1933–34. *Transactions of the Illinois State Academy of Science* 62:181–187.

Brose, David S.
1978   Late Prehistory of the Upper Great Lakes Area. In *Northeast,* edited by Bruce G. Trigger, pp. 569–582. Handbook of North American Indians, vol. 15, William C. Sturtevant, general editor. Smithsonian Institution, Washington, D.C.
1985   The Woodland Period. In *Ancient Art of the American Woodland Indians,* edited by David S. Brose, James A. Brown, and David W. Penney, pp. 43–91. Harry N. Adams, New York.

Brown, James A.
1961   *The Zimmerman Site. A Report on Excavations at the Grand Village of the Kaskaskia, La Salle County, Illinois.* Reports of Investigations No. 9. Illinois State Museum, Springfield.
1965   *The Prairie Peninsula: An Interaction Area in the Eastern United States.* Unpublished Ph.D. dissertation, Department of Anthropology, University of Chicago, Chicago.
1982   What Kind of Economy Did the Oneota Have? In *Oneota Studies,* edited by Guy E. Gibbon, pp. 107–112. Publications in Anthropology No. 1. University of Minnesota, Minneapolis.
1985   The Mississippian Period. In *Ancient Art of the American Woodland Indians,* edited by David S. Brose, James A. Brown, and David W. Penney, pp. 93–145. Harry N. Abrams, New York.
1990   The Oak Forest Site: Investigations into Oneota Subsistence-Settlement in the Cal-Sag Area of Cook County, Illinois. In *At the Edge of Prehistory: Huber Phase Archaeology in the Chicago Area,* edited by James A. Brown and Patricia J. O'Brien, pp. 123–308. Center for American Archeology, Kampsville, Illinois.
1991   *Aboriginal Cultural Adaptations in the Midwestern Prairies.* Garland, New York.
1993   *Oneota Mortuary Contexts.* Paper presented at the 38th annual Midwest Archaeological Conference, Milwaukee, Wisconsin.
1997   The Archaeology of Ancient Religion in the Eastern Woodlands. *Annual Review of Anthropology* 26:465–485.

Brown, James A., and David L. Asch
1990   Cultural Setting: The Oneota Tradition. In *At the Edge of Prehistory: Huber Phase Archaeology in the Chicago Area,* edited by James A. Brown and Patricia J. O'Brien, pp. 145–154. Center for American Archeology, Kampsville, Illinois.

Brown, James A., and Patricia J. O'Brien (editors)
1990   *At the Edge of Prehistory: Huber Phase Archaeology in the Chicago Area.* Center for American Archeology, Kampsville, Illinois.

Brown, James A., and Robert F. Sasso
1992   *Prelude to History on the Eastern Plains.* Ms. on file, Northern Illinois University, DeKalb.

Brown, James A., Roger W. Willis, Mary A. Barth, and George K. Neumann
1967   *The Gentleman Farm Site, La Salle County, Illinois.* Reports of Investigations No. 12. Illinois State Museum, Springfield.

Brown, Judith K.
1970   Economic Organization and the Position of Women among the Iroquois. *Ethnohistory* 17:151–167.

Brown, Margaret K.
1975   *The Zimmerman Site: Further Excavation at the Grand Village of Kaskaskia.* Reports of Investigations No. 32. Illinois State Museum, Springfield.

Browning-Hoffmann, Kathryn
1979   Can Incised Pottery Give Clues to Prehistoric Basketry? *Bulletin and Journal of the Archaeology of New York State* 76:26–34.

Bryson, Reid A.
1966   Air Masses, Streamlines, and the Boreal Forest. *Geographical Bulletin* 8:228–269.

1978   Cultural, Economic, and Climatic Records. In *Climatic Change and Variability,* edited by A. B. Pittock, L. A. Frakes, D. Jenssen, J. A. Peterson, and J. W. Zillman, pp. 316–327. Cambridge University Press, Cambridge.

Bryson, Reid A., David A. Baerreis, and Wayne M. Wendland
1970   The Character of Late-Glacial and Post-Glacial Climatic Changes. In *Pleistocene and Recent Environments of the Central Great Plains,* edited by W. Dort, Jr., and J. K. Jones, pp. 53–74. University of Kansas Press, Lawrence.

Buikstra, Jane E., Lyle W. Konigsberg, and Jill Bullington
1986   Fertility and the Development of Agriculture in the Prehistoric Midwest. *American Antiquity* 51:528–546.

Bunn, Henry T.
1993   Bone Assemblages at Base Camps: A Further Consideration of Carcass Transport and Bone Destruction by the Hadza. In *From Bones to Behavior: Ethnoarchaeological and Experimental Contributions to the Interpretation of Faunal Remains,* edited by Jean Hudson, pp. 156–167. Occasional Paper No. 21. Center for Archaeological Investigations, Southern Illinois University, Carbondale.

Bunzel, Ruth L.
1982   The Personal Element in Design (Pueblo). In *Native North American Art History: Selected Readings,* edited by Zena Pearlstone Mathews and Aldona Jonaitis, pp. 179–205. Peek, Palo Alto, California.

Bushnell, David I., Jr.
1920   *Native Cemeteries and Forms of Burial East of the Mississippi.* Bulletin No. 71. Bureau of American Ethnology, Smithsonian Institution, Washington, D.C.

Caldwell, Joseph R.
1970   New World Archaeology. In *Introductory Readings in Archaeology,* edited by B. M. Fagan, pp. 19–29. Little, Brown and Company, Boston.

Callender, Charles
1978a   Fox. In *Northeast,* edited by Bruce G. Trigger, pp. 636–647. Handbook of North American Indians, vol. 15, William C. Sturtevant, general editor. Smithsonian Institution, Washington, D.C.

1978b   Great Lakes–Riverine Sociopolitical Organization. In *Northeast,* edited by Bruce G. Trigger, pp. 610–621. Handbook of North American Indians, vol. 15, William C. Sturtevant, general editor. Smithsonian Institution, Washington, D.C.

Cannon, Debbi Yee
1987   *Marine Fish Osteology: A Manual for Archaeologists.* Publication No. 18.
         Department of Archaeology, Simon Fraser University, Burnaby, B.C.
Casagrande, Joseph B.
1952   Ojibwa Bear Ceremonialism: The Persistence of a Ritual Attitude. In
         *Acculturation in the Americas: Proceedings and Selected Papers of the
         29th International Congress of Americanists,* edited by Sol Tax, pp.
         113–117. University of Chicago Press, Chicago.
Catlin, George
1926   *North American Indians: Being Letters and Notes on Their Manners,
         Customs, and Conditions, Written during Eight Year's Travel
         amongst the Wildest Tribes of Indians in North America, 1832–1839.*
         John Grant, Edinburgh.
1973[1841] *Letters and Notes on the Manners, Customs, and Conditions of
         the North American Indians,* 2 Vols. Reprint. Dover Publications,
         New York.
Chamberlain, Alexander F.
1890   The Thunder-bird amongst the Algonkins. *American Anthropologist*
         3(1):51–54.
1907   Busk. In *Handbook of American Indians North of Mexico, Part I,*
         edited by Frederick Webb Hodge, pp. 176–178. Bulletin No. 30.
         Bureau of American Ethnology, Smithsonian Institution, Washing-
         ton, D.C.
Chandler, Milford G.
1973   Art and Culture. In *The Art of the Great Lakes Indians,* by the Flint
         Institute of Arts, pp. xv–xxvi. Flint Institute of Arts, Flint, Michigan.
Chapman, Carl H.
1975   *The Archaeology of Missouri,* vol. I. University of Missouri Press,
         Columbia.
Charles, Lucile Hoerr
1948   Regeneration through Drama at Death. *Journal of American Folk-
         lore* 61:151–174.
Claassen, Cheryl P.
1991   Gender, Shellfishing, and the Shell Mound Archaic. In *Engendering
         Archaeology: Women and Prehistory,* edited by Joan M. Gero and
         Margaret W. Conkey, pp. 276–300. Basil Blackwell, Oxford.
Clift, Gene
1953   Discover Lost Indian Village. *Graphic* 1(11):3–9.
Clifton, James A.
1978   Potawatomi. In *Northeast,* edited by Bruce G. Trigger, pp. 725–742.
         Handbook of North American Indians, vol. 15, William C. Sturte-
         vant, general editor. Smithsonian Institution, Washington, D.C.
Cobb, Charles R.
1991   Social Reproduction and the *Longue Duree* in the Prehistory of the
         Midcontinental United States. In *Processual and Postprocessual Ar-
         chaeologies: Multiple Ways of Knowing the Past,* edited by Robert W.
         Preucel, pp. 168–182. Occasional Paper No. 10. Center for Archae-
         ological Investigations, Southern Illinois University, Carbondale.
1993   Archaeological Approaches to the Political Economy of Nonstratified

Societies. In *Archaeological Method and Theory,* vol. 5, edited by Michael B. Schiffer, pp. 43–100. University of Arizona Press, Tucson.

Cobb, Charles R., and Patrick H. Garrow
1996   Woodstock Culture and the Question of Mississippian Emergence. *American Antiquity* 61(1):21–37.

Cobb, Charles R., and Michael S. Nassaney
1995   Interaction and Integration in the Late Woodland Southeast. In *Native American Interactions: Multiscalar Analyses and Interpretations in the Eastern Woodlands,* edited by Michael S. Nassaney and Kenneth E. Sassaman, pp. 205–226. University of Tennessee Press, Knoxville.

Coe, Michael, Dean Snow, and Elizabeth Benson
1986   *Atlas of Ancient America.* Facts on File, New York.

COHMAP Project Members
1988   Climatic Changes of the Last 18,000 Years: Observations and Model Simulations. *Science* 241:1043–1052.

Colburn, Mona L.
1989   Mississippi Faunal Remains from the Lundy Site (11-Jd-140), Jo Daviess County, Illinois. *Illinois Archaeology* 1(1):5–38.

Conant, Roger
1975   *A Field Guide to Reptiles and Amphibians of Eastern and Central North America.* Houghton Mifflin, Boston.

Conant, Roger, and J. T. Collins
1991   *A Field Guide to Reptiles and Amphibians: Eastern and Central North America.* Houghton Mifflin, Boston.

Conklin, N. F., and V. M. Patraka
1977   *Women's Art and Culture.* Women's Studies Curriculum Series, University of Michigan, Ann Arbor.

Cook, E. R., D. W. Stahle, and M. K. Cleaveland
1992   Dendroclimatic Evidence from Eastern North America. In *Climate Since* A.D. *1500,* edited by Raymond S. Bradley and Philip D. Jones, pp. 331–348. Routledge, London and New York.

Conkey, Margaret W., and Joan M. Gero
1991   Tensions, Pluralities, and Engendering Archaeology: An Introduction to Women and Prehistory. In *Engendering Archaeology: Women and Prehistory,* edited by Joan M. Gero and Margaret W. Conkey, pp. 3–30. Basil Blackwell, Oxford.

Costin, Cathy Lynne
1996   Exploring the Relationship between Gender and Craft in Complex Societies: Methodological and Theoretical Issues of Gender Attribution. In *Gender and Archaeology,* edited by Rita P. Wright, pp. 111–140. University of Pennsylvania Press, Philadelphia.

Craig, Joseph, and Joseph M. Galloy
1995   *The Reeves Site (11-Wi-555): Archaeological Investigations at a Langford Tradition Settlement on the DuPage River, Northeastern Illinois (Draft).* Hanson Engineers Incorporated, Springfield, Illinois.

Cremin, William M.
1978   *Paleoethnobotany: Implications for Crab Orchard Exploitation of the Shawnee Hills, Southern Illinois.* Unpublished Ph.D. dissertation, Department of Anthropology, Southern Illinois University, Carbondale.

Culin, Stewart
    1907   Games of the North American Indians. *Twenty-fourth Annual Report of the Bureau of American Ethnology for the Years 1902–1903,* pp. 3–846. Smithsonian Institution, Washington, D.C.
Cummings, Kevin S., and Christine A. Mayer
    1992   *Field Guide to Freshwater Mussels of the Midwest.* Manual 5. Illinois Natural History Survey, Champaign.
Curtis, John T.
    1959   *The Vegetation of Wisconsin.* University of Wisconsin Press, Madison.
Curtis, Martha E.
    1952   The Black Bear and the White-tailed Deer. *Midwest Folklore* 2:177–190. Bloomington, Indiana.
Darling, J. Andrew
    1999   From Hobbes to Rousseau and Back Again. *Science285:537*
Darnell, Regna
    1988   The Implications of Cree Interactional Etiquette. In *Native North American Interaction Patterns,* edited by Regna Darnell and Michael K. Foster, pp. 69–77. Canadian Museum of Civilization, National Museums of Canada, Hull, Quebec.
Daubenmire, Rexford
    1978   *Plant Geography with Special Reference to North America.* Academic Press, New York.
Deetz, James
    1965   *The Dynamics of Stylistic Change in Arikara Ceramics.* Illinois Studies in Anthropology No. 4. University of Illinois Press, Urbana.
    1968   The Inference of Residence and Descent Rules from Archaeological Data. In *New Perspectives in Archaeology,* edited by Sally R. Binford and Lewis R. Binford, pp. 41–48. Aldine, Chicago.
Deliette, Louis
    1934   Memoir concerning the Illinois Country [ca. 1702]. In *The French Foundations 1680–1693,* edited by Theodore C. Pease and Raymond C. Werner, pp. 302–395. Collections, vol. 23. Illinois State Historical Library, Springfield.
DeMallie, Raymond J.
    1988   Lakota Traditionalism: History and Symbol. In *Native North American Interaction Patterns,* edited by Regna Darnell and Michael K. Foster, pp. 2–21. Canadian Museum of Civilization, National Museums of Canada, Hull, Quebec.
Densmore, Frances
    1928   Uses of Plants by the Chippewa Indians. *Forty-fourth Annual Report of the Bureau of American Ethnology for the Years 1926–1927,* pp. 275–397. Smithsonian Institution, Washington, D.C.
    1929   *Chippewa Customs.* Bulletin No. 86. Bureau of American Ethnology, Smithsonian Institution, Washington, D.C.
    1950   Communication with the Dead as Practiced by the American Indians. *Man: A Monthly Record of Anthropological Science* 50:40–41.
De Vore, Steven L.
    1990   The Cribb's Crib Site (13WA105): The Archaeology and Ecology of

an Oneota Village in the Central Des Moines Valley. *Journal of the Iowa Archaeological Society* 37:46–87.

Dial, Adolph L.
  1978   Death in the Life of Native Americans. *Indian Historian* 11(3):32–37.

Dice, L. R.
  1943   *The Biotic Provinces of North America.* University of Michigan Press, Ann Arbor.

Dickason, O. P.
  1974   *Indian Arts in Canada.* Department of Indian Affairs and Northern Development, Ottawa.

Dixon, Roland B.
  1908   Some Aspects of the American Shaman. *Journal of American Folklore* 21:1–12.

Dobbs, Clark A.
  1982   Oneota Origins and Development: The Radiocarbon Evidence. In *Oneota Studies,* edited by Guy E. Gibbon, pp. 91–105. Publications in Anthropology No. 1. University of Minnesota, Minneapolis.

Doershuk, John F.
  1985   *Washington Irving 1985: Subsistence and Settlement at an Upper Mississippian Langford Tradition Site.* Paper presented at the Midwest Archaeological Conference, East Lansing, Michigan.
  1988   *Plenemuk Mound and the Archaeology of Will County.* Illinois Cultural Resources Study No. 3. Illinois Historic Preservation Agency, Springfield.

Doob, Christopher Bates
  1988   *Sociology: An Introduction.* 2nd ed. Holt, Rinehart and Winston, New York.

Dorsey, James Owen
  1883   The Religion of the Omahas and Ponkas. *American Antiquarian* 5(3):271–275.
  1894   A Study of Siouan Cults. *Eleventh Annual Report of the Bureau of American Ethnology for the Years 1889–'90,* pp. 351–544. Smithsonian Institution, Washington, D.C.

Dorwin, John T.
  1971   *The Bowen Site: An Archaeological Study of Culture Process in the Late Prehistory of Central Indiana.* Prehistory Research Series, vol. 4, no. 4. Indiana Historical Society, Indianapolis.

Douglas, John G.
  1976   *Collins: A Late Woodland Ceremonial Complex in the Woodfordian Northeast.* Unpublished Ph.D. dissertation, Department of Anthropology, University of Illinois, Urbana.

Driver, Harold E.
  1961   *Indians of North America.* University of Chicago Press, Chicago.

Drooker, Penelope B.
  1992   *Mississippian Village Textiles at Wickliffe.* University of Alabama Press, Tuscaloosa.
  1997   *The View from Madisonville: Protohistoric Western Fort Ancient Interaction Patterns.* Memoirs No. 31. Museum of Anthropology, University of Michigan, Ann Arbor.

Dugan, Kathleen M.

1985 *The Vision Quest of the Plains Indians: Its Spiritual Significance.* Studies in American Religion, vol. 13. Edwin Mellen Press, Lewiston, New York.

Early, Ann M.

1970 *NAL 1970 Archaeological Survey: The Prehistoric Occupations of the National Accelerator Site.* Report on file, Illinois State Historic Preservation Office, Illinois Historic Preservation Agency, Springfield.

1973 *Upper Mississippian Occupation of the Fox River Valley.* Unpublished Ph.D. dissertation, Department of Anthropology, University of Massachusetts, Amherst.

Eells, Myron

1889 The Thunder Bird. *American Anthropologist* 2(4):329–336.

Ehleringer, James R.

1978 Implications of Quantum Yield Differences on the Distribution of C3 and C4 Grasses. *Oecologia* 31:255–267.

Ember, Carol R., and Melvin Ember

1990 *Anthropology.* 6th ed. Prentice Hall, Englewood Cliffs, New Jersey.

Emerson, Alice M.

1993 The Role of Body Part Utility in Small-Scale Hunting under Two Strategies of Carcass Recovery. In *From Bones to Behavior: Ethnoarchaeological and Experimental Contributions to the Interpretations of Faunal Remains,* edited by Jean Hudson, pp. 138–155. Occasional Paper No. 21. Center for Archaeological Investigations, Southern Illinois University, Carbondale.

Emerson, Thomas E.

1991a The Apple River Mississippian Culture of Northwestern Illinois. In *Cahokia and the Hinterlands: Middle Mississippian Cultures of the Midwest,* edited by Thomas E. Emerson and R. Barry Lewis, pp. 164–182. University of Illinois Press, Urbana.

1991b Some Perspectives on Cahokia and the Northern Mississippian Expansion. In *Cahokia and the Hinterlands: Middle Mississippian Cultures of the Midwest,* edited by Thomas E. Emerson and R. Barry Lewis, pp. 221–236. University of Illinois Press, Urbana.

1999 The Langford Tradition and the Process of Tribalization on the Mississippian Borders. *Midcontinental Journal* 24(1):3–56.

Emerson, Thomas E., and James A. Brown

1992 The Late Prehistory and Protohistory of Illinois. In *Calumet Fleur-De-Lys: Archaeology of Indian and French Contact in the Midcontinent,* edited by John A. Walthall and Thomas E. Emerson, pp. 77–128. Smithsonian Institution Press, Washington, D.C.

Esarey, Duane, and Sharron K. Santure

1990 The Morton Site Oneota Component and the Bold Counselor Phase. In *Archaeological Investigations at the Morton Village and Norris Farms 36 Cemetery,* edited by Sharron K. Santure, Alan D. Harn, and Duane Esarey, pp. 162–166. Reports of Investigations No. 45. Illinois State Museum, Springfield.

Fago, Don
    1982   *Distribution and Relative Abundance of Fishes in Wisconsin. I. Greater Rock River Basin.* Technical Bulletin No. 136. Wisconsin Department of Natural Resources, Madison.

Falassi, Alessandro
    1967   Festival: Definition and Morphology. In *Time out of Time: Essays on the Festival,* edited by Alessandro Falassi, pp. 1–10. University of New Mexico Press, Albuquerque.

Faulkner, Charles H.
    1964   The Radar Site. *Central States Archeological Journal* 11(3):90–96.
    1972   *The Late Prehistoric Occupation of Northwestern Indiana: A Study of the Upper Mississippian Cultures of the Kankakee Valley.* Prehistory Research Series, vol. 5, no. 1. Indiana Historical Society, Indianapolis.

Feest, Christian F.
    1984   Ottawa Bags, Baskets, and Beadwork. In *Beadwork and Textiles of the Ottawa,* by the Harbor Springs Historical Commission, pp. 12–28. Harbor Springs, Michigan.
    1986   *Indians of Northeastern North America.* E. J. Brill, Leiden.

Fehrenbacher, J. B., G. O. Walker, and H. L. Wascher
    1967   *Soils of Illinois.* Bulletin No. 725. Agricultural Experiment Station, University of Illinois, Urbana.

Feinman, Gary, and Jill Neitzel
    1984   Too Many Types: An Overview of Sedentary Prestate Societies in the Americas. In *Advances in Archaeological Method and Theory,* vol. 7, edited by Michael B. Schiffer, pp. 39–102. Academic Press, New York.

Fell, Egbert W.
    1955   *Flora of Winnebago County, Illinois: An Annotated List of the Vascular Plants.* Nature Conservancy, Washington, D.C.

Fell, Egbert W., and George B. Fell
    1958   The Ravine Flora of Winnebago County, Illinois. *Transactions of the Illinois State Academy of Science* 50:83–89.

Fenner, Gloria J.
    1963   The Plum Island Site, La Salle County, Illinois. In *Chicago Area Archaeology,* edited by Elaine A. Bluhm, pp. 1–105. Bulletin No. 4. Illinois Archaeological Survey, University of Illinois, Urbana.

Finney, Fred A., and James B. Stoltman
    1991   The Fred Edwards Site: A Case of Stirling Phase Culture Contact in Southwestern Wisconsin. In *New Perspectives on Cahokia: Views from the Periphery,* edited by James B. Stoltman, pp. 229–252. Monographs in World Archaeology No. 2. Prehistory Press, Madison, Wisconsin.

Fischman, Joshua
    1996   California Social Climbers: Low Water Prompts High Status. *Science* 272:811–812.

Fishel, Richard L.
    1995   *Excavations at the Dixon Site (13WD8): Correctionville Phase Oneota in Northwest Iowa.* Contract Completion Report 442. Office of the State Archaeologist, University of Iowa, Iowa City.

Fitting, James E.
    1975   *The Archaeology of Michigan: A Guide to the Prehistory of the Great*

Lakes Region. Cranbrook Institute of Science, Bloomfield Hills, Michigan.

Fletcher, Alice C.
1904　The Hako: A Pawnee Ceremony. *Twenty-second Annual Report,* Pt. 2, pp. 13–368. Bureau of American Ethnology, Smithsonian Institution, Washington, D.C.
1907　Mourning. In *Handbook of American Indians North of Mexico, Part I,* edited by Frederick Webb Hodge, pp. 951–953. Bulletin No. 30. Bureau of American Ethnology, Smithsonian Institution, Washington, D.C.

Fletcher, Alice C., and Francis La Flesche
1911　The Omaha Tribe. *Twenty-seventh Annual Report of the Bureau of American Ethnology for the Years 1905–1906,* pp. 17–672. Smithsonian Institution, Washington, D.C.

Ford, Pamela J.
1989　Molluscan Assemblages from Archaeological Deposits. *Geoarchaeology: An International Journal* 4(2):157–173.

Foss, Dorothy B., and Paul W. Parmalee
1990　Animal Remains from the Hoxie Farm Site (11CK-4). In *At the Edge of Prehistory: Huber Phase Archaeology in the Chicago Area,* edited by James A. Brown and Patricia J. O'Brien, pp. 108–109. Center for American Archeology, Kampsville, Illinois.

Foucault, Michel
1983　The Subject of Power. In *Michel Foucault: Beyond Structuralism and Hermeneutics,* 2nd ed., edited by Hubert L. Dreyfus and Paul Rabinow, pp. 208–226. University of Chicago Press, Chicago.

Fowler, Melvin L.
1952　The Robinson Reserve Site. *Journal of the Illinois State Archaeological Society* 2(2–3):50–62.

Fowler, Melvin L., and Robert A. Birmingham
1974　An Archaeological Survey of the Rock River Valley in Illinois. In *Preliminary Report of 1973 Historic Sites Survey: Archaeological Reconnaissance of Selected Areas of the State of Illinois, Part I, Section A,* pp. 66–74. Illinois Archaeological Survey, University of Illinois, Urbana.
1975　An Archaeological Survey of the Rock River Valley in Illinois. In *Preliminary Report of 1974 Historic Sites Survey: Archaeological Reconnaissance of Selected Areas of the State of Illinois, Part I, Section A,* pp. 72–78. Illinois Archaeological Survey, University of Illinois, Urbana.

Fowler, Melvin L., and Gordon R. Peters
1972　An Archaeological Survey of the Rock River Valley in Illinois. In *Preliminary Report of 1972 Historic Sites Survey: Archaeological Reconnaissance of Selected Areas of the State of Illinois, Part I, Section B,* pp. 76–81. Illinois Archaeological Survey, University of Illinois, Urbana.

Fritz, John M., and Fred T. Plog
1970　The Nature of Archaeological Explanation. *American Antiquity* 35:405–412.

Gabaccia, Donna R.
1998　*We Are What We Eat: Ethnic Food and the Making of Americans.* Harvard University Press, Cambridge, Massachusetts.

Gajewski, K.
1988   Late Holocene Climate Changes in Eastern North America Estimated from Pollen Data. *Quaternary Research* 29:255–262.

Garland, Elizabeth B.
1991   *The Wymer-West Knoll (20BE132), an Early Mississippian Component on the Lower St. Joseph River in Southwestern Michigan: A Preliminary Report*. Paper presented at the Midwest Archaeological Conference, La Crosse, Wisconsin.

Geis, James W., and William R. Boggess
1968   The Prairie Peninsula: Its Origin and Significance in the Vegetational History of Central Illinois. In *The Quaternary of Illinois,* edited by Robert E. Bergstrom, pp. 89–95. University of Illinois College of Agriculture, Urbana.

Gibbon, Guy E.
1972   Cultural Dynamics and Development of the Oneota Life-way in Wisconsin. *American Antiquity* 37(2):166–185.

1974   A Model of Mississippian Development and Its Implication for the Red Wing Area. In *Aspects of Upper Great Lakes Anthropology: Papers in Honor of Lloyd A. Wilford,* edited by Elden Johnson, pp. 129–137. Minnesota Prehistoric Archaeology Series No. 1. Minnesota Historical Society, St. Paul.

1979   *The Mississippian Occupation of the Red Wing Area*. Minnesota Prehistoric Archaeology Series No. 13. Minnesota Historical Society, St. Paul.

1986   The Mississippian Tradition: Oneota Culture. *Wisconsin Archeologist* 67(3–4):314–338.

1995   Oneota at the Periphery: Trade, Political Power, and Ethnicity in Northern Minnesota and on the Northeastern Plains in the Late Prehistoric Period. In *Oneota Archaeology: Past, Present, and Future,* edited by William Green, pp. 175–199. Office of the State Archaeologist, University of Iowa, Iowa City.

Gibbon, Guy E. (editor)
1982   *Oneota Studies*. Publications in Anthropology No. 1. University of Minnesota, Minneapolis.

Gifford-Gonzalez, Diane
1993   Gaps in Zooarchaeological Analyses of Butchery: Is Gender an Issue? In *From Bones to Behavior: Ethnoarchaeological and Experimental Contributions to the Interpretation of Faunal Remains,* edited by Jean Hudson, pp. 181–199. Occasional Paper No. 21. Center for Archaeological Investigations, Southern Illinois University, Carbondale.

Gilbert, B. Miles
1990   *Mammalian Osteology*. Missouri Archaeological Society, Columbia.

Gilbert, B. Miles, Larry D. Martin, and Howard G. Savage
1985   *Avian Osteology*. B. M. Gilbert, Laramie, Wyoming.

Gill, Sam D.
1987   *Native American Religious Action: A Performance Approach to Religion*. University of South Carolina Press, Columbia.

Gill, Sam D., and Irene F. Sullivan
1992   *Dictionary of Native American Mythology*. Oxford University Press, New York.

Gillespie, Susan D.
1993   Power, Pathways, and Appropriations in Mesoamerican Art. In *Imagery and Creativity: Ethnoaesthetics and Art Worlds in the Americas,* edited by Dorothea S. Whitten and Norman E. Whitten, Jr., pp. 67–108. University of Arizona Press, Tucson.

Gillette, Charles E.
1949   Late Woodland Occupations of the Fisher Site, Will County, Illinois. *Transactions of the Illinois State Academy of Science* 42:35–40.

Gilmore, Melvin R.
1932   The Sacred Bundles of the Arikara. *Papers of the Michigan Academy of Science, Arts, and Letters* 31:33–50.

Glenn, Elizabeth J.
1974   *Physical Affiliations of the Oneota Peoples.* Report No. 7. Office of the State Archaeologist, University of Iowa, Iowa City.

Gluckman, Max
1968   Social Beliefs and Individual Thinking in Tribal Society. In *Theory in Anthropology,* edited by Robert A. Manners and David Kaplan, pp. 453–465. Aldine, New York.

Goldman, Charles R., and Alexander J. Horne
1983   *Limnology.* McGraw-Hill, New York.

Gordon, Arnold L., Stephen E. Zebiak, and Kirk Bryan
1992   Climate Variability and the Atlantic Ocean. *EOS* 73:161–165.

Goudie, Andrew
1992   *Environmental Change.* 3rd ed. Clarendon, New York.

Gradwohl, David M.
1974   Archaeology of the Central Des Moines River Valley: A Preliminary Summary. In *Aspects of Upper Great Lakes Anthropology: Papers in Honor of Lloyd A. Wilford,* edited by Elden Johnson, pp. 90–102. Minnesota Prehistoric Archaeology Series No. 11. Minnesota Historical Society, St. Paul.
1982   *Shelling Corn in the Prairie-Plains: Archaeological Evidence and Ethnographic Parallels beyond the Pun.* Smithsonian Contributions to Anthropology No. 30. Smithsonian Institution, Washington, D.C.

Grantham, D. R.
1980   *Soil Survey of Winnebago and Boone Counties, Illinois.* United States Department of Agriculture, Soil Conservation Service, Illinois Agricultural Experiment Station. The Service, Washington, D.C.

Grayson, Donald K.
1984   *Quantitative Zooarchaeology: Topics in the Analysis of Archaeological Faunas.* Academic Press, Orlando, Florida.

Green, William
1987   *Between Hopewell and Mississippian: Late Woodland in the Prairie Peninsula as Viewed from the Western Illinois Uplands.* Unpublished Ph.D. dissertation, Department of Anthropology, University of Wisconsin, Madison.

Greller, Andrew M.
1988   Deciduous Forest. In *North American Terrestrial Vegetation,* edited by Michael G. Barbour and William D. Billings, pp. 287–316. Cambridge University Press, Cambridge.

Grieder, Terence
    1975   The Interpretation of Ancient Symbols. *American Anthropologist* 77:849–855.
Griffin, James B.
    1943   *The Fort Ancient Aspect: Its Cultural and Chronological Position in Mississippi Valley Archaeology.* University of Michigan Press, Ann Arbor.
    1960   A Hypothesis for the Prehistory of the Winnebago. In *Culture in History: Essays in Honor of Paul Radin,* edited by Stanley Diamond, pp. 809–868. Columbia University Press, New York.
    1967   Eastern North American Archaeology: A Summary. *Science* 156:175–191.
    1992   Fort Ancient Has No Class: The Absence of an Elite Group in Mississippian Societies in the Central Ohio Valley. In *Lords of the Southeast: Social Inequality and the Native Elites of Southeastern North America,* edited by Alex W. Barker and Timothy R. Pauketat, pp. 53–59. Archeological Papers No. 3. American Anthropological Association, Washington, D.C.
    1993   Cahokia Interaction with Contemporary Southeastern and Eastern Societies. *Midcontinental Journal of Archaeology* 18(1):3–17.
Griffin, John W.
    1944   New Evidence from the Fisher Site. *Transactions of the Illinois State Academy of Science* 37:37–40.
    1946   *The Upper Mississippian Occupation of the Fisher Site.* Unpublished Master's thesis, Department of Anthropology, University of Chicago, Chicago.
    1948   Upper Mississippi at the Fisher Site. *American Antiquity* 14(2):124–126.
Grinnell, George B.
    1893   Pawnee Mythology. *Journal of American Folklore* 6:113–130.
Grist, N. P., T. C. Morelock, C. M. Tucker, and W. F. English
    1950   *Missouri: Its Resources, People, and Institutions.* Curators of the University of Missouri, Columbia.
Guss, David M.
    1989   *To Weave and Sing: Art, Symbol, and Narrative in the South American Rain Forest.* University of California Press, Berkeley.
Hadlock, Wendell S.
    1947   War among the Northeastern Woodland Indians. *American Anthropologist* 405:204–221.
Hale, Horatio
    1963   *The Iroquois Book of Rites.* University of Toronto Press, Toronto.
Hall, Robert L.
    1962   *The Archaeology of Carcajou Point.* University of Wisconsin Press, Madison.
    1973   *The Cahokia Presence outside of the American Bottom.* Paper presented at the Central States Anthropological Society Meetings, St. Louis, Missouri.
    1977   An Anthropocentric Perspective for Eastern United States Prehistory. *American Antiquity* 42:499–518.

1986 Upper Mississippi and Middle Mississippi Relationships. *Wisconsin Archeologist* 67(3–4):365–370.

1987a Type Description of Starved Rock Collared. *Wisconsin Archeologist* 68(1):65–70.

1987b Calumet Ceremonialism, Mourning Ritual, and Mechanisms of Inter-Tribal Trade. In *Mirror and Metaphor: Material and Social Constructions of Reality,* edited by D. W. Ingersoll, Jr., and G. Bronitsky, pp. 29–43. University Press of America, Lanham, Maryland.

1991 Cahokia Identity and Interaction Models of Cahokia Mississippian. In *Cahokia and the Hinterlands: Middle Mississippian Cultures of the Midwest,* edited by Thomas E. Emerson and R. Barry Lewis, pp. 3–34. University of Illinois Press, Urbana.

1993 Red Banks, Oneota, and the Winnebago: Views from a Distant Rock. *Wisconsin Archeologist* 74(1–4):10–79.

1997 *An Archaeology of the Soul: North American Indian Belief and Ritual.* University of Illinois Press, Urbana.

Hallowell, A. Irving

1926 Bear Ceremonialism in the Northern Hemisphere. *American Anthropologist* 28:1–175.

1934 Some Empirical Aspects of Northern Saulteaux Religion. *American Anthropologist* 36:389–404.

1947 Myth, Culture, and Personality. *American Anthropologist* 49:544–556.

1952 Ojibwa Personality and Acculturation. In *Acculturation in the Americas: Proceedings and Selected Papers of the 29th International Congress of Americanists,* edited by Sol Tax, pp. 105–112. University of Chicago Press, Chicago.

1967 Ojibwa World View. In *The North American Indians: A Sourcebook,* edited by Roger C. Owen, James J. F. Deetz, and Anthony D. Fisher, pp. 208–235. Macmillan, New York.

1992 *The Ojibwa of Berens River, Manitoba: Ethnography into History.* Harcourt Brace Jovanovich College Publishers, Fort Worth, Texas.

Harn, Alan D.

1980 *The Prehistory of Dickson Mounds: The Dickson Excavation.* Reports of Investigations No. 36. Illinois State Museum, Springfield.

Harrington, Mark Raymond

1914 *Sacred Bundles of the Sac and Fox Indians.* Anthropological Publications, vol. 4, no. 2. University of Pennsylvania, Philadelphia.

1941 Indian Tribes of the Plains II. *Masterkey* 15(5):168–177.

Harrod, Howard L.

1987 *Renewing the World: Plains Indian Religion and Morality.* University of Arizona Press, Tucson.

Hart, John P.

1990 Modeling Oneota Agricultural Production: A Cross-Cultural Evaluation. *Current Anthropology* 31:569–577.

Hart, John P., and Robert J. Jeske

1987 *Report on a Systematic Archaeological Survey of Portions of the Illinois-Michigan Canal National Heritage Corridor, in Cook, Will,*

Du Page, Grundy, and La Salle Counties, Illinois. Report submitted to the National Park Service, Evanston, Illinois.

1991   Models of Prehistoric Site Location for the Upper Illinois River Valley. *Illinois Archaeology* 3(1):3–22.

Hartland, E. Sidney
1912   Death and Disposal of the Dead. In *Encyclopaedia of Religion and Ethics,* edited by James Hastings, pp. 411–444. T. & T. Clark, Edinburgh.

Hartmann, Ernest
1998   *Dreams and Nightmares: The New Theory on the Origin and Meaning of Dreams.* Plenum Trade, New York.

Harvey, Amy E.
1979   *Oneota Culture in Northwestern Iowa.* Report No. 12. Office of the State Archaeologist, University of Iowa, Iowa City.

Hastorf, Christine A., and Sissel Johannessen
1991   Understanding Changing People/Plant Relationships in the Prehispanic Andes. In *Processual and Postprocessual Archaeologies: Multiple Ways of Knowing the Past,* edited by Robert W. Preucel, pp. 140–155. Occasional Paper No. 10. Center for Archaeological Investigations, Southern Illinois University, Carbondale.

Henderson, A. Gwynn, David Pollack, and Christopher A. Turnbow
1992   Chronology and Cultural Patterns. In *Fort Ancient Cultural Dynamics in the Middle Ohio Valley,* edited by A. Gwynn Henderson, pp. 253–280. Monographs in World Archaeology No. 8. Prehistory Press, Madison, Wisconsin.

Henning, Dale R.
1970   Development and Interrelationships of Oneota Culture in the Lower Missouri River Valley. *Missouri Archaeologist* 32:1–180.

1995   Oneota Evolution and Interactions: A Perspective from the Wever Terrace, Southeast Iowa. In *Oneota Archaeology: Past, Present, and Future,* edited by William Green, pp. 65–88. Report No. 20. Office of the State Archaeologist, University of Iowa, Iowa City.

Henshaw, H. W.
1910   Pictographs. In *Handbook of American Indians North of Mexico, Part II,* edited by Frederick Webb Hodge, pp. 242–245. Bulletin No. 30. Bureau of American Ethnology, Smithsonian Institution, Washington, D.C.

Herman, Mary W.
1967   The Social Aspects of Huron Property. In *The North American Indians: A Sourcebook,* edited by Roger C. Owen, James J. F. Deetz, and Anthony D. Fisher, pp. 581–597. Macmillan, New York.

Herold, Elaine Bluhm, Patricia J. O'Brien, and David J. Wenner, Jr.
1990   Hoxie Farm and Huber: Two Upper Mississippian Archaeological Sites in Cook County, Illinois. In *At the Edge of Prehistory: Huber Phase Archaeology in the Chicago Area,* edited by James A. Brown and Patricia J. O'Brien, pp. 3–119. Center for American Archeology, Kampsville, Illinois.

Hewitt, J. N. B.
1889   Sacred Numbers among the Iroquois. *American Anthropologist*

2:165–166.

1895 The Iroquoian Concept of the Soul. *Journal of American Folklore* 8(28):107–116.

1902 Orenda and a Definition of Religion. *American Anthropologist* 4:33–46.

1910 Potawatomi. In *Handbook of American Indians North of Mexico, Part I,* edited by Frederick Webb Hodge, pp. 289–291. Bulletin No. 30. Bureau of American Ethnology, Smithsonian Institution, Washington, D.C.

1911 Mythology. In *Handbook of American Indians North of Mexico, Part II,* edited by Frederick Webb Hodge, pp. 964–972. Bulletin No. 30. Bureau of American Ethnology, Smithsonian Institution, Washington, D.C.

Higgins, Michael J.

1980 *An Analysis of the Faunal Remains from the Schwerdt Site, a Late Prehistoric Encampment in Allegan County, Michigan.* Unpublished Master's thesis, Department of Anthropology, Western Michigan University, Kalamazoo.

Highwater, J.

1983 *Arts of the Indian Americas: Leaves from the Sacred Tree.* Harper & Row, Publishers, New York.

Hodder, Ian

1991 Postprocessual Archaeology and the Current Debate. In *Processual and Postprocessual Archaeologies: Multiple Ways of Knowing the Past,* edited by Robert W. Preucel, pp. 30–41. Occasional Paper No. 10. Center for Archaeological Investigations, Southern Illinois University, Carbondale.

1992 *Theory and Practice in Archaeology.* Routledge, London and New York.

Hodder, Ian, Michael Shanks, Alexandra Alexandri, Victor Buchli, John Carman, Jonathan Last, and Gavin Lucas (eds.)

1995 *Interpreting Archaeology.* Routledge, London and New York.

Hodge, Frederick Webb (editor)

1910–11 *Handbook of American Indians North of Mexico, Parts I and II.* Bulletin No. 30. Bureau of American Ethnology, Smithsonian Institution, Washington, D.C.

Hoffman, Walter James

1891 The Midewiwin or "Grand Medicine Society" of the Ojibwa. *Seventh Annual Report of the Bureau of American Ethnology for the Years 1885–86,* pp. 143–300. Smithsonian Institution, Washington, D.C.

1896 The Menomini Indians. *Fourteenth Annual Report of the Bureau of American Ethnology,* Pt. 2, pp. 3–328. Smithsonian Institution, Washington, D.C.

Hoffmeister, Donald F.

1989 *Mammals of Illinois.* University of Illinois Press, Urbana.

Hollinger, R. Eric, and Dale R. Henning

1998 *The Cultural Context of Oneota Incised Stone Art.* Paper presented at the Midwest Archaeological Conference, Muncie, Indiana.

Holmes, William Henry
    1883   Art in Shell of the Ancient Americans. *Second Annual Report of the Bureau of American Ethnology,* pp. 179–305. Smithsonian Institution, Washington, D.C.
    1903   Aboriginal Pottery of the Eastern United States. *Twentieth Annual Report of the Bureau of American Ethnology,* pp. 1–237. Smithsonian Institution, Washington, D.C.
    1911   Cross. In *Handbook of American Indians North of Mexico, Part I,* edited by Frederick Webb Hodge, pp. 365–367. Bulletin No. 30. Bureau of American Ethnology, Smithsonian Institution, Washington, D.C.

Holsbeke, Mireille
    1997   The Object as Mediator: On the Transcendental Meaning of Art in Traditional Cultures. In *The Object as Mediator,* edited by Mireille Holsbeke, pp. 11–18. Etnografisch Museum Antwerp.

Horner, George R.
    1947   An Upper Mississippi House-Pit from the Fisher Village Site: Further Evidence. *Transactions of the Illinois State Academy of Science* 40:26–29.

Hough, Walter
    1911   Eagle. In *Handbook of American Indians North of Mexico, Part I,* edited by Frederick Webb Hodge, pp. 409–410. Bulletin No. 30. Bureau of American Ethnology, Smithsonian Institution, Washington, D.C.

Howard, James H.
    1960   When They Worship the Underwater Panther: A Prairie Potawatomi Bundle Ceremony. *Southwestern Journal of Anthropology* 16(2):217–224.

Hudson, Charles
    1976   *The Southeastern Indians.* University of Tennessee Press, Knoxville.

Huff, F. A., and S. A. Changnon, Jr.
    1963   *Drought Climatology of Illinois.* Illinois State Water Survey Bulletin 50, Champaign.

Hultkrantz, Åke
    1981   *Belief and Worship in Native North America,* edited by Charles Vecsey. Syracuse University Press, Syracuse, New York.
    1983   *The Study of American Indian Religions,* edited by Christopher Vecsey. Crossroad Publishing, New York, and Scholars Press, Chico, California.
    1986   The Peril of Visions: Changes of Vision Patterns among the Wind River Shoshoni. *History of Religions* 26(1):34–46.

Hunt, C. B.
    1977   *Natural Regions of the United States and Canada.* W. H. Freeman, San Francisco.

Hurlburt, Isobel
    1977   *Faunal Remains from Fort White Earth NW Co. (1810–1813).* Provincial Museum of Alberta, Human History Occasional Paper No. 1. Alberta Culture, Historical Resources Division, Edmonton.

Hurley, William Michael
1970 *The Wisconsin Effigy Mound Tradition.* Unpublished Ph. D. dissertation, Department of Anthropology, University of Wisconsin, Madison.
Illinois Department of Natural Resources, Division of Energy and Environmental Assessment
1996 *The Rock River Country: An Inventory of the Region's Resources.* Illinois Department of Natural Resources, Office of Realty and Environmental Planning, Springfield.
Illinois Technical Advisory Committee on Water Resources
1967 *Water for Illinois: A Plan for Action.* Illinois Technical Advisory Committee on Water Resources, Springfield.
Ingersoll, Jr., D. W., and G. Bronitsky
1987 Introduction. In *Mirror and Metaphor: Material and Social Constructions of Reality,* edited by D. W. Ingersoll, Jr., and G. Bronitsky, pp. 1–16. University Press of America, Lanham, Maryland.
Ingold, Tim
1993 Globes and Spheres: The Topology of Environmentalism. In *Environmentalism: The View from Anthropology,* edited by Kay Milton, pp. 31–42. Routledge, London and New York.
Jackson, Douglas K.
1992a Ceramics. In *The Sponemann Site 2: The Mississippian and Oneota Occupations (11-Ms-517),* by Douglas K. Jackson, Andrew C. Fortier, and Joyce A. Williams, pp. 125–215. American Bottom Archaeology FAI-270 Site Reports 24. University of Illinois Press, Urbana.
1992b Interpretation. In *The Sponemann Site 2: The Mississippian and Oneota Occupations (11-Ms-517),* by Douglas K. Jackson, Andrew C. Fortier, and Joyce A. Williams, pp. 511–516. American Bottom Archaeology FAI-270 Site Reports 24. University of Illinois Press, Urbana.
Jackson, Douglas K., Andrew C. Fortier, and Joyce A. Williams
1992 Research Design and Analytical Methods. In *The Sponemann Site 2: The Mississippian and Oneota Occupations (11-Ms-517),* by Douglas K. Jackson, Andrew C. Fortier, and Joyce A. Williams, pp. 29–44. American Bottom Archaeology FAI-270 Site Reports 24. University of Illinois Press, Urbana.
Jackson, Hartley H. T.
1961 *Mammals of Wisconsin.* University of Wisconsin Press, Madison.
Jackson, Jean E.
1983 *The Fish People: Linguistic Exogamy and Tukanoan Identity in Northwest Amazonia.* Cambridge University Press, Cambridge.
James, E. O.
1927 The Concept of the Soul in North America. *Folk-Lore* 38:338–357.
Jans-Langel, Carmen, K. Kris Hirst, and Xang Jun Shan
1995 Faunal Remains. In *Excavations at the Dixon Site (13WD8): Correctionville Phase Oneota in Northwest Iowa,* by Richard L. Fishel, pp. 56–69. Contract Completion Report 442. Office of the State Archaeologist, University of Iowa, Iowa City.
Jennings, Jesse D.
1974 *Prehistory of North America.* 2nd ed. McGraw-Hill, New York.

Jeske, Robert J.
  1989   Horticultural Technology and Social Interaction at the Edge of the Prairie Peninsula. *Illinois Archaeology* 1(2):103–120.
  1990   Langford Tradition Subsistence, Settlement, and Technology. *Midcontinental Journal of Archaeology* 15(2):221–249.

Jeske, Robert J., and John P. Hart
  1988   *Report on Test Excavations at Four Sites in the Illinois and Michigan Canal National Heritage Corridor, La Salle and Grundy Counties, Illinois.* Contribution No. 6. Northwestern Archaeological Center, Northwestern University, Evanston.

Johnson, A., and T. Earle
  1987   *The Evolution of Human Society: From Forager Group to Agrarian State.* Stanford University Press, Stanford.

Johnston, Basil H.
  1995   *The Manitous: The Spiritual World of the Ojibway.* HarperCollins, New York.

Jolley, Robert L.
  1983   North American Historic Sites Zooarchaeology. *Historical Archaeology* 17(2):64–79.

Jones, Colin, and Roy Porter (editors)
  1994   *Reassessing Foucault: Power, Medicine, and the Body.* Routledge, London and New York.

Jones, James R. III
  1989   *Degrees of Acculturation at Two 18th Century Aboriginal Villages near Lafayette, Tippecanoe County, Indiana: Ethnohistoric and Archaeological Perspectives.* Unpublished Ph.D. dissertation, Department of Anthropology, Indiana University, Bloomington.

Jones, J. K., Jr., D. C. Carter, H. H. Genoways, R. S. Hoffman, and D. W. Rice
  1982   *Revised Checklist of North American Mammals North of Mexico.* Occasional Papers 80. Texas Tech University Museum, Lubbock.

Jones, William
  1905   The Algonkin Manitou. *Journal of American Folklore* 18:183–190.

Keene, Arthur S.
  1981   *Prehistoric Foraging in a Temperate Forest: A Linear Programming Model.* Academic Press, New York.
  1983   Biology, Behavior, and Borrowing: A Critical Examination of Optimal Foraging Theory in Archaeology. In *Archaeological Hammers and Theories,* edited by James A. Moore and Arthur S. Keene, pp. 137–155. Academic Press, New York.

Kelly, John E., Fred A. Finney, Dale L. McElrath, and Steven J. Ozuk
  1984   Late Woodland Period. In *American Bottom Archaeology,* edited by Charles J. Bareis and James W. Porter, pp. 104–127. University of Illinois Press, Urbana.

Kelly, Lucretia S.
  1990   Oneota Faunal Remains. In *Archaeological Data Recovery at Five Prehistoric Sites, Lake Red Rock, Marion County, Iowa,* vol. 1, by Michael J. McNerney and Charles R. Moffat, pp. 369–399. Report No. 133. Cultural Resources Management, American Resources Group, Carbondale, Illinois.

1992   Faunal Remains. In *The Sponemann Site 2: The Mississippian and Oneota Occupations (11-Ms-517)*, by Douglas K. Jackson, Andrew C. Fortier, and Joyce A. Williams, pp. 497–504. American Bottom Archaeology FAI-270 Site Reports 24. University of Illinois Press, Urbana.

Kempton, John P., Richard C. Berg, and Leon R. Follmer
1985   Revision of the Stratigraphy and Nomenclature of Glacial Deposits in Central Northern Illinois. In *Illinoian and Wisconsinan Stratigraphy and Environments in Northern Illinois: The Altonian Revised*, pp. 1–19. Illinois State Geological Survey Division Guidebook 19, Illinois Department of Energy and Natural Resources, Champaign.

Kepecs, Susan
1997   Introduction to New Approaches to Combining the Archaeological and Historical Records. *Journal of Archaeological Method and Theory* 4(3/4):193–198.

Keyes, Charles Reuben
1927   Prehistoric Man in Iowa. *Palimpest* 8(6):215–229. State Historical Society of Iowa, Iowa City.

Kind, Robert, and Lynne Goldstein
1982   Early Vegetation and Its Effects on Man. In *Archaeology in the Southeastern Wisconsin Glaciated Region: Phase I*. University of Wisconsin-Milwaukee.
Archaeological Research Laboratory Reports of Investigations 64.

Kindscher, Kelly
1987   *Edible Wild Plants of the Prairie: An Ethnobotanical Guide*. University Press of Kansas, Lawrence.

King, Frances B.
1984   *Plants, People, and Paleoecology: Biotic Communities and Aboriginal Plant Usage in Illinois*. Scientific Papers Vol. 20. Illinois State Museum, Springfield.

King, J. C. H.
1982   *Thunderbird and Lightening: Indian Life in Northeastern North America, 1600–1900*. British Museum, London.

Kinietz, W. Vernon
1940   *The Indians of the Western Great Lakes, 1615–1760*. Occasional Contributions from the Museum of Anthropology of the University of Michigan No. 10. University of Michigan Press, Ann Arbor.

Klein, Laura F., and Lillian A. Ackerman
1995   Introduction. In *Women and Power in Native North America*, edited by Laura F. Klein and Lillian A. Ackerman, pp. 3–16. University of Oklahoma Press, Norman and London.

Klein, Richard G., and Kathryn Cruz-Uribe
1984   *The Analysis of Animal Bones from Archaeological Sites*. University of Chicago Press, Chicago.

Knapp, A. Bernard (editor)
1992   *Archaeology, Annales, and Ethnohistory*. Cambridge University Press, Cambridge.

Knox, James C.
1983   Responses of River Systems to Holocene Climates. In *Late-Quaternary Environments of the United States*, vol. 2, *The Holocene*, edited

by H. E. Wright, Jr., pp. 26–41. University of Minnesota Press, Minneapolis.

1984   Fluvial Responses to Small Scale Climate Changes. In *Developments and Applications of Geomorphology,* edited by J. E. Costa and P. J. Fleisher, pp. 318–342. Springer-Verlag, Berlin.

1985   Responses of Floods to Holocene Climatic Change in the Upper Mississippi Valley. *Quaternary Research* 23:287–300.

1988   Climatic Influences on Upper Mississippi Valley Floods. In *Flood Geomorphology,* edited by V. R. Baker, R. C. Kochel, and P. C. Patton, pp. 279–300. Wiley, New York.

Koch, Amy
1995   The McIntosh Fauna: Late Prehistoric Exploitation of Lake and Prairie Habitats in the Nebraska Sand Hills. *Plains Anthropologist* 40(151):39–60.

Kohl, Philip L.
1989   The Use and Abuse of World Systems Theory: The Case of the "Pristine" West Asian State. In *Archaeological Thought in America,* edited by C. C. Lamberg-Karlovsky, pp. 218–240. Cambridge University Press, Cambridge.

Kowalewski, Stephen A.
1995   Large-Scale Ecology in Aboriginal Eastern North America. In *Native American Interactions: Multiscalar Anayses and Interpretations in the Eastern Woodlands,* edited by Michael S. Nassaney and Kenneth E. Sassaman, pp. 147–173. University of Tennessee Press, Knoxville.

Kreisa, Paul P.
1993   Oneota Burial Patterns in Eastern Wisconsin. *Midcontinental Journal of Archaeology* 18(1):35–60.

Kullen, Douglas
1994   The Comstock Trace: A Huber Phase Earthwork and Habitation Site near Joliet, Will County, Illinois. *Midcontinental Journal of Archaeology* 19(1):3–38.

La Flesche, Francis
1889   Death and Funeral Customs among the Omahas. *Journal of American Folklore* 2:3–11.

Lame Deer, John (Fire), and Richard Erdoes
1972   *Lame Deer, Seeker of Visions.* Simon and Schuster, New York.

Landes, Ruth
1970   *The Prairie Potawatomi: Tradition and Ritual in the Twentieth Century.* University of Wisconsin Press, Madison.

Langdon, E. Jean Matteson
1992   Introduction: Shamanism and Anthropology. In *Portals of Power: Shamanism in South America,* edited by E. J. M. Matteson and G. Baer, pp. 1–21. University of New Mexico Press, Albuquerque.

Langford, George
1927   The Fisher Mound Group: Successive Aboriginal Occupations near the Mouth of the Illinois River. *American Anthropologist* 29(3):153–206.

1928   Stratified Indian Mounds in Will County. *Transactions of the Illinois State Academy of Science* 20:247–253.

1930　The Fisher Mound and Village Site. *Transactions of the Illinois State Academy of Science* 22:79–92.

Lapham, I. A.
1973　*The Antiquities of Wisconsin, as Surveyed and Described by I. A. Lapham.* AMS Press, New York.

Leach, Edmund
1976　*Culture and Communication: The Logic by Which Symbols Are Connected.* Cambridge University Press, Cambridge.

Lears, T. J. Jackson
1985　The Concept of Cultural Hegemony: Problems and Possibilities. *American Historical Review* 90(3):567–593.

LeBlanc, Steven A.
1973　Two Points of Logic concerning Data, Hypotheses, General Laws, and Systems. In *Research and Theory in Current Archeology,* edited by Charles L. Redman, pp. 199–214. John Wiley & Sons, New York.

Lee, Dorothy
1957　Cultural Factors in Dietary Choice. *American Journal of Clinical Nutrition* 5(2).

Leechman, Douglas
1951　Bone Grease. *American Antiquity* 16(4):355–356.

Leone, Mark P.
1986　Symbolic, Structural, and Critical Archaeology. In *American Archaeology Past and Future: A Celebration of the Society for American Archaeology, 1935–1985,* edited by David J. Meltzer, Don D. Fowler, and Jeremy A. Sabloff, pp. 415–438. Smithsonian Institution Press, Washington.

Levin, Jack, and James Alan Fox
1991　*Elementary Statistics in Social Research.* 5th ed. HarperCollins, New York.

Levinson, David
1996　*Religion: A Cross-Cultural Encyclopedia.* ABC-CLIO, Santa Barbara, California.

Levi-Strauss, Claude
1963　*Structural Anthropology.* Basic Books, New York.

Lewellen, Ted C.
1983　*Political Anthropology: An Introduction.* Bergin & Garvey, Massachusetts.

Lienhardt, Godfrey
1968　Belief and Knowledge. In *Theory in Anthropology,* edited by Robert A. Manners and David Kaplan, pp. 438–453. Aldine, New York.

Lightfoot, Kent G., and Antoinette Martinez
1995　Frontiers and Boundaries in Archaeological Perspective. *Annual Review of Anthropology* 24:471–492.

Lincoln, Bruce
1994　A Lakota Sun Dance and the Problematics of Sociocosmic Reunion. *History of Religions* 33:1–14.

Link, Adolph W.
1995　Symbolism of Certain Oneota Designs and Use of Lifeform Decora-

tion on Upper Mississippi Ceramics. *Wisconsin Archeologist* 76(1–2):2–26.

Lowie, Robert H.
1914   Ceremonialism in North America. *American Anthropologist* 16:602–631.

Lurie, Rochelle
1987   *Robinson Reserve: A Langford Tradition Habitation and Mound Site along the Des Plaines River in Chicago.* Paper presented at the Annual Meeting of the American Anthropological Association, Chicago.
1993   *Robinson Reserve Revisited.* Paper presented at the Midwest Archaeological Conference, Milwaukee, Wisconsin.

Lyman, R. Lee
1994a   Quantitative Units and Terminology in Zooarchaeology. *American Antiquity* 59(1):36–71.
1994b   *Vertebrate Taphonomy.* Cambridge University Press, Cambridge.

McConaughy, Mark A., Terrance J. Martin, and Frances B. King
1993   Late Late Woodland/Mississippian Period Component. In *Rench: A Stratified Site in the Central Illinois River Valley,* edited by Mark A. McConaughy, pp. 76–130. Reports of Investigations No. 49. Illinois State Museum, Springfield.

McCullough, Robert G.
1991   *A Reanalysis of Ceramics from the Bowen Site: Implications for Defining the Oliver Phase of Central Indiana.* Unpublished Master's thesis, Department of Anthropology, Ball State University, Muncie, Indiana.

McGimsey, C. R., M. A. Grahm, E. K. Schroeder, R. W. Graham, M. D. Wiant, and R. Druhot
1985   *An Overview and Predictive Model of Cultural and Paleobiological Resources in the S.C.C. Study Area, Northern Illinois.* Archaeological Program Technical Report No. 85-197-4. Illinois State Museum Society, Springfield.

McGuire, R. H.
1989   The Greater Southwest as a Periphery of Mesoamerica. *In Centre and Periphery: Comparative Studies in Archeology,* edited by T. C. Champion, pp. 40–66. Unwin Hyman, Cambridge.

McIntosh, Wm. Alex
1996   *Sociologies of Food and Nutrition.* Plenum Press, New York.

McKern, Will C.
1931   Wisconsin Pottery. *American Anthropologist* 33(3):283–290.
1933   Local Types and the Regional Distribution of Pottery-Bearing Cultures. *Transactions of the Illinois State Academy of Science* 25(4):84–86.
1935   Certain Culture Classification Problems in Middle Western Archaeology. In *The Indianapolis Archaeological Conference: A Symposium upon the Archaeological Problems of the North Central United States Area.* Circular No. 17. Committee on State Archaeological Surveys, National Research Council, Washington, D.C.
1939   The Midwestern Taxonomic Method as an Aid to Archaeological Culture Study. *American Antiquity* 4:301–313.

1945   Preliminary Report on the Upper Mississippi Phase in Wisconsin. *Bulletin of the Public Museum of the City of Milwaukee* 16(3):109–285. Milwaukee, Wisconsin.

1956   On Willey and Phillips' "Method and Theory in American Archaeology." *American Anthropologist* 58:360–361.

Maher, Thomas O.

1991   Sponemann Phase Ceramics. In *The Sponemann Site: The Formative Emergent Mississippian Sponemann Phase Occupations,* by Andrew C. Fortier, Thomas O. Maher, and Joyce A. Williams, pp. 157–330. American Bottom Archaeology FAI-270 Site Reports 23. University of Illinois Press, Urbana.

Malinowski, Bronislaw

1968   Malinowski on the Kula. In *Economic Anthropology: Readings in Theory and Analysis,* edited by Edward E. LeClair, Jr., and Harold K. Schneider, pp. 17–39. Holt, Rinehart and Winston, New York.

Mallam, R. Clark

1976   *The Iowa Effigy Mound Manifestation: An Interpretive Model.* Report No. 9. Office of the State Archaeologist, University of Iowa, Iowa City.

Mallery, Garrick

1893   Picture-Writing of the American Indians. *Tenth Annual Report of the Bureau of American Ethnology for the Years 1888–89,* pp. 4–822. Government Printing Office, Washington, D.C.

Maltz, Daniel, and JoAllyn Archambault

1995   Gender and Power in Native North America. In *Women and Power in Native North America,* edited by Laura F. Klein and Lillian A. Ackerman, pp. 230–249. University of Oklahoma Press, Norman.

Mansfield, Victor N.

1981   Mandalas and Mesoamerican Pecked Circles. *Current Anthropology* 22(3):269–284.

Markman, Charles W.

1984   *The Cooke Site: A Middle Woodland–Emergent Mississippian Site in Cook County, Illinois.* Paper presented at the Midwest Archaeological Conference, Evanston, Illinois.

1991a   Above the American Bottom: The Late Woodland–Mississippian Transition in Northeast Illinois. In *New Perspectives on Cahokia: Views from the Periphery,* edited by James B. Stoltman. Monographs in World Archaeology No. 2. Prehistory Press, Madison, Wisconsin.

1991b   *Chicago before Prehistory: The Prehistoric Archaeology of a Modern Metropolitan Area.* Studies in Illinois Archaeology No. 7. Illinois Historic Preservation Agency, Springfield.

Marquardt, William H.

1992   Dialectical Archaeology. In *Archaeology Method and Theory,* vol. 4, edited by Michael B. Schiffer, pp. 101–140. Academic Press, New York.

Marshall, Fiona

1993   Food Sharing and the Faunal Record. In *From Bones to Behavior: Ethnoarchaeological and Experimental Contributions to the Interpretations of Faunal Remains,* edited by Jean Hudson, pp. 228–246. Occasional Paper No. 21. Center for Archaeological Investigations, Southern Illinois University, Carbondale.

Marshall, Fiona, and Tom Pilgram
  1991   Meat versus Within-Bone Nutrients: Another Look at the Meaning
          of Body Part Representation in Archaeological Sites. *Journal of Ar-*
          chaeological Science 18:149–163.
  1993   NISP vs. MNI in Quantification of Body-Part Representation.
          American Antiquity 58(2):261–269.
Martin, Terrance J.
  1996   Wais-ke-shaw at Windrose: Animal Exploitation in the "Country of
          Muskrats." In *Investigating the Archaeological Record of the Great*
          Lakes State: Essays in Honor of Elizabeth Baldwin Garland, edited by
          Margaret B. Holman, Janet G. Brashler, and Kathryn E. Parker, pp.
          455–500. New Issues Press, Kalamazoo, Michigan.
Martin, Terrance J., and Mary Carol Masulis
  1993   Faunal Remains from the Weaver Component. In *Rench: A Strati-*
          fied Site in the Central Illinois River Valley, edited by Mark A. Mc-
          Conaughy, pp. 274–307. Reports of Investigations No. 49. Illinois
          State Museum, Springfield.
Martin, Terrance J., and J. C. Richmond
  1994   *A Preliminary Report on Animal Remains Recovered during 1991*
          from Grid D at the Zimmerman Site. Zimmerman Site West Re-
          search for 1991. Ms. on file, Public Service Archaeology Program,
          Urbana.
Mason, Otis Tufton
  1904   *Aboriginal American Basketry: Studies in a Textile Art without Ma-*
          chinery. Annual Report of the Board of Regents of the Smithsonian
          Institution for 1902. Washington, D.C.
Mason, Ronald J.
  1981   *Great Lakes Archaeology.* Academic Press, New York.
Mead, James F., Roslyn B. Alfin-Slater, David R. Howton, and George Popjak
  1986   *Lipids: Chemistry, Biochemistry, and Nutrition.* Plenum Press,
          New York.
Mehrer, Mark W.
  1991   Letter Report for the Phase II Investigations at the McKeown Site
          (11-Wt-215). Submitted to the Illinois Department of Transporta-
          tion, Springfield.
Merriman, R. O.
  1926   The Bison and the Fur Trade. *Queen's Quarterly: A Canadian Re-*
          view 34:78–96.
Michalik, Laura K.
  1982   An Ecological Perspective on the Huber Phase Subsistence-Settle-
          ment System. In *Oneota Studies,* edited by Guy E. Gibbon, pp.
          29–54. Publications in Anthropology No. 1. University of Min-
          nesota, Minneapolis.
Michalik, Laura K., and James A. Brown
  1990   Ceramic Artifacts. In *At the Edge of Prehistory: Huber Phase Archaeology*
          in the Chicago Area, edited by James A. Brown and Patricia J. O'Brien,
          pp. 199–217. Center for American Archeology, Kampsville, Illinois.
Michelson, Truman
  1930   Notes on the Great Sacred Pack of the Thunder Gens of the Fox In-

dians. In *Contributions to Fox Ethnology II,* by Truman Michelson, pp. 47–183. Bulletin No. 95. Bureau of American Ethnology, Smithsonian Institution, Washington, D.C.

Miller, Daniel

1989 The Limits of Dominance. In *Domination and Resistance,* edited by D. Miller, M. Rowlands, and C. Tilley, pp. 63–79. Unwin Hyman, London.

Milner, George R.

1990 *Cultural Dynamics, Data, and Debate: Perspectives from Late Prehistoric Western Illinois.* Paper presented at Mississippian Transformation: Social Change in the Late Prehistoric Midwest, special conference, Purdue University, West Lafayette, Indiana.

1999 Warfare in Prehistoric and Early Historic Eastern North America. *Journal of Archaeological Research* 7(2):105–151.

Milner, George R., Virginia G. Smith, and Eve Anderson

1991 Warfare in Late Prehistoric West-Central Illinois. *American Antiquity* 56(4):581–603.

Milner, George R., Thomas E. Emerson, Mark W. Mehrer, Joyce A. Williams, and Duane Esarey

1984 Mississippian and Oneota Period. In *American Bottom Archaeology,* edited by Charles J. Bareis and James W. Porter, pp. 158–186. University of Illinois Press, Urbana.

Mitchell, W. D.

1948 *Unit Hydrographs in Illinois.* Illinois Department of Public Works and Buildings, Division of Waterways, Urbana.

Moffat, Charles R., and Brad Koldehoff

1990a Excavations at the Wildcat Creek Site (13MA209). In *Archaeological Data Recovery at Five Prehistoric Sites, Lake Red Rock, Marion County, Iowa,* vol. I, edited by Michael J. McNerney and Charles R. Moffat, pp. 63–221. Report No. 133. Cultural Resources Management, American Resources Group, Carbondale, Illinois.

1990b Investigations at the Dawson Site (13MA207). In *Archaeological Data Recovery at Five Prehistoric Sites, Lake Red Rock, Marion County, Iowa,* vol. I, edited by Michael J. McNerney and Charles R. Moffat, pp. 223–312. Report No. 133. Cultural Resources Management, American Resources Group, Carbondale, Illinois.

1990c Overview of Oneota Studies at Lake Red Rock. In *Archaeological Data Recovery at Five Prehistoric Sites, Lake Red Rock, Marion County, Iowa,* vol. I, edited by Michael J. McNerney and Charles R. Moffat, pp. 417–465. Report No. 133. Cultural Resources Management, American Resources Group, Carbondale, Illinois.

Mooney, James

1896 The Ghost-Dance Religion and the Sioux Outbreak of 1890. *Fourteenth Annual Report of the Bureau of American Ethnology for the Years 1892–93,* Pt. 2, pp. 641–1136. Smithsonian Institution, Washington, D.C.

1910 Skin and Skin Dressing. In *Handbook of American Indians North of Mexico, Part II,* edited by Frederick Webb Hodge, pp. 591–594. Bulletin No. 30. Bureau of American Ethnology, Smithsonian Institution, Washington, D.C.

Moran, J. M., and M. D. Morgan
1995   *Essentials of Weather.* Prentice Hall, New Jersey.

Morgan, David T.
1985   Ceramic Assemblage. In *The Hill Creek Homestead and the Late Mississippian Settlement in the Lower Illinois Valley,* edited by M. D. Conner, pp. 16–54. Research Series Vol. 1. Center for American Archeology, Kampsville Archeological Center, Kampsville, Illinois.

Morrow, Toby
1994   A Key to the Identification of Chipped-Stone Raw Materials Found on Archaeological Sites in Iowa. *Journal of the Iowa Archaeological Society* 41:108–129.

Moss, B.
1980   *Ecology of Fresh Waters.* Blackwell Scientific Publications, Oxford.

Moyle, P. B., and J. J. Cech, Jr.
1988   *Fishes: An Introduction to Ichthyology.* Prentice Hall, New Jersey.

Murdock, George P.
1955   Universals of Culture. In *Readings in Anthropology,* edited by A. Adamson Hoebel, Jesse D. Jennings, and Elmer R. Smith, pp. 4–5. McGraw-Hill, New York.

Murdock, George P., and Caterina Provost
1973   Factors in the Division of Labor by Sex: A Cross-Cultural Analysis. *Ethnology* 9:203–225.

Nagy, Imre
1994   Cheyenne Shields and Their Cosmological Background. *American Indian Art Magazine* 19(3):39–47, 104.

Nanda, Serena
1994   *Cultural Anthropology.* Wadsworth, Belmont, California.

Nassaney, Michael S., and Kenneth E. Sassaman
1995   Introduction: Understanding Native American Interactions. In *Native American Interactions: Multiscalar Analyses and Interpretations in the Eastern Woodlands,* edited by Michael S. Nassaney and Kenneth E. Sassaman, pp. xix–xxxviii. University of Tennessee Press, Knoxville.

Needham, James G., and Paul R. Needham
1962   *A Guide to the Study of Fresh-water Biology.* 5th ed. McGraw-Hill, New York.

Neely, R. Dan, and Carla G. Heister
1987   *The Natural Resources of Illinois: Introduction and Guide.* Special Publication 6. Illinois Natural History Survey, Department of Energy and Natural Resources, Champaign.

Neill, Edward D.
1884   Life among the Mandans and Gros Ventres Eighty Years Ago: As Described by Apartner of the North West Company. *American Antiquarian* 6(4):248–253.

Neihardt, John G.
1979   *Black Elk Speaks.* University of Nebraska Press, Lincoln.

Neff, Hector
1992   Ceramics and Evolution. In *Archaeological Method and Theory,* vol.4,

edited by Michael B. Schiffer, pp. 141–194. Academic Press, New York.

Neusius, Sarah W.
1990   Archaeozoology. In *At the Edge of Prehistory: Huber Phase Archaeology in the Chicago Area,* edited by James A. Brown and Patricia J. O'Brien, pp. 266–279. Center for American Archeology, Kampsville, Illinois.

Niering, William A.
1989   *Wetlands.* Alfred A. Knopf, New York.

Oberlander, Theodore M., Robert A. Muller
1987   *Essentials of Physical Geography Today.* 2nd ed. Random House, New York.

O'Brien, Michael J., and W. Raymond Wood
1998   *The Prehistory of Missouri.* University of Missouri Press, Columbia.

O'Brien, Patricia J.
1972   *A Formal Analysis of Cahokia Ceramics from the Powell Tract.* Monograph No. 3. Illinois Archaeological Survey, Urbana.
1993   Steed-Kisker: The Western Periphery of the Mississippian Tradition. *Midcontinental Journal of Archaeology* 18(1):61–79.

Ocvirk, Otto G., Robert O. Bone, Robert E. Stinson, and Philip R. Wigg
1968   *Art Fundamentals: Theory and Practice.* Wm. C. Brown, Dubuque, Iowa.

Ode, P. J., L. L. Tieszen, and J. C. Lerman
1980   The Seasonal Contribution of C3 and C4 Plant Species to Primary Production in a Mixed Prairie. *Ecology* 61:1304–1311.

Oliver, James S.
1993   Carcass Processing by the Hadza: Bone Breakage from Butchery to Consumption. In *From Bones to Behavior: Ethnoarchaeological and Experimental Contributions to the Interpretations of Faunal Remains,* edited by Jean Hudson, pp. 200–227. Occasional Paper No. 21. Center for Archaeological Investigations, Southern Illinois University, Carbondale.

Olsen, Stanley J.
1960   *Post-cranial Skeletal Characters of Bison and Bos.* Papers of the Peabody Museum of Archaeology and Ethnology, vol. 35, no. 4. Peabody Museum, Cambridge, Massachusetts.
1968   *Fish, Amphibian, and Reptile Remains from Archaeological Sites.* Papers of the Peabody Museum of Archaeology and Ethnology, vol. 56, no. 2. Peabody Museum, Cambridge, Massachusetts.

O'Meara, J. Tim
1989   Anthropology as Empirical Science. *American Anthropologist* 91:354–369.

Orr, Ellison
1914   Indian Pottery of the Oneota or Upper Iowa River Valley in Northeastern Iowa. *Iowa Academy of Science Proceedings* 21:231–239.

Overstreet, David F.
1978   Oneota Settlement Patterns in Eastern Wisconsin. In *Mississippian Settlement Patterns,* edited by Bruce D. Smith, pp. 21–49. Academic Press, New York.
1995   The Eastern Wisconsin Oneota Regional Continuity. In *Oneota Archaeology: Past, Present, and Future,* edited by William Green, pp.

33–64. Report No. 20. Office of the State Archaeologist, University of Iowa, Iowa City.

Ozuk, Steven J.
1987   Patrick Phase Ceramics. In *The Range Site: Archaic through Late Woodland Occupations,* by J. E. Kelly, A. C. Fortier, S. J. Ozuk, and J. A. Williams, pp. 230–304. American Bottom Archaeology FAI-270 Site Reports 16. University of Illinois Press, Urbana.

Page, J. L.
1949   *Climate of Illinois.* Bulletin No. 532. Agricultural Experiment Station, University of Illinois, Urbana.

Page, L. M., and C. E. Johnston
1990   Spawning in the Creek Chubsucker, *Erimyzon oblongus,* with a Review of Spawning Behavior in Suckers (Catostomidae). *Environmental Biology of Fishes* 27:265–272.

Paget, A. M.
1909   *The People of the Plains.* Ryerson Press, Toronto.

Parmalee, Paul W.
1959   Use of Mammalian Skulls and Mandibles by Prehistoric Indians of Illinois. *Transactions of the Illinois State Academy of Science* 52(3–4):85–95.

1961   Faunal Materials from the Zimmerman Site (Ls^{v}13), La Salle County, Illinois. In *The Zimmerman Site: A Report on Excavations at the Grand Village of Kaskaskia, LaSalle County, Illinois,* edited by James A. Brown, pp. 79–81. Reports of Investigations No. 9. Illinois State Museum, Springfield.

1962   The Faunal Complex of the Fisher Site, Illinois. *American Midland Naturalist* 68(2):399–408.

1964   Vertebrate Remains from an Historic Archaeological Site in Rock Island County, Illinois. *Transactions of the Illinois State Academy of Science* 57(3):167–174.

1967   *The Fresh-water Mussels of Illinois.* Popular Science Series 8. Illinois State Museum, Springfield.

1972a   Vertebrate Remains from the Griesmer Site, Lake County, Indiana. In *The Late Prehistoric Occupation of Northwestern Indiana: A Study of the Upper Mississippi Cultures of the Kankakee Valley,* by Charles H. Faulkner, pp. 199–201. Prehistoric Research Series, vol. 5, no. 2. Indiana Historical Society, Indianapolis.

1972b   Vertebrate Remains from the Fifield Site, Porter County, Indiana. In *A Study of the Upper Mississippi Cultures of the Kankakee Valley,* by Charles H. Faulkner, pp. 202–205. Prehistoric Research Series, vol. 5, no. 2. Indiana Historical Society, Indianapolis.

1977   The Avifauna from Prehistoric Arikara Sites in South Dakota. *Plains Anthropologist* 22(77):189–222.

1990   Vertebrate Remains from the Huber Site (11CK-1), Cook County, Illinois. In *At the Edge of Prehistory: Huber Phase Archaeology in the Chicago Area,* edited by James A. Brown and Patricia J. O'Brien, pp. 104–107. Center for American Archeology, Kampsville, Illinois.

Parmalee, Paul W., and Arthur E. Bogan
1980a   A Summary of the Animal Remains from the Noble-Wieting Site

(11ML28), McLean County, Illinois. *Transactions of the Illinois State Academy of Science* 73(4):1–6.

1980b   Vertebrate Remains from Early European and Historic Indian Occupations at the Waterman Site, Randolph County, Illinois. *Transactions of the Illinois State Academy of Science* 73(3):49–54.

Parmalee, Paul W., and Walter E. Klippel

1974   Freshwater Mussels as a Prehistoric Food Source. *American Antiquity* 39:421–434.

1983   The Role of Native Animals in the Food Economy of the Historic Kickapoo in Central Illinois. In *Lulu Linear Punctated: Essays in Honor of George Irving Quimby*, edited by Robert C. Dunnell and Donald K. Grayson, pp. 253–324. Anthropological Papers No. 72. Museum of Anthropology, University of Michigan, Ann Arbor.

Patterson, Thomas C.

1995   *Toward a Social History of Archaeology in the United States*. Harcourt Brace College Publishers, Fort Worth, Texas.

Pauketat, Timothy R.

1994   *The Ascent of the Chiefs: Cahokia and Mississippian Politics in Native North America*. University of Alabama Press, Tuscaloosa.

Pauketat, Timothy R., and Thomas E. Emerson

1991   The Ideology of Authority and the Power of the Pot. *American Anthropologist* 93:919–941.

1997   Introduction: Domination and Ideology in the Mississippian World. In *Cahokia: Domination and Ideology in the Mississippian World*, edited by Timothy R. Pauketat and Thomas E. Emerson, pp. 1–29. University of Nebraska Press, Lincoln and London.

Payne, J. N.

1942   Groundwater Aquifers. In *Geology and Mineral Resources of the Marseilles, Ottawa, and Streator Quadrangles*, edited by H. B. Willman and J. N. Payne, pp. 281–286. Bulletin No. 66. Illinois State Geological Survey, Urbana.

Paynter, Robert W.

1989   The Archaeology of Equality and Inequality. *Annual Review of Anthropology* 18:369–399.

Paynter, Robert W., and Randall H. McGuire

1991   The Archaeology of Inequality: Material Culture, Domination, and Resistance. In *The Archaeology of Inequality,* edited by Randall H. McGuire and Robert Paynter, pp. 1–27. Basil Blackwell, Oxford.

Peale, Titian R.

1871   *On the Uses of the Brain and Marrow of Animals among the Indians of North America*. Annual Report for 1870, pp. 390–391. Smithsonian Institution, Washington, D.C.

Penman, John T.

1988   Neo-boreal Climatic Influences on the Late Prehistoric Agricultural Groups of the Upper Mississippi Valley. *Geoarchaeology* 3:139–145.

Penney, David W.

1985   Continuities of Imagery and Symbolism in the Art of the Woodlands. In *Ancient Art of the American Woodland Indians,* edited by

David S. Brose, James A. Brown, and David W. Penney, pp. 147–198. Harry N. Abrams, New York.

Perkins, Dexter, Jr., and Patricia Daly
1968   A Hunters' Village in Neolithic Turkey. *Scientific American* 219(5):96–106.

Pettingill, O. S., Jr.
1985   *Ornithology in Laboratory and Field.* 5th ed. Academic Press, Orlando.

Piddocke, Stuart
1968   The Potlatch System of the Southern Kwakiutl: A New Perspective. In *Economic Anthropology: Readings in Theory and Analysis,* edited by Edward E. LeClair, Jr., and Harold K. Schneider, pp. 283–299. Holt, Rinehart and Winston, New York.

Piotrowski, Zygmunt A., and Albert M. Biele
1986   *Dreams: A Key to Self-Knowledge.* Lawrence Erlbaum Associates, Hillsdale, New Jersey.

Plog, Stephen
1990   Agriculture, Sedentism, and Environment in the Evolution of Political Systems. In *The Evolution of Political Systems,* edited by Stedman Upham, pp. 177–199. Cambridge University Press, Cambridge.

Pollack, David, and A. Gwynn Henderson
1992   Toward a Model of Fort Ancient Society. In *Fort Ancient Cultural Dynamics in the Middle Ohio Valley,* edited by A. Gwynn Henderson, pp. 281–294. Monographs in World Archaeology No. 8. Prehistory Press, Madison, Wisconsin.

Pond, Samuel W.
1986   *The Dakota or Sioux in Minnesota as They Were in 1834.* Minnesota Historical Society Press, St. Paul.

Powers, William K.
1981   On Mandalas and Native American World Views. *Current Anthropology* 22(4):443.
1987   *Beyond the Vision: Essays on American Indian Culture.* University of Oklahoma Press, Norman.

Purdue, James R., and Bonnie W. Styles
1987   Changes in the Mammalian Fauna of Illinois and Missouri during the Late Pleistocene and Holocene. In *Late Quaternary Mammalian Biogeography and Environments of the Great Plains and Prairies,* edited by R. W. Graham, H. A. Semken, Jr., and M. A. Graham, pp. 144–174. Scientific Papers Vol. 21. Illinois State Museum, Springfield.

Rackerby, Frank E., and Stuart Struever
1968   The Horton Site: A Casebook in Urgent Archaeology. *Bulletin of the Field Museum of Natural History* 39(3):10–13.

Radin, Paul
1911   Some Aspects of Winnebago Archeology. *American Anthropologist,* n.s. 13:517–538.
1923   The Winnebago Tribe. *Thirty-seventh Annual Report of the Bureau of American Ethnology for the Years 1915–1916,* pp. 33–560. Smithsonian Institution, Washington, D.C.

Rajnovich, Grace
 1989   Visions in the Quest for Medicine: An Interpretation of the Indian Pictographs of the Canadian Shield. *Midcontinental Journal of Archaeology* 14(2):179–225.
Rands, Robert L.
 1994   Ceramic Analysis and Synthesis: Searching for New Levels of Understanding. *Reviews in Anthropology* 23:75–85.
Reidhead, Van A.
 1980   The Economics of Subsistence Change: Test of an Optimization Model. In *Modeling Change in Prehistoric Subsistence Economies,* edited by Timothy K. Earle and Andrew L. Christenson, pp. 141–186. Academic Press, New York.
 1981   *A Linear Programming Model of Prehistoric Subsistence Optimization: A Southeastern Indiana Example.* Prehistory Research Series, vol. 6. Indiana Historical Society, Indianapolis.
Richards, John D.
 1992   *Ceramics and Culture at Aztalan: A Late Prehistoric Village in Southeast Wisconsin.* Unpublished Ph.D. dissertation, Department of Anthropology, University of Wisconsin-Milwaukee.
Ridington, Robin, and Tonia Ridington
 1970   The Inner Eye of Shamanism and Totemism. *History of Religions* 10(1):49–61.
Riggs, Stephen R.
 1883   Mythology of the Dakotas. *American Antiquarian and Oriental Journal* 5(2):147–149.
Ringrose, T. J.
 1993   Bone Counts and Statistics: A Critique. *Journal of Archaeological Science* 20:121–157.
Robison, Neil D.
 1987   Zooarchaeology: Its History and Development. In *The Zooarchaeology of Eastern North America: History, Method and Theory, and Bibliography,* edited by Arthur E. Bogan and Neil D. Robison, pp. 1–26. Miscellaneous Paper No. 12. Tennessee Anthropological Association, Knoxville.
Rogers, J. Daniel, and Samuel M. Wilson (editors)
 1993   *Ethnohistory and Archaeology: Approaches to Postcontact Change in the Americas.* Plenum Press, New York.
Root, Dolores
 1983   Information Exchange and the Spatial Configurations of Egalitarian Societies. In *Archaeological Hammers and Theories,* edited by James A. Moore and Arthur S. Keene, pp. 193–219. Academic Press, New York.
Roper, Donna C.
 1979   *Archaeological Survey and Settlement Pattern Models in Central Illinois.* Scientific Papers Vol. 16. Illinois State Museum, Springfield.
Rosman, Abraham, and Paula G. Rubel
 1995   *The Tapestry of Culture: An Introduction to Cultural Anthropology.* 5th ed. McGraw-Hill, New York.

Rostlund, Erhard
   1952   *Freshwater Fish and Fishing in Native North America.* University of California Press, Berkeley.

Rowe, C. W.
   1956   *The Effigy Mound Culture of Wisconsin.* Publications in Anthropology No. 3. Milwaukee Public Museum, Milwaukee, Wisconsin.

Ruhe, R. V.
   1983   Aspects of Holocene Pedology in the United States. In *Late-Quaternary Environments of the United States,* vol. 2, *The Holocene,* edited by H. E. Wright, Jr., pp. 12–25. University of Minnesota Press, Minneapolis.

Rye, Owen S.
   1981   *Pottery Technology.* Taraxacum, Washington, D.C.

Sabata, L. R.
   1995   *Soil Survey of Whiteside County, Illinois.* United States Department of Agriculture, Soil Conservation Service, Illinois Agricultural Experiment Station. Soil Conservation Service, Washington, D.C.

Sala, O. E., W. J. Parton, L. A. Joyce, and W. K. Laurenroth
   1988   Primary Production of the Central Grassland Region of the United States. *Ecology* 69(1):40–45.

Salisbury, R. D., and H. H. Barrows
   1918   *The Environment of Camp Grant.* Bulletin No. 39. Illinois State Geological Survey, Urbana.

Salvador, Mari Lyn
   1967   Food for the Holy Ghost: Ritual Exchange in Azorean Festivals. In *Time out of Time: Essays on the Festival,* edited by Alessandro Falassi, pp. 244–260. University of New Mexico Press, Albuquerque.

Sampson, Kelvin W.
   1988   Conventionalized Figures on Late Woodland Ceramics. *Wisconsin Archeologist* 69(3):163–188.

Sampson, Kelvin, and Duane Esarey
   1993   A Survey of Elaborate Mississippian Copper Artifacts from Illinois. In *Highways to the Past: Essays on Illinois Archaeology in Honor of Charles J. Bareis,* edited by Thomas E. Emerson, Andrew C. Fortier, and Dale L. McElrath, pp. 452–480. *Journal of the Illinois Archaeological Survey,* vol. 5(1–2).

Santure, Sharron K.
   1990   Summary Excavations and Analyses. In *Archaeological Investigations at the Morton Village and Norris Farms 36 Cemetery,* edited by Sharron K. Santure, Alan D. Harn, and Duane Esarey, pp. 160–161. Reports of Investigations No. 45. Illinois State Museum, Springfield.

Santure, Sharron K., and Duane Esarey
   1990   Analysis of Artifacts from the Oneota Mortuary Component. In *Archaeological Investigations at the Morton Village and Norris Farms 36 Cemetery,* edited by Sharron K. Santure, Alan D. Harn, and Duane Esarey, pp. 75–110. Reports of Investigations No. 45. Illinois State Museum, Springfield.

Santure, Sharron K., Alan D. Harn, and Duane Esarey (editors)
   1990   *Archaeological Investigations at the Morton Village and Norris Farms*

36 Cemetery. Reports of Investigations No. 45. Illinois State Museum, Springfield.

Sassaman, Kenneth E.
1992 Gender and Technology at the Archaic-Woodland "Transition." In *Exploring Gender through Archaeology: Selected Papers from the 1991 Boone Conference,* edited by Cheryl Claassen, pp. 71–80. Monographs in World Archaeology No. 11. Prehistory Press, Madison, Wisconsin.
1993 *Early Pottery in the Southeast: Tradition and Innovation in Cooking Technology.* University of Alabama Press, Tuscaloosa.
1995 The Cultural Diversity of Interactions among Mid-Holocene Societies of the American Southeast. In *Native American Interactions: Multiscalar Analyses and Interpretations in the Eastern Woodlands,* edited by Michael S. Nassaney and Kenneth E. Sassaman, pp. 174–204. University of Tennessee Press, Knoxville.

Saunders, Nicholas J.
1998 *Icons of Power: Feline Symbolism in the Americas.* Routledge, New York.

Schilt, A. Rose
1977 *Noble-Weiting: An Early Upper Mississippian Village.* Unpublished Master's thesis, Department of Anthropology and Sociology, Illinois State University, Normal.

Schuberth, C. J.
1986 *A View of the Past: An Introduction to Illinois Geology.* Illinois State Museum, Springfield.

Schurr, Mark K., and Margaret J. Schoeninger
1995 Associations between Agricultural Intensification and Social Complexity: An Example from the Prehistoric Ohio Valley. *Journal of Anthropological Archaeology* 14:315–339.

Schuster, Carl, and Edmund Carpenter
1996 *Patterns That Connect: Social Symbolism in Ancient and Tribal Art.* Harry N. Abrams, New York.

Scott, Michael J.
1994 Faunal Remains from the Midway Village Site. *Wisconsin Archeologist* 75(3–4):393–421.

Semken, Holmes A., Jr.
1983 Holocene Mammalian Biogeography and Climatic Change in the Eastern and Central United States. In *Late-Quaternary Environments of the United States,* vol. 2, *The Holocene,* edited by H. E. Wright, Jr., pp. 182–207. University of Minnesota Press, Minneapolis.

Shanks, Michael, and Christopher Tilley
1992 *Re-Constructing Archaeology: Theory and Practice.* 2nd ed. Routledge, London and New York.

Shay, C. Thomas
1978 Late Prehistoric Bison and Deer Use in the Eastern Prairie-Forest Border. In *Bison Procurement and Utilization: A Symposium,* edited by Leslie B. Davis and Michael Wilson, pp. 194–212. Plains Anthropologist, Memoir 14.

Shelford, Victor E.
1963   *The Ecology of North America.* University of Illinois Press, Urbana.

Shepard, Anna O.
1971   *Ceramics for the Archaeologist.* Publication No. 609. Carnegie Institution of Washington, Washington, D.C.

Sims, P. L.
1988   Grasslands. In *North American Terrestrial Vegetation,* edited by Michael G. Barbour and William D. Billings, pp. 266–286. Cambridge University Press, Cambridge.

Skinner, Alanson B.
1913   Social Life and Ceremonial Bundles of the Menomini Indians. *Anthropological Papers of the American Museum of Natural History* 13(1):1–165.

1914a   The Algonkin and the Thunderbird. *American Museum Journal* 14(2):71–72.

1914b   Bear Customs of the Cree and Other Algonkin Indians of Northern Ontario. *Papers and Records* 12:203–209. Ontario Historical Society, Ottawa.

1914c   Political Organization, Cults, and Ceremonies of the Plains-Ojibway and Plains-Cree Indians. *Anthropological Papers of the American Museum of Natural History* 11(6):475–542.

1915   Societies of the Ioway, Kansa, and Ponca Indians. *Anthropological Papers of the American Museum of Natural History* 11(9)679–801.

1921   *Material Culture of the Menomini.* Indian Notes and Monographs. Museum of the American Indian, New York.

1923   Observations on the Ethnology of the Sauk Indians. *Bulletin of the Public Museum of the City of Milwaukee* 5(1). Milwaukee, Wisconsin.

1924   The Mascoutens or Prairie Potawatomi Indians. *Bulletin of the Public Museum of the City of Milwaukee* 6(1):1–262. Milwaukee, Wisconsin.

1925   Observations on the Ethnology of the Sauk Indians. *Bulletin of the Public Museum of the City of Milwaukee* 5(3):119–180. Milwaukee, Wisconsin.

1926   Ethnology of the Ioway Indians. *Bulletin of the Public Museum of the City of Milwaukee* 5(4):181–354. Milwaukee, Wisconsin.

1927   The Mascoutens or Prairie Potawatomi Indians: Mythology and Folklore. *Bulletin of the Public Museum of the City of Milwaukee* 6(3):327–411. Milwaukee, Wisconsin.

Skinner, Robert R.
1953   The Oakwood Mound, an Upper Mississippi Component. *Journal of the Illinois Archaeological Society* 3(1):2–14.

Smith, Hale G.
1951   *The Crable Site, Fulton County, Illinois.* Anthropological Papers No. 7. Museum of Anthropology, University of Michigan, Ann Arbor.

Smith, Philip W.
1961   *The Amphibians and Reptiles of Illinois.* Bulletin 28(1). Illinois Natural History Survey, Urbana.

1979   *The Fishes of Illinois.* University of Illinois Press, Urbana.

Snow, Dean R.
1995   Migration in Prehistory: The Northern Iroquoian Case. *American Antiquity* 60(1):59–79.

Snyder, Lynn M.
1991   Barking Mutton: Ethnohistoric, Ethnographic, Archaeological, and Nutritional Evidence Pertaining to the Dog as a Native American Food Resource on the Plains. In *Beamers, Bobwhites, and Blue-Points: Tributes to the Career of Paul W. Parmalee,* edited by James R. Purdue, Walter E. Klippel, and Bonnie W. Styles, pp. 359–378. Scientific Papers Vol. 23. Illinois State Museum, Springfield.

Sober, Elliott, and David Sloan Wilson
1998   *Unto Others: The Evolution and Psychology of Unselfish Behavior.* Harvard University Press, Cambridge.

Speck, Frank G.
1955   *The Iroquois: A Study in Cultural Evolution.* Bulletin 23. Cranbrook Institute of Science, Bloomfield Hills, Michigan.

Spector, Janet D.
1998   Male/Female Task Differentiation among the Hidatsa: Toward the Development of an Archaeological Approach to the Study of Gender. In *Reader in Gender Archaeology,* edited by Kelley Hays-Gilpin and David S. Whitley, pp. 145–158. Routledge, London and New York.

Spence, Lewis
1911   Cherokees. In *Encyclopaedia of Religion and Ethics,* edited by James Hastings, vol. 3, pp. 503–508. Scribner's and T. & T. Clark, New York and Edinburgh.

Speth, John D.
1991   Some Unexplored Aspects of Mutualistic Plains-Pueblo Food Exchange. In *Farmers, Hunters, and Colonists: Interaction between the Southwest and the Southern Plains,* edited by Katherine A. Spielmann, pp. 18–35. University of Arizona Press, Tucson.

Spielmann, Katherine A.
1991   Interaction among Nonhierarchical Societies. In *Farmers, Hunters, and Colonists: Interaction between the Southwest and the Southern Plains,* edited by Katherine A. Spielmann, pp. 1–17. University of Arizona Press, Tucson.

Spindler, Louise S.
1967   Women in Menomini Culture. In *The North American Indians: A Sourcebook,* edited by Roger C. Owen, James J. F. Deetz, and Anthony D. Fisher, pp. 598–605. Macmillan, New York.
1989   Great Lakes: Menomini. In *Witchcraft and Sorcery of the American Native Peoples,* edited by Deward E. Walker, Jr., pp. 39–74. University of Idaho Press, Moscow, Idaho.

Spores, Ronald
1980   New World Ethnohistory and Archaeology, 1970–1980. *Annual Review of Anthropology* 9:575–603.

Springer, James Warren
1984   Site Distribution, Environmental Adaptation, and Environmental Change along the Northern Edge of the Prairie Peninsula. *Wisconsin Archeologist* 66:1–46.

Staeck, John Paul
    1993   Chief's Daughters, Marriage Patterns, and the Construction of Past
            Identities: Some Suggestions on Alternative Methods for Modeling
            the Past. *Wisconsin Archeologist* 74(1–4):370–399.
    1995   Oneota Archaeology Past, Present, and Future: In the Beginning,
            Again. In *Oneota Archaeology: Past, Present, and Future,* edited by
            William Green, pp. 3–6. Report No. 20. Office of the State Archae-
            ologist, University of Iowa, Iowa City.
Stahle, David W., and Malcolm K. Cleaveland
    1992   Reconstruction and Analysis of Spring Rainfall over the Southeastern
            U.S. for the Past 1000 Years. *Bulletin of the American Meteorological
            Society* 73:1947–1961.
Steltenkamp, Michael F.
    1993   *Black Elk: Holy Man of the Oglala.* University of Oklahoma Press,
            Norman.
Steponaitis, Vincas P.
    1983   *Ceramics, Chronology, and Community Patterns: An Archaeological
            Study at Moundville.* Academic Press, New York.
Stevenson, Katherine Phyllis
    1985   *Oneota Subsistence Related Behavior in the Driftless Area: A Study of the
            Valley View Site near LaCrosse, Wisconsin.* Unpublished Ph.D. disserta-
            tion, Department of Anthropology, University of Wisconsin, Madison.
Stoltman, James B.
    1986   The Appearance of the Mississippian Cultural Tradition in the Upper
            Mississippi Valley. In *Prehistoric Mound Builders of the Mississippi
            Valley,* edited by James B. Stoltman, pp. 26–34. Putnam Museum,
            Davenport.
    1991a   Introduction. In *New Perspectives on Cahokia: Views from the Periph-
            ery,* edited by James B. Stoltman, pp. vii–viii. Monographs in World
            Archaeology No. 2. Prehistory Press, Madison, Wisconsin.
    1991b   Cahokia As Seen from the Peripheries. In *New Perspectives on Ca-
            hokia: Views from the Periphery,* edited by James B. Stoltman, pp.
            349–354. Monographs in World Archaeology No. 2. Prehistory
            Press, Madison, Wisconsin.
Stoltman, James B., and David A. Baerreis
    1983   The Evolution of Human Ecosystems in the Eastern United States.
            In *Late-Quaternary Environments of the United States,* vol. 2, *The
            Holocene,* edited by H. E. Wright, Jr., pp. 252–268. University of
            Minnesota Press, Minneapolis.
Stothers, David M.
    1995   The "Michigan Owasco" and the Iroquois Co-Tradition: Late
            Woodland Conflict, Conquest, and Cultural Realignment in the
            Western Lower Great Lakes. *Northeast Anthropology* 49:5–41.
    1999   Late Woodland Models for Cultural Development in Southern
            Michigan. In *Retrieving Michigan's Buried Past: The Archaeology of
            the Great Lakes State,* edited by John Halsey, pp. 194–211. Bulletin
            64. Cranbrook Institute of Science, Bloomfield Hills, Michigan.
Stothers, David M., and James R. Graves
    1983   Cultural Continuity and Change: The Western Basin, Ontario Iro-

quois, and Sandusky Traditions: A 1982 Perspective. *Archaeology of Eastern North America* 11:109–142.

Stothers, David M., and G. Michael Pratt

1980   Cultural Continuity and Change in the Region of the Western Lake Erie Basin: The Sandusky Tradition. *Toledo Area Aboriginal Research Bulletin* 9:1–38.

1981   New Perspectives on the Late Woodland Cultures of the Western Lake Erie Region. *Midcontinental Journal of Archaeology* 6(1):91–121.

Stothers, David M., James R. Graves, and Susan B. Conway

1984   The Weiser Site: A Sandusky Tradition Village in Transition. *Michigan Archaeologist* 26(4):59–89.

Studenmund, Sarah

1988   *Excavations at Propheter Site on the Upper Rock River, Whiteside County.* Paper presented at the 26th Annual Workshop on Illinois Archaeology, Dickson Mounds, Illinois.

Stuiver, M., and P. J. Reimer

1993   Extended ^{14}C Database and Revised CALIB Radiocarbon Calibration Program. *Radiocarbon* 35:215–230.

Styles, Bonnie W.

1981   *Faunal Exploitation and Resource Selection: Early Late Woodland Subsistence in the Lower Illinois Valley.* Scientific Papers No. 3. Northwestern University Archeological Program, Evanston, Illinois.

1993   Discussion: Social Interaction. In *From Bones to Behavior: Ethnoarchaeological and Experimental Contributions to the Interpretation of Faunal Remains,* edited by Jean Hudson, pp. 263–270. Occasional Paper No. 21. Center for Archaeological Investigations, Southern Illinois University, Carbondale.

1994   The Value of Archaeological Faunal Remains for Paleodietary Reconstruction: A Case Study for the Midwestern United States. In *Paleonutrition: The Diet and Health of Prehistoric Americans,* edited by Kristin D. Sobdik, pp. 34–54. Occasional Paper No. 22. Center for Archaeological Investigations, Southern Illinois University, Carbondale.

Styles, Bonnie W., and Frances B. King

1990   Faunal and Floral Remains from the Bold Counselor Phase Village. In *Archaeological Investigations at the Morton Village and Norris Farms 36 Cemetery,* edited by Sharron K. Santure, Alan D. Harn, and Duane Esarey, pp. 57–65. Reports of Investigations No. 45. Illinois State Museum, Springfield.

Sullivan, Lawrence E.

1986   Sound and Senses: Toward a Hermeneutics of Performance. *History of Religions* 26(1):1–33.

1988   *Icanchu's Drum: An Orientation to Meaning in South American Religions.* Macmillan, New York.

Swanton, John R.

1910   Thunderbird. In *Handbook of American Indians North of Mexico, Part II,* edited by Frederick Webb Hodge, pp. 746–747. Bulletin

No. 30. Bureau of American Ethnology, Smithsonian Institution, Washington, D.C.

1943   Are Wars Inevitable? Smithsonian Institution War Background Studies, no. 12. Washington, D.C.

1979   *The Indians of the Southeastern United States.* Reprinted. Smithsonian Institution Press, Washington, D.C. Originally published 1946, Bulletin No. 137, Bureau of American Ethnology, Smithsonian Institution, Washington, D.C.

1996   *Source Material on the History and Ethnology of the Caddo Indians.* University of Oklahoma Press, Norman and London.

Swartz, B. K., Jr.
1973   *Indiana's Prehistoric Past.* Ball State University, Muncie, Indiana.

Talalay, Laurie, Donald R. Keller, and Patrick J. Munson
1984   Hickory Nuts, Walnuts, Butternuts, and Hazelnuts: Observations and Experiments Relevant to Their Aboriginal Exploitation in Eastern North America. In *Experiments and Observations on Aboriginal Wild Food Utilization in Eastern North America,* edited by Patrick J. Munson, pp. 338–359. Prehistory Research Series, vol. 6, no. 2, Indiana Historical Society, Indianapolis.

Tankersley, Kenneth B.
1986   Bison Exploitation by Late Fort Ancient Peoples in the Central Ohio River Valley. *North American Archaeologist* 7(4):289–303.

Tanner, Adrian
1979   *Bringing Home Animals: Religious Ideology and Mode of Production of the Mistassini Cree Hunters.* St. Martin's Press, New York.

Taylor, Colin F.
1991   The Plains. In *The Native Americans: The Indigenous People of North America,* edited by Colin F. Taylor, pp. 62–99. Smithsonian Publishers, New York.

Teller, Walter Magnes
1976   *On the River: A Variety of Canoe and Small Boat Voyages.* Rutgers University Press, New Brunswick, New Jersey.

Theler, James L.
1983   *Woodland Tradition Economic Strategies: Animal Resource Utilization in South-western Wisconsin and Northeastern Iowa.* Unpublished Ph.D. dissertation, Department of Anthropology, University of Wisconsin, Madison.

1989   The Pammel Creek Site Faunal Remains. *Wisconsin Archeologist* 70(1–2):157–242.

1994   Oneota Faunal Remains from Seven Sites in the La Crosse, Wisconsin, Area. *Wisconsin Archeologist* 75(3–4):343–392.

Thomas, Cyrus
1907   Mortuary Customs. In *Handbook of American Indians North of Mexico, Part I,* edited by Frederick Webb Hodge, pp. 945–947. Bulletin No. 30. Bureau of American Ethnology, Smithsonian Institution, Washington, D.C.

Thomas, Louis-Vincent
1987   Funeral Rites. In *The Encyclopedia of Religions,* vol. 5, edited by Mircea Eliade, pp. 450–459. Simon and Schuster, New York.

Tiffany, Joseph A.

1979   An Overview of Oneota Sites in Southeastern Iowa: A Perspective from the Ceramic Analysis of the Schmeiser Site, 13DM101, Des Moines County, Iowa. *Proceedings of the Iowa Academy of Science* 86:89–101.

1982   Site Catchment Analysis of Southeast Iowa Oneota Sites. In *Oneota Studies,* edited by Guy E. Gibbon, pp. 1–14. Publications in Anthropology No. 1. University of Minnesota, Minneapolis.

Tilley, Christopher (editor)

1993   *Interpretative Archaeology.* Berg, London.

Tooker, Elisabeth

1964   *An Ethnography of the Huron Indians, 1615–1649.* Bulletin No. 190. Bureau of American Ethnology, Smithsonian Institution, Washington, D.C.

1979   *ative North American Spirituality of the Eastern Woodlands: Sacred Myths, Dreams, Visions, Speeches, Healing Formulas, Rituals, and Ceremonials.* Paulist Press, New York.

Transeau, Edgar N.

1935   The Prairie Peninsula. *Ecology* 16(3):423–437.

Trenberth, K. E., G. W. Branstator, and P. A. Arkin

1988   Origins of the 1988 North American Drought. *Science* 242:1640–1645.

Trewartha, G. T.

1968   *An Introduction to Climate.* McGraw-Hill, New York.

Trigger, Bruce G.

1969   *The Huron: Farmers of the North.* Holt, Rinehart and Winston, New York.

1980   Archaeology and the Image of the American Indian. *American Antiquity* 45:662–676.

1984   Archaeology at the Crossroads: What's New? *Annual Review of Anthropology* 13:275–300.

1986a   Ethnohistory: The Unfinished Edifice. *Ethnohistory* 33(3):253–267.

1986b   Prehistoric Archaeology and American Society. In *American Archaeology Past and Future: A Celebration of the Society for American Archaeology, 1935–1985,* edited by David J. Meltzer, Don D. Fowler, and Jeremy A. Sabloff, pp. 187–215. Smithsonian Institution Press, Washington, D.C.

1989   History and Contemporary American Archaeology: A Critical Analysis. In *Archaeological Thought in America,* edited by C. C. Lamberg-Karlovsky, pp. 19–34. Cambridge University Press, Cambridge.

1990   Maintaining Economic Equality in Opposition to Complexity: An Iroquoian Case Study. In *The Evolution of Political Systems,* edited by Steadman Upham, pp. 119–145. Cambridge University Press, Cambridge.

Turnbow, Christopher A., and A. Gwynn Henderson

1992   Ceramics and Other Baked Clay Objects. In *Fort Ancient Cultural Dynamics in the Middle Ohio Valley,* edited by A. Gwynn Henderson, pp. 295–382. Monographs in World Archaeology No. 8. Prehistory Press, Madison, Wisconsin.

Turner, Jonathan H.
  1972   *Patterns of Social Organization*. McGraw-Hill, New York.
Turner, Lucien M.
  1894   Ethnology of the Ungava District, Hudson Bay Territory. *Eleventh Annual Report of the Bureau of American Ethnology for the Years 1889–'90*, pp. 159-350. Smithsonian Institution, Washington, D.C.
Ubelaker, Douglas H., and Waldo R. Wedel
  1975   Bird Bones, Burials, and Bundles in Plains Archaeology. *American Antiquity* 40(4):445–452.
Underhill, Ruth M.
  1957   Religion among American Indians. *Annals of the American Academy of Political and Social Science* 311:127–136.
  1971   *Red Man's America: A History of Indians in the United States*. Rev. ed. University of Chicago Press, Chicago and London.
Upham, Steadman
  1990   Decoupling the Processes of Political Evolution. In *The Evolution of Political Systems,* edited by Steadman Upham, pp. 1–17. Cambridge University Press, Cambridge.
Vaughan, Terry A.
  1986   *Mammalogy*. 3rd ed. Saunders College Publishing, Fort Worth, Texas.
Vehik, Susan C.
  1977   Bone Fragments and Bone Grease Manufacturing: A Review of Their Archaeological Use and Potential. *Plains Anthropologist* 22(77):169–182.
Vialles, Noelie
  1994   *Animal to Edible*. Cambridge University Press, Cambridge.
Villa, Dana R.
  1992   Postmodernism and the Public Sphere. *American Political Science Review* 86(3):712–721.
Vogel, Joseph O.
  1975   Trends in Cahokia Ceramics: Preliminary Study of the Collections from Tracts 15A and 15B. In *Perspectives in Cahokia Archaeology,* edited by James A. Brown, pp. 32–125. Bulletin No. 10. Illinois Archaeological Survey, University of Illinois, Urbana.
Wade, D. E., and D. R. Wade
  1977   *Introduction to Flora of Ogle County*. Occasional Paper No. 24. Taft Campus, Northern Illinois University, Oregon.
Wallace, Anthony F. C.
  1949   The Role of the Bear in Delaware Society. *Pennsylvania Archaeologist* 19(1–2):37–46.
  1958   Dreams and the Wishes of the Soul: A Type of Psychoanalytic Theory among the Seventeenth Century Iroquois. *American Anthropologist* 60:234–248.
  1966   *Religion, An Anthropological View*. Random House, New York.
  1969   *The Death and Rebirth of the Seneca*. Vintage Books, New York.
Watson, Patty Jo, and Mary C. Kennedy
  1991   The Development of Horticulture in the Eastern Woodlands of North America: Women's Role. In *Engendering Archaeology: Women and Prehistory,* edited by Joan M. Gero and Margaret W. Conkey,

pp. 255–275. Basil Blackwell, Oxford.

Watson, Patty Jo, Steven A. LeBlanc, and Charles L. Redman
1971   *Explanation in Archeology: An Explicitly Scientific Approach.* Columbia University Press, New York.

Weatherford, Jack
1991   *Native Roots: How the Indians Enriched America.* Fawcett Columbine, New York.

Weaver, John E.
1954   *North American Prairie.* Johnson, Lincoln, Nebraska.
1968   *Prairie Plants and Their Environment.* University of Nebraska Press, Lincoln.

Webster, Gary S.
1983   Optimality, Apple Pie, and the Broad-Spectrum Revolution. *Anthropology* 7(2):43–60.

Wedel, Mildred M.
1959   Oneota Sites on the Upper Iowa River. *Missouri Archaeologist* 21(2–4).
1963   Notes on Oneota Classification. *Wisconsin Archeologist* 44:118–122.

Wedel, Waldo R.
1986   *Central Plains Prehistory: Holocene Environments and Culture Change in the Republican River Basin.* University of Nebraska Press, Lincoln.

Wendland, Wayne M.
1978   Holocene Man in North America: The Ecological Setting and Climatic Background. *Plains Anthropologist* 23:273–287.
1983   Illinois Climate: A History of Climatic Changes and Their Effect on Early Settlement. *Living Museum* 45:26–29.

Whelan, Mary K.
1987   *The Archaeological Analysis of a 19th Century Dakota Indian Economy.* Unpublished Ph.D. dissertation, Department of Anthropology, University of Minnesota, Minneapolis.
1993   Dakota Indian Economics and the Nineteenth-Century Fur Trade. *Ethnohistory* 40(2):246–276.

Whitaker, John O., Jr., and William J. Hamilton, Jr.
1998   *Mammals of the Eastern United States.* Cornell University Press, Ithaca, New York.

White, John K.
1985   Ceramics. In *Deer Track: A Late Woodland Village in the Mississippi Valley,* edited by C. R. McGimsey and M. D. Conner, pp. 27–43. Technical Report No. 1. Center for American Archaeology, Kampsville, Illinois.

White, Leslie A.
1949   *The Science of Culture: A Study of Man and Civilization.* Farrar, Straus, and Giroux, New York.
1959   *The Evolution of Culture.* McGraw-Hill, New York.

White, Richard
1984   Native Americans and the Environment. In *Scholars and the Indian Experience: Critical Reviews of Recent Writing in the Social Sciences,* edited by W. R. Swagerty, pp. 179–204. Indiana University Press, Bloomington.

Whiteford, Andrew Hunter
    1977   Fiber Bags of the Great Lakes Indians. *American Indian Art Magazine* 2(2):52–64, 85.

Whitman, William
    1937   *The Oto.* Columbia University Contributions to Anthropology Vol. 28. Columbia University Press, New York.

Whitten, Dorothea S., and Norman E. Whitten, Jr.
    1993   Introduction. In *Imagery and Creativity: Ethnoaesthetics and Art Worlds in the Americas,* edited by D. S. Whitten and N. E. Whitten, Jr., pp. 3–44. University of Arizona Press, Tucson.

Whitten, Norman E., Jr.
    1985   *Sicuanga Runa: The Other Side of Development in Amazonian Ecuador.* University of Illinois Press, Urbana.

Willey, Gordon R.
    1971   *An Introduction to American Archaeology,* vol. 2, *South America.* Prentice-Hall, Englewood Cliffs, New Jersey.

Willey, Gordon R., and Philip Phillips
    1955   Method and Theory in American Archaeology. *American Anthropologist* 57(4):723–819.
    1958   *Method and Theory in American Archaeology.* University of Chicago Press, Chicago.

Willey, Gordon R., and Jeremy A. Sabloff
    1974   *A History of American Archaeology.* W. H. Freeman, San Francisco.

Willis, Roy
    1990   Introduction. In *Signifying Animals: Human Meaning in the Natural World,* edited by Roy Willis, pp. 1–24. Unwin Hyman, London.

Willman, H. B., E. Atherton, T. C. Buschbach, C. Collinson, J. C. Frye, M. E. Hopkins, J. A. Lineback, and J. A. Simon
    1975   *Handbook of Illinois Stratigraphy.* Bulletin No. 95. Illinois State Geological Survey, Urbana.

Willman, H. B., and D. R. Kolata
    1978   *The Platteville and Galena Groups in Northern Illinois.* Circular No. 502. Illinois State Geological Survey, Urbana.

Willoughby, Charles C.
    1897   An Analysis of the Decorations upon Pottery from the Mississippi Valley. *Journal of American Folklore* 10:9–20.

Wilson, Edward O.
    1998   Integrated Science and the Coming Century of the Environment. *Science* 279:2048–2049.

Wilson, Gilbert L.
    1928   Hidatsa Eagle Trapping. *Anthropological Papers of the American Museum of Natural History* 30(4):100–245.

Wilson, Lee Anne
    1982   Bird and Feline Motifs on Great Lakes Pouches. In *Native North American Art History: Selected Readings,* edited by Zena Pearlstone Mathews and Aldona Jonaitis, pp. 429–443. Peek, Palo Alto, California.

Wing, Elizabeth S., and Antoinette B. Brown
  1979   *Paleonutrition: Method and Theory in Prehistoric Foodways.* Academic Press, New York.
Wintemberg, W. J.
  1928   Representations of the Thunder Bird in Indian Art. *Thirty-sixth Annual Archaeological Report,* pp. 27–39. Report of the Ministry of Education, Toronto.
Winters, Howard D.
  1969   *The Riverton Culture: A Second Millenium Occupation in the Central Wabash Valley.* Reports of Investigations No. 13. Illinois State Museum, Springfield.
Wissler, Clark
  1907   Some Protective Designs of the Sioux. *Anthropological Papers of the American Museum of Natural History* 1:21–53.
  1910   Material Culture of the Blackfoot Indians. *Anthropological Papers of the American Museum of Natural History* 5:1–175.
Witthoft, John
  1949   *Green Corn Ceremonialism in the Eastern Woodlands.* Occasional Contributions from the Museum of Anthropology of the University of Michigan No. 13. University of Michigan Press, Ann Arbor.
Wolforth, T. R., K. Kaufmann, and D. Moore
  1995   *A Phase II Archaeological Investigation of a Portion of Site 11-Le-35, Lee County, Illinois.* Contract Archaeology Program Project Completion Report No. 6. Northern Illinois University.
Woolworth, Alan R., and Douglas A. Birk
  1968   Description of Artifacts. In *Voices from the Rapids: An Underwater Search for Fur Trade Artifacts, 1960–73,* edited by Robert C. Wheeler, Walter A. Kenyon, Alan R. Woolworth, and Douglas A. Birk, pp. 55–93. Minnesota Historical Society, St. Paul.
Wooton, R. J.
  1990   *Ecology of Teleost Fishes.* Chapman and Hall, New York.
Wright, H. E., Jr.
  1968   History of the Prairie Peninsula. In *The Quaternary of Illinois,* edited by Robert E. Bergstrom, pp. 78–88. University of Illinois College of Agriculture, Urbana.
Wright, James V.
  1987   Archaeological Evidence for the Use of Furbearers in North America. In *Wild Furbearer Management and Conservation in North America,* edited by Milan Novak, James A. Baker, Martyn E. Obbard, and Bruce Malloch, pp. 3–12. Ministry of Natural Resources, Toronto.
Wright, Rita P.
  1991   Woman's Labor and Pottery Production in Prehistory. In *Engendering Archaeology: Women and Prehistory,* edited by Joan M. Gero and Margaret W. Conkey, pp. 194–223. Basil Blackwell, Oxford.
  1996   Introduction: Gendered Ways of Knowing in Archaeology. In *Gender and Archaeology,* edited by Rita P. Wright, pp. 1–19. University of Pennsylvania Press, Philadelphia.
Wylie, Alison
  1998   The Interplay of Evidential Constraints and Political Interests:

Recent Archaeological Research on Gender. In *Reader in Gender Archaeology*, edited by Kelley Hays-Gilpin and David S. Whitley, pp. 57–84. Routledge, London and New York.

Yarrow, H. C.
1881   A Further Contribution to the Study of the Mortuary Customs of the North American Indians. *First Annual Report of the Bureau of American Ethnology for the Years 1879–80*, pp. 87–203. Smithsonian Institution, Washington, D.C.

Zawacki, A. A., and G. Hausfater
1969   *Early Vegetation of the Lower Illinois Valley.* Reports of Investigations No. 17. Illinois State Museum, Springfield.

Zierhut, N. W.
1967   Bone Breaking Activities of the Calling Lake Cree. *Alberta Anthropologist* 1(3):33–37.

Index